D0937349

THE OLD BRETHREN

THE OLD BRETHREN

James H. Lehman

THE BRETHREN PRESS ⧗ ELGIN, ILLINOIS

THE OLD BRETHREN

Published by Pillar Books for The Brethren Press

The Brethren Press edition published August 1976

ISBN 0-87178-650-8

Copyright © 1976 by James H. Lehman

All Rights Reserved

Library of Congress Catalogue Card number: 76-20274

Printed in the United States of America

THE BRETHREN PRESS
14151 Dundee Avenue
Elgin, Illinois 60120, U.S.A.

graphic design by ANTHONY BASILE

CONTENTS

Introduction 9

1. The Old Brethren 17
2. The Book As It Reads 43
3. The Ordinances of the Lord 65
4. The Fraternal Spirit of Worship 93
5. The Ancient Order
   of the Brethren 139
6. Two Brethren from Ohio 165
7. A Bold and Masterful Elder 187
8. A Virginia Slave 215
9. Two Doctors and a Fisherman ..237
10. Two Gifts of the Spirit 261
11. Vintage Brethren in the East ...289
12. Venturesome Brethren
    in the "West" 315
13. Geography, Dress, Schism, and
    Die Grosse Versammlung 339

Notes 365
Index 379

Introduction

When Wilbur Brumbaugh asked me to write this book, I almost said no. He wanted curriculum material on Brethren heritage for high school age persons, and I presumed correctly that he asked me because I was purported to know something about young people, not because I knew anything about Brethren history. I graduated from Bethany Theological Seminary relatively untouched by that part of its curriculum. While the one course I had was well presented, it touched neither my imagination nor my heart. And at the time Wilbur asked, I was losing interest in youth work and have since left it. So I almost said no; and I must confess that I said yes finally because there was a small stipend and I was flattered to be asked.

Out of poor motives, good events sometimes issue, and I was surprised to find that, not only was I interested in Brethren history, I was fascinated. What began as a dutiful work project for hire turned out beyond all my expectations to be a labor of love and the most satisfying thing I have done. In the process I probably learned as much about myself as I did about the Brethren. Here is the fruit of that labor, and I hope you enjoy reading it as much as I enjoyed writing it.

I quickly decided that I did not want to write for young people only, but for adults as well; and I rationalized that by saying that youth today read at the same level as most adults anyway. I also have had a long-standing dislike for "hip" youth material where the adult writer tries to be "with it." I decided to write something that is generally readable and interesting to me and trust that youth would have the good sense to recognize its merit if it had any. I feel that adults and youth are sufficiently within the same world to use the same material; whether these thoughts are correct or not, the editor was good enough to let me have a go at it on that basis.

I saw no way to survey all of Brethren history in thirteen chapters and have anything more than just that—a survey. History has always been more interesting to me when it is concrete, when I can know the personalities, however noble and peculiar, and experience the events, however strange. Obviously I could not do that for all of Brethren history. So I decided to choose one ten-year period and go into that in depth, assuming that acquainting the reader thoroughly with one small sector of Brethren history would go a longer way toward his understanding than giving him a little bit about everything. And my intuition told me that it would be more interesting as well. I assumed further that a fuller knowledge of a small period would give some hints about other times, since change among the Brethren was neither disjunctive nor instantaneous.

I cannot claim originality for this apprach. It was

used in my freshman course in Western civilization at Juniata College in the early sixties. The course had the extravagant title *Great Epochs of World Culture* and was to its lasting credit one of the few courses even the football players liked. Instead of surveying all of Western culture, a task anyone who has been a freshman will know is impossible, it examined four epochs in depth and assumed that an intelligent student could begin to guess at the historical development within which they lay and at least have a framework upon which to hang later learning and from which to pursue further research. I liked the approach and decided that if it could interest football players it would probably work for anyone.

I chose the 1840s somewhat arbitrarily. I wanted a decade from the so-called "wilderness period," when, according to some historians, the Brethren were ignorant and narrow, so that I could show that while they lived in the wilderness and were unschooled, they were neither ignorant nor unattractive. On the contrary, they were warm and vigorous, very much to be respected, and quite worthy to be learned from. The 1840s were convenient because they were not so far back that little research material existed. It turned out that this decade was a good choice because it was the last decade before the beginning of the cultural changes that today make the Church of the Brethren so different from the Brethren of that day.

In treating the period, I frequently include events that occurred before or after the decade. I found it impossible to restrict the account rigidly. When such events are recounted, they are in reference to something or someone within the decade and are for the purpose of illumination or background or to make a narrative fragment complete.

Wilbur Brumbaugh, the editor of the Church of the Brethren Heritage Learning Program, accepted the book as I wanted to write it; for that, for asking me in the first place, and for enduring my not always predict-able work habits, I especially thank him. Dennis Slabaugh, a student at Bethany Theological Seminary, gave me valuable research assistance. Edith Bonsack Barnes, who is one of the unsung laborers in Brethren historical research and who has unstintingly volunteered a day a week for years to the Brethren Historical Library at Elgin, obligingly allowed me to interrupt her fre-quently with questions. I soon learned that if I needed something which had resisted all my researches, it was a mistake not to ask Edith, who would quietly tell me how to find it. Edith also proofread all cited material in my manuscript and checked my footnotes for accuracy—a large labor from which I was glad to be relieved and for which I am very grateful. Gwendolyn Bobb, who has charge of the historical library, and Mildred Heckert, who does considerable work there, endured my constant presence, piles of books and papers, and frequent borrowings with equanimity. My appreciation goes also to Maria Johnson, who in the evenings and on Satur-days typed most of the manuscript, and to Chris Missele, who typed the last chapter and the concluding commentary. I should like to thank the professors who taught that freshman course: Steven Barbash, who is gone from Juniata and who has, I am sure, long since forgotten me; Betty Ann Cherry, who is still there and a friend I especially enjoy on my infrequent return visits; and Elmer Mass, who is likely, wherever he is, still going his bemused and friendly way.

Finally, I want to thank my wife Peg and sister Susan, who during the month of July absolved me of all household responsibilities so I might secrete myself in the basement and write, who read parts of the manuscript, who were candid in their reactions and constant in their support; and my small son Joshua, who calmly tolerated my repeated disappearance into the basement. To my wife I am especially thankful for so graciously holding household and family together while I was spending more time in the nineteenth century than the twentieth.

I have long wanted to write a book and now have done so. It is my first and I hope not my last, for I have thoroughly enjoyed doing it.

James H. Lehman
Elgin, Illinois
August, 1975

CHAPTER
1

Chapter One
The Old Brethren

This book is in a general way a history, in a more particular way an anecdotal history, and in a still more specific way not a history at all. I wish to take you, the reader, out of our present time into the world of the Brethren in the 1840s. I am not, first of all, interested in having you learn facts about their world, although to know that world you will have to know something about it. Accordingly there are some places, persons, practices, beliefs, events, and dates I will want you to remember. Nor am I interested only in having you feel what it was like to be Brethren, although that, above all else, is necessary to the book's success. I want you, when you have put down this book, to appreciate affectionately the unique and vigorous qualities you have encountered and to accept with candor and forgiveness what you do not like.

Each of us is tempted, when we regard the past, to feel nostalgia or disdain. I hope you suffer neither as you

Love Feast among the Dunkers

read the book. The Brethren were who they were. Their time obviously cannot be brought back, even by an attempt to appropriate their life-style; nor can their failings be undone. We, likewise, are who we are, faced with the sometimes impossible task of coping with a complicated present and an uncertain future. There is much we can learn from a people as vital and distinctive as they were, and there is much that we have to muddle out for ourselves unguided by a past no longer retrievable.

You will quickly see that my temptation is to feel nostalgia, for my heart has been mostly warmed by these "Old Brethren." Having had for a grandfather a bearded, plain-coated elder whom I and others loved, has more than a little to do with this. So my aim is to kindle in you the same delight. However, I invite you to be candid as you read. Though I want you to like the Old Brethren, I want you even more to know them frankly for the singular and warm-hearted as well as stiff-backed and sectarian human beings they were.

This first chapter is an anecdotal introduction presenting five vignettes drawn from their life. Each has been excerpted from the writings of someone else and in the last case from someone who was very much alive in the decade. Read them with enjoyment and with an eye toward what they reveal about the Old Brethren.

Elder John Metzger

Long years ago, 1758, it is said from Holland there came to Pennsylvania a young husband and wife unable to pay their fare for the Atlantic voyage. As the laws then permitted, these two young people were sold to different parties for a time equal in value to the cost of their ocean trip. After serving their time they were then free, and happy as larks. They made their way into the interior of the State, worked, saved and raised a family.

December 20, 1807, in Blair County, there was born a
grandson, whose name was entered in the old family Bible as John Metzger. In 1819, when John was twelve
years old, his parents located near Dayton, Ohio, at that
time a small village. When twenty-one years old John
took to himself a wife in the person of Hannah Ulery. A
little later they both entered the Church . . . by confession and baptism. In 1834 they moved to Tippecanoe
County, Ind., and the next year, when John was twenty-
eight years old, he was called to the ministry. His schooling was scant, very much so. In those pioneer days
schools were few. In raising a family it was not so much
a matter of educating the boys and girls as producing
enough for them to eat and wear. However, John during
his teens learned to read and do some writing. He knew
a little about arithmetic, but nothing about grammar,
geography or history. To his credit he could read and
speak both the German and the English, one about as
well as the other. But unlike some preachers we meet
with now and then, he had the preaching spirit in the
superlative degree, and with the Bible open before him
he felt that there was a place in the world for him, and
that God being his Helper he was going to find it.

His first preaching service was in a sawmill and there
were six persons present to hear his maiden sermon. For
him in a thinly settled community that was a good
beginning. Having six people to tell the neighbors about
the sermon meant a much larger congregation at the
next service. It was not long until we hear of his
preaching in different parts of the State. He went for
miles to fill appointments in localities where there were
but few members, making most of his trips on horseback
but sometimes, when the roads through the dense forest
were almost impassable even for a horse, he would walk
rather than disappoint a congregation. Now and then,
on reaching a stream overflowing to its banks, he would
remove all his clothes, tie them into a bundle and with
his Bible in the pack, and hold the bundle high above his

head, while wading the stream, the water often coming up to his neck. On the other side he would dress and go his way rejoicing.

Everywhere he went the people heard him gladly, for they looked upon him as a man of God with a message. Under his marvelous preaching men and women were converted and baptized regardless of weather conditions. With him conversion was not a mere matter of joining the church. It was a matter of salvation and to neglect it meant condemnation and eternal separation from God. It was in this sense that he preached the Gospel and he made those who listened to him feel that there was something in the act of turning to God. In those days there were ungodly men who presumed to dictate as to whether their wives should join certain churches. A few of these rough characters threatened Brother Metzger with bodily injuries if he attempted to baptize their wives. With such he would try to reason, but some of them remained obstinate, and would not listen to reason. Under such circumstances our pioneer John the Baptist, so to speak, would unhesitatingly do his duty, and proceeded to baptize all who demanded the sacred and initiatory rite, though some of it was done in the very face of threats.

In 1842 he was ordained to the eldership and six years later moved to Clinton County, Ind. Seeing the need of a more suitable place for meetings than small uncomfortable schoolhouses, he built for his residence a log house twenty-five by forty feet, so arranged that part of it could be used for preaching services. After collecting the logs, about eighty in number, he drove, in the winter, one hundred miles to purchase the needed hardware for his building. The house once ready he announced services and the people coming from every direction easily filled the chapel part and the large porch besides. Here a church was organized and he broadened out still more and more in his work. Wishing to take up work in a still larger field, in 1861, he located near Cerro Gordo, Piatt

County, Ill., where a large and influential congregation soon came into existence. While looking after his well-cultivated farm and his flourishing congregation he preached and traveled extensively in Illinois and Indiana, and even in other states. In their covered buggy he and his wife made many trips to Tippecanoe, Ind., and it is said that he preached in every schoolhouse between the two points, more than a hundred miles apart . . . .

In some ways Elder John Metzger, or Johnny Metzger, as people generally spoke of him, was a remarkable man. The Brotherhood never had another preacher just like him. He had a personality all his own, and an ideal personality it was. He was a well-built man, possessing a fine face, always beaming with love and cheerfulness. His eyes were sparkling, his face large, complexion fair, and his hair as black as a raven, and just wavy enough to make him attractive. His voice was strong, well-modulated, at all times under control and on still evenings could be heard a mile distant. Many times he was heard quite distinctly for several hundred yards. When thoroughly warmed up in a discourse he had a way of gracefully swinging his head so as to cause his long black locks to seem fairly alive as they swept to and fro in the air. All this seemed wholly befitting the man and his message. When he had before him a mixed assembly he would sometimes preach about forty minutes, then excuse himself to the English part of the congregation and say that he must now preach in German. This he would do with the same grace, efficiency, and power displayed in his first discourse. Those who understood both tongues said that he could talk as fluently in one language as in the other . . . .

Under his preaching hundreds of people came to the church and demanded baptism at his hands. But how is it, some one is ready to ask, that a man without even a common school education could exert such an influence over the public? With Elder Metzger there were several

things that more than made up for his lack of schooling.
He was a thoroughgoing believer in the doctrines and
claims of the church as he had accepted them, and that
he lived as he preached. Probably his great strength was
in his marvelous spontaneity, ability to act intelligently
. . . on the spur of the moment. His flashes of thought, in
the sweep of his native oratory, almost like flashes of
lightning and peals of thunder, gave to such preachers as
John Umstad, John Metzger and others of the past
generations, a power that can be acquired at no seat of
learning . . . .[1]

The Brethren followed a migratory pattern west
across Pennsylvania into Ohio and Kentucky and then
on to Indiana and Illinois. This is as far west as they had
gotten by 1850, excepting one church in Iowa and one in
Missouri. Elder Metzger's pilgrimage was repeated by
many of his brethren. He was virtually unschooled as
were most of the preachers and nearly all of the
members. While many ministers had little oratorical
skill, his unlettered but folksy grace as a preacher was
not uncommon.

Like most people on the frontier, the Brethren were
uneducated from necessity; there were few schools and
little time away from work to attend them. However, the
Brethren were also unschooled by choice, believing that
education beyond primary school led to worldliness and
the eventual disintegration of the church. Many
Brethren were not as excessive as Yelles Cassel, but few
would have welcomed young Abraham's eagerness for
books. Abraham H. Cassel was born in 1820, so these
incidents were occurring in the decade just prior to the
1840s.

Yelles and Abraham Cassel
Yelles Cassel was a Brethren farmer in Montgomery

Traveler's garb

Abraham Harley Cassel as an older man

County, Pennsylvania, with a small farm of seventy or eighty acres. It has been said of Pennsylvania farmers of that period and could be said of Yelles that they were devoted to two things—their farms and their religion. In the evenings, after a day of the severest toil, the men sat about the blaze of the log fire in the kitchen and shelled corn or mended harness, while the women spun, knitted, and sewed. For most the Bible was their only literary fare except the sermons by a farmer-preacher. Their life was ordered by seedtime and harvest. Abraham said of his father, "He could scarcely read the Bible right well with mother's assistance and that was about all he ever did read. He never read a newspaper in his life." The elder Cassel was adamantly opposed to formal education. Abraham wrote in later years, "There was only three months school in a year and that was in the depths of winter, and no public road to get there; but my father was so prejudiced against education that he would not have allowed me to go even if I could . . . . I could read, write and cypher before I was nine years old; but by the time I was eleven I was through several arithmetics . . . . My sister . . . . taught me the a b c's, she did not know much more herself; and from then on I had but very little assistance . . . ."

His sister, Sally, along with the other children, had been given some schooling because their father wanted them to be able to read, but he believed in having his children raised in pious ignorance. Her minimal tutoring of Abraham fell on fertile ground. The boy was bright. In addition, he had an independent spirit. He so impressed several people, including Mr. Isaac Wampole, a prominent citizen of Philadelphia who had a residence in the country, that they interceded with his father to send Abraham to school. Wampole even offered to pay all costs. Similar offers were made by others. The reluctant father relented, but took no responsibility for the possible consequence of the action, saying, "I tried to bring you up according to my conscientious convictions, but I see I can't, as you will learn in spite of all my op-position. Therefore, learn, and if it leads you to evil, the fault is not mine." Thus, at the age of eleven, Abraham Cassel began six months of formal schooling which was all he ever got.

"As soon as I could read and write I became the possessor of a small Walker's Pronouncing Dictionary, which I had the occasion to use more than any other book in my life." With this and his sister's help he managed to learn English. It was difficult to learn to speak English because he seldom heard it in public.

Abraham's interest in books and learning increased, even though his father gave him extra work to do on the farm in order to limit the amount of time available for reading. His Uncle George Cassel, different from his father, was sometimes indirectly helpful to him. "Uncle George took pride in giving his children an education, and to encourage them he would frequently buy them little penny or two-penny books of pedlars when they came around. These I would borrow and study word for word until I was master of them." He must have enjoyed the penny books because in 1830 he sent in an order for twenty dozen, ". . . I want every kind of penny books that's in the world. . . . I want 12 dozens of them longley ones and 8 dozens of the square ones—and I wish you would pick them out with the nicest kovers for me . . ."

When storekeeper Thomas J. White heard about the father's opposition to Abraham's studying and reading, he gave the boy a gift of candles which he could use to read in his room. When his father discovered this he re-quired the eager boy to go to bed without getting a light for his candle from the stove downstairs. "It was not long until a Yankee pedlar, who had his home with one of my friends, who knew my case very well, came to our house—he was a highly educated gentleman and sym-pathized with me all he could. He told me that he had recently read in a newspaper of a peculiar kind of matches being invented in Paris, by which a candle could be lit without fire—and that he was going to New York soon and would, if possible, get some of them for me. He succeeded in getting them, paid 25 cents for a box containing 75 matches . . ." The matches, the first ever seen in the area, and candles were locked in an old desk in his room and Abraham spent many nights reading.

Another problem was finding books. There were no English books in the home, only a German Bible and a few old hymnbooks. Neither were there many books in the neighborhood. A Dr. Fonfield and a few friends heard about the problem and assisted where possible, but as they lived some distance away they could not do much. Abraham managed to get textbooks he felt to be most important. He spent all possible money on books and was punished by the family by being given less money. To make extra money, he picked cherries for neighbors and gathered herbs for Dr. Fonfield who paid him treble their value because of the laudable use he made of the money.[2]

Abraham Cassel, despite his lack of formal education, went on to amass an extraordinary private library. Even for the Brethren of the latter half of the century, when education was more acceptable, his interests were exceptional. But for the 1830s and 1840s when he was a young man, his love for books was irregular.

In 1864, Elder John Kline of the Linville Creek Church in Rockingham County, Virginia, was shot to death by Rebel supporters several miles from his house just after he had returned from Yearly Meeting. He was at the time one of the most prominent men in the Brotherhood, having served as moderator of Yearly Meeting for four years running. In the 1840s Elder Kline was just coming into his full leadership strength. One of his peculiarities was his long trips. Many elders and ministers traveled because congregations were scattered, but no one matched Elder Kline. He traveled thousands of miles in his lifetime, keeping a careful diary of nearly every event. The following is an excerpt from his diary, recounting portions of a trip he took in 1844. The description of him and his companion was written by the editor of his diary, Benjamin Funk, as a preface to an earlier trip, but it is appropriate to this trip as well.

Elder John Kline's Trip

These two brethren were well-mounted. Their horses were good travelers, not only as to gait, but *bottom* as well. This, in common *parlance*, meant great power of endurance. . . . The two travelers did not know what weather they might have to contend with on a journey which was to occupy . . . weeks. Umbrellas were rare in that day; but even if they had been abundant, they were too much "after the fashion" to have been used by these unfashionable brethren. Instead umbrellas were not used by the Brotherhood, at least in Virginia, until many years after this.

A **Great Coat**, made of heavy and compact stuff, with long skirts reaching to the feet, and a large cape attached, covering completely the shoulders, and buttoning over the breast, constituted a covering defying both rain and storm. Superadded to this was a very broadbrimmed hat of solid felt. Every saddle in that day was provided with what was called a *coat-pad*. This was a flat leather pad fastened to the saddle just behind the seat, and furnished with straps and buckles so as to hold an overcoat, when properly rolled up and fastened, in perfect order whilst traveling. Leather saddlebags well stocked with changes of clean underwear completed the outfit.

Thus equipped, these two brethren started on their journey.[3]

Tuesday, September 17, 1844. Brother George R. Hedrick and I start from my home this morning, on horseback, for Ohio. We dine at William Fitzwater's, in Brock's Gap, and arrive in the evening at Isaac Dasher's on the South Fork, Hardy County, Virginia where we stay over night. . . .

Friday, September 20. Today we passed through what is called the Glades and the Wilderness, to the Briery Mountain. A very lonely road; but the companionship of a man and a brother like George Hedrick makes solitude enjoyable. Only those who have experienced the agreeableness of a bright, serene, calm and contented mind and heart, such as I find in Brother Hedrick, can ever realize the pleasure of such company. . . . We fed our horses and took breakfast at Smith's tavern, in Preston County, Virginia; took dinner at Bransonville and find ourselves here at Brother Jacob Thomas's, where we are spending the night. . . .

Sunday, September 22. Go to George's Creek Meetinghouse. We have forenoon and afternoon meeting. Second Corinthians 6 is read in the forenoon meeting. In the 3 o'clock meeting Luke 14 is read. I speak on the great supper, from the sixteenth to the twenth-fourth verse. . . .

Wednesday, September 25. Breakfast and feed in Darlington at Dunlap's tavern. Then on to New Middletown to Daniel Summer's; and this evening reach Brother Henry Kurtz's in Columbiana County,* where we stay all night.

Thursday, September 26. Meeting at Brother Haas's. Hebrews 8 is read. Love feast this evening. Come back to Brother Kurtz's and stay all night. Paul has told us more than once of the joy he felt, and how his heart was refreshed on meeting dear brethren and sisters whom he had not seen for a time. In meeting the brethren and sisters here and elsewhere we experience much of the

---

* Kurtz's farm was five miles south of Poland in Springfield Township. That area was originally a part of Columbiana County but was broken off in 1846 and formed a new county called Mahoning—J.H.L.

same feeling. They everywhere make us feel at home, and show us more love and give us more attention than we deserve. What a blessed thing it is to be filled with the love of Christ! This implants love in the heart for the Brethren. John says: "We know that we have passed out of death into life, because we love the brethren." This is the first-fruits of the tree of life in our hearts. . . .

Monday, October 14. Westward through Greenville to Brother Emanuel Flory's in Darke County, where we dine and feed; then on to Winchester in Indiana, and stay all night at Acker's tavern. We are now in Randolph County, Indiana. If we were among false brethren in this new country, as Paul says he once was in the land in which he traveled, situated as we are in respect to bad roads, a long way from our homes, with no means of conveyance except the backs of our horses to carry us to Virginia, the prospect of our stay here, and our hopes of safe return, might be gloomy indeed. But, thanks to the good Lord, we are not among false brethren. Our Brethren are true Brethren wherever we find them. There may be some hypocrites, God knows; but I know of none. Brother Hedrick and I have repeatedly discoursed on this subject in our travels together, and neither he nor I have in a single instance met with a brother or sister that has not, in our presence at least, shown something of the gentleness and meekness of Christ. We are made to feel at home wherever we go among them, and these considerations strengthen our faith and encourage the assurance that the Gospel which we as a band of Christians preach and practice, and which works mightly in the hearts of the dear Brethren everywhere, is of God. "By their fruits ye shall know them. . . ."

Monday, October 28. Go to Dayton, and after spending some time in visiting the factories and other points of interest in the city, we start towards Cincinnati, and stay all night in Miamisburg, at Zimmer's tavern. . . .

Sunday, November 3. On through Logan on the

Hocking River; then down the same river to Warren's tavern, near Athens, in Athens County, where we stay all night. The Hocking Valley is a fine, rich country, and I feel to encourage some of our younger people to come here and get good cheap homes. In this way they might establish the church here, and thus prepare the way of the Lord as John did in the wilderness of Judea. What an opening there is here for good, industrious people. . . .

Monday, November 11. Home today. Find all well, but some sickness in the neighborhood around. On the journey from which I have just returned, I traveled 1,271 miles on horseback, one beast carrying me safely all that distance. The roads we traveled were in many places just as nature formed them, the hand of man having done but little more than cut the timber out and remove impassable obstructions. We crossed high and rugged mountains, and forded dangerous streams. But in the West* the people are waking up to the importance of improving the public roads. The abundant natural wealth of that country, when properly developed by wise industry, will respond in such lavish abundance that there will be no lack of means to build the best of roads, and in every respect to raise the country generally to that state of beauty by high culture, which ministers to the comfort and usefulness of its people. . . .

I feel like saying to the Brethren everywhere that now is the time to sow the pure seeds of Gospel Truth in the West. . . .

John Kline's and John Metzger's interest in evangelism (sowing the "pure seed of Gospel truth in the West") was unusual. The Brethren at that time were very low key. They did not aggressively seek converts and had a hearty distrust for camp meetings and revival meetings. Elder Sturgis' straightforward conversion on his own initiative was the most common way of entering the frater-

* The "West" for John Kline was Indiana—J.H.L.

nity. Elder Gibson's reply when young Sturgis asked for
a book of doctrine and practice is revealing.

Elder D. B. Sturgis

It is said that late one afternoon, about 1833, while
raking cornstalks in the field, for burning, Elder Isham
Gibson was approached by a neatly dressed young man
known in the sparsely settled community as Dr. Sturgis,
or more fully Daniel B. Sturgis. Elder Gisbon had
known the young man a few years, and had often had
him in his congregation when preaching, and had con-
versed with him several times. The father of young
Sturgis was once a wealthy farmer, but losing his splendid possession by going on security bonds, he moved to
eastern Tennessee where Daniel was born June 17, 1811.
Another move when the boy was three years old brought
the family to Montgomery County, Ohio, and still
another in 1822 to Green County, Ill., near the
Macoupin County line, and about eighty miles
northwest of Vandalia, at that time the new capital of
the state. Illinois was then very sparsely settled. Only
two years before two men had been paid twenty-five
dollars to move the state records from Kaskaskia to a
hunter's ranch eighty-five miles, and so new was the
county that the men had to use their axes in opening
through the woods a way wide enough for the small cart
containing the valuable cargo. This ranch became Vandalia and was the nearest post office for the Sturgis
family. Mail was received twice a year. The nearest grist
mill was twelve miles distant.

There were no schools in the community and the
bright boy, ever eager for information, had to study of
nights by the blazing light of the fireplace. When Daniel
was fourteen years old his father died, leaving the
mother and two daughters to the support of the lad. Un-
daunted by the handicap he determined to make
something of himself. He worked during the day and
studied of nights, reading everything he could get hold

Elder D.B. Sturgis

of, even infidel books. One Sunday morning when about nineteen, barefoot, thinly clad, wearing a broken straw hat, he met up with Elder Gibson, who was on his way to one of his appointments, and greeted him about thus: "Well, I presume you are like all the other preachers." "In what way?" said Gibson. "Neither believe nor practice what the gospel teaches" was the reply. "What part of the gospel do you refer to?" the elder asked. The young man then named the church ordinances and some other points. Gibson assured him that he believed, taught, and practiced all of them. And thus the conversation continued until the place of meeting was reached. The boy had become so interested that he decided, in spite of his rude appearance, to enter the house, but keep out of sight as much as possible. As the sermon proceeded he became so entranced that the end of the discourse found him well up in front. Realizing his ridiculous appearance he made quick work of getting out, mounting his horse and disappearing.

That sermon took hold of him and he never got away from it. He kept up his studies, passed, without a teacher, an examination for teaching, entered the schoolroom, and took up the study of medicine. In a little while he was serving as a farmer, teacher and country doctor. This was the situation when he approached Elder Gibson in the cornfield. He had become interested in the elder and his church, and now we find him approaching Gibson saying that if his church has a discipline he would like to get the loan of the book. Gibson assured him that the church had such a book, and on going with him into the house handed him the small black book taken from the mantel. On opening the book the doctor explained, "Elder, this is the New Testament." "Very well," said Gibson, "That is our discipline." A little later at the age of twenty-two he entered the church by confession and baptism, Gibson performing the rite. At twenty-five he was called to the ministry, and at thirty ordained, Elder George Wolfe delivering the charge.

[Here is the ordination certificate:]

> This is to clarify that at a meeting appointed at Bro. Isham Gibson's, on Apple Creek, in Morgan County, Illinois, by the request of the church, Daniel B. Sturgis was ordained a bishop of the church of Fraternity of Baptist, by the laying on of hands of the Presbytery [see Chapter Three p. 86] on the eleventh day of September, in the year of our Lord, 1841. Given under our hands the day and date above written.
>
> George Wolfe
> Isham Gibson

When the Brethren did seek to bring someone into the church, it was usually done in restrained personal visits with people in the community whom they had sometimes known for years. That was the case with Aunt Rachel Stoner, and the joy her decision brought was apparently felt beyond the bounds of this world. The following is taken from a letter written on Friday evening, July 12, 1840, by Sophia Lightner of the Pipe Creek Church in Maryland to her uncle, John Bonsack at Stoners Store, Virginia, Roanoke County. It has never before been published.[6] I have reproduced it with Sophia's inimitable spelling intact and have added comments in brackets only where she obviously lost her battle with the English language. Her warm heart was exceeded only by her delightful syntax.

Sophia's Letter

. . . dear Uncle I have great joy to tell you, for if the Angle in heaven rejoises, we poor mortals may, and the cause of joy was this, Old Aunt Rachel Stoner was baptized last Tuesday a week. She had the meeting in her house, and Upton helped to fix the water and dam it up

This woman is younger and the photo is more recent, but Aunt
Rachel's baptism must have been something like this

in the meadow back of there orchard. She stood it very
well, and appeared very happy afterward. O she said
God be praised in time and in eternity for what he has
done for her. She said thies ten years she had a load on
her heart and now it was removed. She said I should give
her love to you, and tell you that when you was to see
her, you gave her so nuch incouragement. You tole her
if she would let the Breatherine [Brethren] know, they
would help. Last fall when Sarah [Sarah Righter Major]
was with us, we went to see her and she said if God
would spare her till warmer weather she would try to get
further. Well, some time after you left in the spring, I
dreamed I was with her and reminded her of the promis
she made and I thought we wept together. After I woke I
still had to think of my dream, and it seemed as if
something still said I must now do as I dremp. I went
and we soon got to discoursing and I tole her I would
help her and tell the breatherine if she wisht me to do so.
She said I should, and they visited her and her desire
where [were] fulfilled. I will also let you know that old
Grandmother Cuney is dead. . . .

The "Breatherine" sometimes referred to themselves
as the *Old* Brethren. Especially in later decades when the
church was in turmoil, they would look back on
Sophia's day when the fellowship was warm and united
and the elders venerable and firm. Then they would
speak fondly of the Old Brethren.

CHAPTER
2

Chapter Two
The Book As It Reads

The Brethren were a peculiar people—not strange or mysterious, although by those who did not know them they were thought to be both—but separate and distinctive. They came to this country in two groups, landing in 1719 and 1729, from a little noticed beginning in Schwarzenau, Germany, in 1708. They brought with them their German language and German culture and retained both well into the latter half of the nineteenth century. If their culture was of the Old World, their economics and agriculture were of the new. They quietly and rather uneventfully made themselves at home, enjoying the religious freedom, following the frontier, and growing in numbers. Their faith was of neither world for they believed that the New Testament enjoined them to shun this world. They were industrious and honest, the former quality leading frequently to prosperity and seldom to excessive wealth, the latter to solid reputations. It was not uncommon to

Das Evangelium des Matthäus.

Das 1. Capitel.

Christi Geschlechts = Register, Empfängniß, Name und Geburt.

Dieß ist das buch von der geburt JESU Christi, der da ist ein sohn Davids, des sohns Abraham.

2. Abraham * zeugete Isaac; Isaac † zeugete Jacob; Jacob ‡ zeugete Juda und seine Brüder;

*1Mof.21,2.3. †1Mof.25,26. ‡1Mof.29,35.

3. Juda * zeugete Pharez und Saram, von der Thamar; Pharez † zeugete Hezron, Hezron zeugete ‡ Ram; *1Mof.38,29.30. †1Chron.2,5.9. ‡Ruth4,19.

4. Ram zeugete * Aminadab, Aminadab zeugete Nahasson, Nahasson zeugete Salma;

*1Chron.2,10.

5. Salma zeugete Boas, * von der Rahab; Boas zeugete Obed, † von der Ruth; Obed zeugete ‡ Jesse; *Ruth4,21. Jof.2,1. †Ruth4,17. ‡Ruth4,22.

6. Jesse * zeugete den König David, der König David † zeugete Salomo, von dem weibe des Uria. *1Chron.2,15. †2Sam.12,24.

7. Salomo * zeugete Roboam, Roboam † zeugete Abia, Abia zeugete Assa; *1Kön.11,43. †1Chron.3,10.

8. Assa zeugete *Josaphat, Josaphat zeugete †Joram, Joram zeugete ‡Osia; *1Kön.15,24. †1Kön.22,51. ‡1Chron.3,11.

9. Osia zeugete *Jotham, Jotham zeugete †Achas, Achas zeugete ‡Ezechia; *2Kön.15,7. †2Kön.16,1. ‡2Kön.16,20.

10. Ezechia zeugete * Manasse, Manasse zeugete † Amon, Amon zeugete ‡Josia; *2Kön.20,21. †2Kön.21,18. ‡2Kön.21,24.

11. Josia zeugete * Jechonia und seine brüder, um die zeit der babylonischen gefangenschaft. *1Chron.3,15.

12. Nach der babylonischen gefangenschaft zeugete Jechonia * Sealthiel, Sealthiel zeugete Zorobabel; *1Chron.3,17.

13. Zorobabel zeugete Abiud, Abiud zeugete Eliachim, Eliachim zeugete Asor;

14. Asor zeugete Zadoch; Zadoch zeugete Achin; Achin zeugete Eliud.

15. Eliud zeugete Eleasar; Eleasar zeugete Matthan; Matthan zeugete Jacob;

16. Jacob zeugete Joseph, den mann Maria, von welcher ist geboren JESUS, der da heißt *Christus.] *c.27,17.22.

17. Alle glieder von Abraham bis auf David sind vierzehn glieder. Von David bis auf die babyloni=

A page from Luther's translation of the New Testament, published in 1836 by Henry Kurtz.

hear it said, "A Dunker's word is as good as his bond," and it was.

By name, they were frequently called German Baptists, from their country of origin and their distinctive baptism. This was made a part of their legal name in 1836 when the Yearly Meeting agreed upon Fraternity of German Baptists. In 1871 the Yearly Meeting changed this to German Baptist Brethren; and in 1908 the church, now English in language and increasingly American in culture, dropped the German and the Baptist and settled simply upon Church of the Brethren, which name continues to this day. Outsiders called them Dunkers after the word tunken, a German verb meaning to dip. Tunker was a more German version of the word, and Dunkard a more vulgar. They were sometimes called Old or Ancient Brethren to distinguish them from the New or River Brethren, who were like them in external appearances, different in some practices, and more recent in origin. Among themselves, they had no other name but Brethren.

From their beginning the Brethren took the New Testament at its word. They were serious on this point for they took their religion straight, unadulterated, and uninterrupted. H. R. Holsinger, who was forced to leave the church in 1882, looked back on the Brethren in 1901 and wrote:

> In the first place, what they believe and teach may be comprehended in the statement that they accept the New Testament as their creed and discipline. That is, the New Testament as it is, and not as they would have it, or as they understand it, but as it reads. They believe that the Book is inspired by God, has been preserved by His almighty power, and translated into various languages through his direct instrumentality; that the Book means

what it says, and says what it means, nothing more and
nothing less, and is not to be added to nor taken from,
and will suffer no deviations. That is Tunkerism, briefly
but accurately stated.[1]

The Brethren believed the New Testament contained
God's will for His people; it was therefore the task of the
Christian to take what he found there, believe it, and as
simply as possible practice it. The New Testament was
the discipline of the church. That was the difference
between the Brethren and some of their Christian
neighbors whom they called "worldly."

There were few Christian churches in the 1840s who
would not have agreed that the New Testament was
God's word, to be taken seriously as it was found.
However, some would have added to the New Testament corpus traditions long practiced, doctrines going
beyond the Scripture, and a well-defined creed. From
their earliest days the Brethren avoided all these and
would say with particular pride that they had no creed.
There are churches in our present day who would agree
that traditions and interpretation should not be allowed
to dilute the Scripture. They have said that the *word* is
divinely inspired, must be taken as it is, and disciplines
all thought; the Brethren would have agreed with these
churches but for one difference in emphasis.

They were more concerned with the way it disciplined
practice than *thought*. The niceties of doctrinal clarity
were far less important than the necessity for correct
practice. It was the duty of the church to ascertain from
the New Testament how the Christian should live and
how the church should be than to do so and to be so.
The Brethren were more disturbed if someone deviated
from the practices of the church than if he formed a
slightly peculiar theological idea. The latter rarely

happened, however, for unanimity in practice tended to produce consensus on doctrine, especially since intellectual inquiries into matters of faith were discouraged. The minutes of the Yearly Meetings for the 1840s are full of questions of practice; there are few issues of doctrine. The Brethren were a practical people; it was not only what you *thought* about Jesus Christ but what you *did* when you joined his church. Peter Nead wrote in 1834:

> I have stated, that it is the duty of the believer to unite himself to that church which has no other rule for her government but the New Testament, not in word only, but in deed; for there are many who say they have no other rule but the New Testament, and yet do not keep house in the church agreeably to that blessed book. . . .[2]

There is nowhere that the Brethren systematically spelled out their faith. Peter Nead published several works which elucidate the faith and practice of the Brethren in a rambling sort of way. After having said that the New Testament was at the heart of the matter and Jesus Christ the focus of faith, the Brethren had much that was important and nothing that was dominant. This was one of their virtues for they had nothing out of which to create a fanatical religion. There are, however, several basic convictions they held and a number of indispensible practices they followed. The remainder of this chapter I will address to their convictions.

Nonconformity to the World

The World, what is this? Not that *world which God has made, and behold it was all very good*; which we may use, so as not to abuse it; 1. Cor. 7:31—not that world, which is divinely regulated by times, seasons and other natural laws, in which the day is given us for labor, and the night for rest, the seedtime for sowing, and the harvest-time for gathering in the fruits of the earth, and to which regulation all, the saint as well as the sinner ... must conform, or suffer the penalty of transgression. No—not that world is meant, when ... the apostle says to believers, *Be not conformed to this world* ... but that present evil world of mankind, which has been deceived by Satan into disobedience and proud rebellion against God and his laws, and which has so readily and foolishly imbibed that wicked principle of their deceiver—*pride*;—this world it is, to which we are not to be conformed. ... there is nothing more frequently inculcated, nothing more strongly enforced in the New Testament than the contrast between this world and the kingdom or church of Christ. ...[3]

If there was anything the Brethren were tempted to take too seriously, it was nonconformity. While they had not yet done so in the 1840s, by the end of the century they were so concerned about the matter that they had discussed at Annual Meeting style of hair and cut of coat. While Brethren successfully avoided the idolatry of a creed, they may be said to have nearly succumbed to an idolatry in this conviction. However, in the 1840s they had not yet fallen into their later rigidities, and nonconformity was both flexible as a practice and vital as a heartfelt concern.

The Brethren recognized with unusual vigilance how easily the good things of this world can become the sole object of attention to the exclusion of our deeper and ultimately more satisfying relations with God and others. The "world" was an ill-defined, emotion-laden term, but it meant to the Brethren at least three things: (1) the unnecessary adornment that persons add to the otherwise acceptable material richness of our Earth; (2)

Self-denial sometimes
made the Brethren stern

the cultural refinements that people add to the otherwise straightforward relations to be had between persons; and (3) the ceremony with which people cloud their relations with God. In the first case, a material creation which God meant to be enjoyed and managed with good stewardship becomes an end in itself. In the second case, relations between persons meant to be loving and honest became self-centered and adorned with false manners. Finally relations with God became cluttered with culture and tradition that obscure the simplicity of His love and majesty of His power. In short, persons became centered on this world in their materials, their relations, and their religion. This the Brethren did not want to do. The New Testament commanded them not to: "And be not conformed to this world: but be ye transformed by the renewing of your mind, that ye may prove what is that good, and acceptable, and perfect will of God" (Rom. 12:2 KJV).

Peter Nead wrote: "The riches, honors, and pleasures of this world are very tempting, and that the people of God be not overcome, let them be humble, keep down at the feet of Jesus, and they are safe."[4] The Brethren resisted the world by keeping their homes simple and spartanly furnished (without carpets, fancy furniture, and the like), their meetinghouses low, roughhewn, and bare of design or device, and their clothing dark, simple, and unadorned. "It is very dangerous and certainly unbecoming . . . to imitate the world in its costly and unnecessarily adorning of the body, such conduct is indicative of a high mind," wrote Elder Nead.[5]

Ironically, by avoiding expensive luxuries, the Brethren inevitably became prosperous. They avoided the *adornments* of the world quite successfully in the 1840s only to begin to be faced with the temptations of its *riches*. They seem to have been known almost universally as prosperous. Not being spent for luxuries, the fruits of their hard work accumulated. It must be said, however, that while rich Dunker farmers were not unheard of and Brethren gatherings were known for the abundance of pies, pickles, apple butter, and homemade bread, there are few accounts of millionaires or unrestrained greed. They sometimes helped their non-Brethren neighbors and were especially careful to care for their own poor.

On the whole the Brethren in the 1840s survived the worst temptations of prosperity rather well and were still free to enjoy the abundance their newly developed land provided. They stayed free of adornment without becoming barren. It helped that they lived near the frontier where everyone had to live simply. In the latter part of the century, conveniences and luxuries were more readily available with the consequence that for awhile their nonconformity became more rigid and then began to diminish. If the unsullied life-style of the 1840s was partly necessary, it was in larger part chosen.

Paul Nead also wrote: "The people of God are a distinct and separate people, from the world—that is, they are of another character and party, engaged in a calling which is opposed to the sinful maxims, customs, and practices of the world;. . . ."[6] While riches and material luxuries are tempting, their temptation is obvious, the "sinful maxims, customs, and practices" that complicate human relations are more subtle. A man might resist the temptation to buy carpets but complicate his conversation with banal pleasantries or false courtesy. The Brethren valued straightforwardness, encouraged each other to be uncomplicated in business matters, and generally said what they meant. More formal society found the Brethren crude or at least uncultured, but entirely trustworthy. What they lacked in broad knowledge and fashionable manners, they made up for in simple hospitality and natural courtesy.

Finally, in order not to complicate relations with God, they avoided creeds, kept their worship simple and unliturgical, did not allow a trained ministry, and forbade musical instruments.

Moderation was the appropriate expression of nonconformity. "Let your moderation be known unto all men" (Phil. 4:5 KJV). Material abundance was not wrong but greed and showiness were. Courtesy was obviously to be desired, but elaborate manners not. Singing was enjoyed; instruments were too much. Even in the use of tobacco and alcohol, the Brethren were not as much concerned with total abstinence as Brethren of recent decades have been, but they were known as a consistently sober and clean living folk. There were, however, some things which were rather strictly forbidden—higher education, culture and the fine arts, professional careers and service in civil government. In these instances, not moderation, but avoidance, was counseled.

Again, Peter Nead: "It was pride that necessitated nonconformity. Now all those who plead for the foolish and giddy fashions of the world . . . must surely have a proud heart, and not willing to walk in the path of self-denial. . . . 'for that which is highly esteemed among men is abomination in the sight of God' (Luke 16:15)"[7]

The Brethren knew that any earthly good, whether material, human, or religious, can be put in the place of its creator and used by a person to justify himself or demonstrate his merit. That is pride—forgetting God, taking His creation for one's own, and esteeming oneself for the success or mastery one has in it. If that is not an abomination, it is at least an empty pleasure. The belief that persons given half a chance will do that was the theological basis for nonconformity, though in practice it was sometimes the spareness of frontier life or the pressure of the church that made it work. This conviction made their self-denial sometimes harsh, but it also provided for a balanced life-style.

Defenselessness

In regard to our being altogether defenseless, not to withstand the evil, but overcome evil with good. Considered, that the nearer we follow the bright example of the Lamb of God, who willingly suffered the cross, and prayed for his enemies; who, though heir of all things, had on earth not where to lay his head—the more we shall fulfill our high calling and obtain grace to deny ourselves for Christ's and his gospel's sake, even to the loss of our property, our liberty, and our lives[8]

In 1831, Elder George Wolfe moved from Union County to Adams County, Illinois, some seventeen miles east of Quincy. J. H. Moore, in his book *Some Brethren Pathfinders*, described an event that occurred shortly thereafter:

Elder Wolfe and his people had not been in Adams County very long before a draft was levied for men to do military service in the Black Hawk War. He and some of his brethren were drafted. He at once mounted his horse and rode off to the Capital to have a talk with the governor. He so greatly impressed the governor with his fine, pleasing and intelligent personality that he is said to have been received with marked cordiality. The governor listened to his story, how he had come from the east, settled in Illinois when it was yet a wilderness, how he had built up and nourished a body of law-abiding Christian people on New Testament principles, that as they understood these principles, they could not and would not accept military service, and if there was no way to avoid, or be excused from military duties, they would have to return to the places whence they came. But the governor at once told him that he and his people need not leave the State, that they should remain right where they were, for added the governor, we need people like you to produce supplies for those engaged in the service. The governor turned to his desk and quickly wrote an exemption notice excusing the elder and all his members from active military service. Returning home with this document, he read it to his people. It made a sensation in the neighborhood for a few weeks.[9]

Aside from demonstrating Elder Wolfe's boldness, the story is a good example of the defenselessness the Brethren have held to throughout their history.

Now to harm intentionally and purposely a fellow-creature in any way, is directly and absolutely contrary to this principle [love to all mankind]. Hence the Brethren have always felt it their solemn duty to abstain from all revengeful actions, from all war and bloodshed, and from doing *violence* to *any man*, either in his person or in his character or any way whatever.[10]

Quite simply the Brethren opposed violence of any kind, and permitted no member to engage in it, either in protection of self, family, and property, or in military service. This was in the beginning and remains the official position of the Brethren. However, in the 1970s a member may enter the military and remain in the church. In the 1840s no member served in the military. Henry Kurtz wrote:

While there are some and perhaps many among our Brethren ... who *before* they became members, had been serving and *mustering* in the *militia*, and a few even may have been actively engaged in *military service* and

IN WAR, we can safely say, that no brother, who was in
full use of his mental facilities, ever could be found in
the military ranks.[11]

Defenselessness was made a test of membership. When
an applicant was brought before the church council to
be examined he was asked to declare his agreement with
this principle.

Obviously, this principle was tested only in war time.
The U.S. government maintained neither a large standing army nor a draft during peacetime. It was relatively
easy for the Brethren to keep their young men from
entering the army or the state militia when to do so was
voluntary. But wartime brought mandatory service for
all eligible men. It was backed up with the threat of fines
and imprisonment. In that instance the Brethren would
go (and still do) to the government and request a special
dispensation. George Wolfe was fortunate to receive an
outright exemption. Usually the government required
the payment of money at least in exchange for exemption. And sometimes no exemption was granted and
prison or military duty were the only alternatives. The
period of the 1840s saw no conscription so the
Brethren's position was not being tested. The Brethren
were little troubled between the Revolutionary War and
the Civil War. However, in both those wars some
Brethren suffered for their adherence to their unusual
doctrine. The 1831 incident was a rare occurrence during
the first half of the eighteenth century.

The Brethren were careful not to construe their
defenselessness as disrespect toward the civil government. They believed that God ordained the government
and its leaders for the order of this world and for
restraining its evil. They paid their taxes and obeyed its
strictures in every instance—unless it ordered them to
do something contrary to the New Testament. In that

event they obeyed this higher authority. For the most part the Brethren were respected and appreciated because except for this doctrine they were model citizens and entirely law-abiding. The governor was obviously impressed with Elder Wolfe and his people.

The Sermon on the Mount is where the Brethren found their instruction in defenselessness: (Matt. 5:38-39 and 43-44 KJV)

> Ye have heard that it hath been said, an eye for an eye, and a tooth for a tooth: But I say unto you, that ye resist not evil; but whosoever shall smite thee on thy right cheek, turn to him the other also.

> Ye have heard that it hath been said, Thou shalt love thy neighbour, and hate thine enemy. But I say unto you, Love your enemies, bless them that curse you, do good to them that hate you, and pray for them which despitefully use you, and persecute you.

But they also turned to another Scripture: (2 Cor. 10:3-4 KJV):

> For the weapons of our warfare are not carnal, but mighty through God to the pulling down of strong holds; Casting down imaginations and every high thing that exalteth itself against the knowledge of God, and bring into captivity every thought to the obedience of Christ.

Defenselessness had its active side as well, wherein spiritual "weapons" were used to destroy "imaginations." Henry Kurtz cites a Quaker writer and agrees with him, ". . . a state of subjugated passions is the great characteristic mark of a true Christian . . ."[12] The erstwhile soldiers of men upon entering the church are to be soldiers of Christ, subjugating passions not persons. What the Brethren lacked in violence toward others, they sometimes made up for in stringent discipline of themselves.

The doctrine of defenselessness turns on the nature and use of power. The Brethren, of course, had no quarrel with using physical (material and human) power in pursuing their agriculture and establishing their homes, although they practiced gentleness with animals. They used and endorsed personal and spiritual power (persuasion, prayer, and exhortation), sometimes of great force, in dealing with each other. But they refused to use physical power against another human being.

Nonlitigation

There was another sort of power the Brethren were enjoined not to use—legal power. Any resort to the law was strictly forbidden both between members and nonmembers. The Brethren took Matthew 18:15-17 literally.

> Moreover if thy brother shall trespass against thee, go and tell him his fault between thee and him alone; if he shall hear thee, thou hast gained thy brother.
>
> But if he will not hear thee, then take with thee one or two more, that in the mouth of two or three witnesses every word may be established.
>
> And if he shall neglect to hear them, tell it unto the church: but if he neglect to hear the church, let him be unto thee as a heathen and a publican. (KJV)

When a dispute, even a serious one, arose between two members it was the plaintiff's first responsibility to go to his antagonist. If the man or woman refused to hear him, the next step was to take one or two other persons with him and try again. If this did not succeed, he then put the matter before the church. If the church in council was unable to effect a reconciliation, the offending member was "put into avoidance" (excommunicated). If he continued to be stubborn (for instance, he owed the other member a large sum of money), the creditor was still not allowed to sue in civil court.

If one of the Brethren had a complaint against a nonmember, and the man did not respond to the brother's requests, there was nothing he could do to enforce his complaint. And if a suit was brought against one of the Brethren, he was expected not to defend himself.

Peter Nead states the position:

> When we speak thus concerning the law, some infer that we mean that the children of God are to oppose the civil powers. But not so—for I say it is right, and agreeable to the will of God, that as long as there are lawless and disobedient persons on the earth, that there should exist a civil authority; and when I say that the children of God are not under the law, I mean that they are not to make use of the law, so as to compel any of their fellow mortals into measures, or to bring any of them unto punishment. No, no—the children of God must not take vengeance of any man.[13]

Nonswearing

When a new member was received into the church, he was asked to declare his agreement with three principles. Two of them, defenselessness and nonconformity, we have already discussed. The third was the refusal of the Brethren to use oaths—called by them the principle of nonswearing. While this was not as obvious a part of Brethren life as nonconformity or trine immersion, it was so important that it was one of the three principles referred to in the membership examination. Their reason for opposing oaths was a simple and straightforward acceptance of Jesus' words in the Sermon on the Mount. (Matt. 5:33-37 KJV)

> Again, ye have heard that it hath been said by them of old time, Thou shalt not forswear thyself, but shalt perform unto the Lord thine oaths;
>
> But I say unto you, Swear not at all; neither by heaven; for it is God's throne:
>
> Nor by the earth; for it is his footstool: neither by Jerusalem; for it is the city of the great King.
>
> Neither shalt thou swear by thy head, because thou canst not make one hair white or black.
>
> But let your communication be, Yea, yea; Nay, nay: for whatsoever is more than these cometh of evil.

When the Brethren required of each other no swearing they were not thinking primarily of profanity. That a brother or sister should not be profane went almost without saying, was clearly called for in the third commandment, and was to be expected of the unworldly softspoken Brethren. They were much more concerned with the swearing of oaths in court. The Brethren believed a man should always be honest and sincere so that his *yes* could always be taken truly for a *yes* and his *no* for a *no*. Peter Nead wrote, "The followers of Christ ought to be men of truth, so that their word may be received without an oath." He also said in regard to the above passage from Matthew, "This is so plain that it needs no comment."[14] While the Brethren were concerned not to take God's name in vain they were also concerned for the basic honesty that they felt a Christian life should reflect. Apparently, they were consistent enough in living by this precept to have earned a reputation for being exceedingly trustworthy people, whose *yea* was a reliable *yea*.

Commentary

Nearly everything the Brethren held was directed toward an action or practice. Being a member of the Fraternity meant not only believing the truth as the New Testament revealed it, but living it directly. The convictions discussed in this chapter were not doctrines only; they were elements of a life-style which the Brethren believed Christ called for. They ruled the members' practical relations with each other, with the civil government and with the secular society. That is what this chapter has been about. The next chapter will be about the special practices that shaped and expressed the inner life of the church—the things the Brethren did together and for each other. These, like their convictions, were defined directly by the New Testament and were a straightforward attempt to do what the book said.

CHAPTER 3

Chapter Three
The Ordinances of the Lord

T he church, which is the body of Christ, will be found in a state of self-denial, walking in all the ordinances and commandments of the Lord, blameless.[1]

Baptism

. . . it is very necessary, before entering the water, for the Administrator to kneel down with the candidate, and supplicate a throne of mercy; after which, let the Administrator lead the subject into the water, and when they arrive to a suitable place, let the candidate kneel down in the water. . . . After the candidate has bowed himself, he must then make a good profession, before God and many witnesses, as Paul tells us Timothy did, (1 Tim. 6:12). . . . the Administrator will then proceed to baptize the believer, in the name of the Father, and of the Son, and of the Holy Ghost, by immersing him three times in the water.[2]

Baptism was important and distinctive in the 1840s.

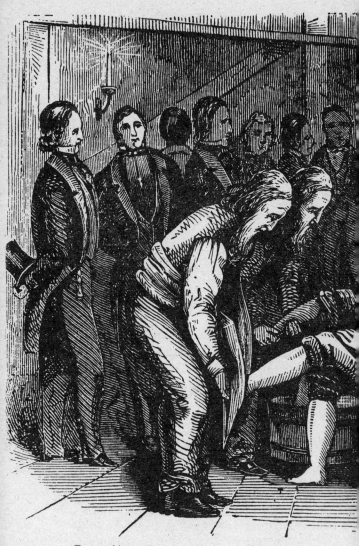

Feet washing, a Brethren rite preceding Communion.

When outsiders thought of the Brethren they thought of their peculiar baptism. Both the formal name German Baptists and the slang names Dunker or Dunkard were derived from this practice. It must have been a curious sight to neighbors and nearby townspeople to see the brethren and sisters, long beards and bonnets, gathered about a meadow stream watching the elder immerse a new brother or sister. This method was strange to Christians of other denominations. Sometimes they would debate the Brethren over trine immersion. One particularly colorful debate took place in 1853 between James Quinter and a Lutheran minister. H. R. Holsinger recounts that:

> I attended a four-days discussion on baptism between Elder Quinter and Joseph Fitchner, a Lutheran preacher. The debate was held in the vicinity of Claysburg, Blair County, Pennsylvania, in the winter of 1853. In this discussion Elder Quinter showed his Christian manhood and strength of purpose to perfection. It was, in the estimation of the writer, a fiery ordeal, almost equal to martyrdom. It appeared as though Mr. Fitchner was determined to break down his opponent by provocation. He taunted him, mocked him, ridiculed him, and did everything that he thought might provoke Brother Quinter and throw him off his guard, but Brother Quinter appeared to be clothed with a coat of mail, proof against the darts of his enemy. Nothing but the grace of God could sustain a man under such trial.
>
> Brother S. B. Furry, of Martinsburg, Pennsylvania, who also attended the debate says of Mr. Fitchner's manner of discussion: "He simply misrepresented and ridiculed his opponent. In reference to Paul's baptism, he said, 'Paul could not have been immersed; why, he was so sick, he could not even raise his head.' As he said this, he let himself down almost to the pulpit to give

emphasis to his assertion. On another occasion, Quinter asked permission to correct some of Fitchner's misstatements. Fitchner stepped back, leaned against the wall, and granted permission. Quinter proceeded very mildly when he was suddenly cut short by Fitchner stepping forward, and, with defiant gesture, crying out, "I will not yield my stand if hell resist."

I will add one more incident. Fitchner said he would now "give out" a Tunker hymn, and this is his hymn:

> Ho, every son and daughter,
> Here's salvation in the water,
> Come and be immersed,
> O, come and be immersed!

And as he repeated these words he would duck his head down to his knees, in the most dramatic style, in derision of the Tunker mode of baptism.[3]

Not all debaters were this abusive; most opponents were courteous. The Brethren always won, at least when a Brother retold the story. I presume that the opponent's constituency believed *he* won.

That immersion was the proper and only method the Brethren were wholly convinced, and to marshal their arguments they appealed to some well-respected sources. Peter Nead quoted John Calvin, Martin Luther, and John Wesley. Henry Kurtz published excerpts from the noted historian Philip Scharf. The evidence seemed to support the Brethren case. Their argument centered on two points: (1) the Greek word for baptize means to dip into or cover over with water completely; and (2) John's baptism of Jesus was a complete immersion in the Jordan River after which he came "straightway . . . up out of the water" (Mark 1:10). It was a good argument, made even better by the words of prominent non-Brethren. But argument aside, immersion was right by tradition, for the original eight began that way by immersion in the Eder River at Schwarzenau in 1708.

That it should be a three-fold (trine) immersion was not so clear-cut. Elder Nead argued from the great commission that they should immerse once in the name of each member of the trinity. "Go ye therefore, and teach all nations, baptizing them in the name of the Father, and of the Son, and of the Holy Ghost" (Matt. 28:19 KJV). Beyond this they had little evidence except their own tradition.

There was one further detail the Brethren carefully adhered to—immersion was forward, not backward like the American Baptists. Peter Nead says:

> We can read nowhere in the Bible, or Testament, of any of the institutions or appointments of God being observed by presenting themselves before God upon their backs. . . . therefore, kneeling and falling upon the face will be observed in the administration of this sacred ordinance.[4]

Three times, face-forward, in the water, from a kneeling position remains the practice of the Church of the Brethren to this day, the important difference being that now the Brethren accept persons into membership on the basis of a baptism in another denomination.

The age of the candidate was no less important than the method. Persons were baptized only upon a mature choice. They usually waited until their early twenties or until marriage. They had to be ready to take up their adult lives, exercise independent judgment, and put behind worldly ways and youthful rambunctiousness. Children were not baptized. The Brethren wanted Christians who were there on their own choice, not their

Baptism in 1850

parents. It was a serious one and the person usually understood what was expected before making it. Baptism was for believers.

A careful order was followed, when baptism was administered. Yearly Meeting defined that order in 1848 (Article 3). It was still used in 1953 when I was baptized.

> First, the applicant to be examined by two or more brethren; then, the case to be brought before the church council, before whom the applicant is to declare his agreement with us, in regard to the principles of being defenseless, non-swearing, and not conforming to the world; then, in meeting, or at the water, to read from Matt. 18, verses 10 to 22, in public, the candidates being asked if they will be governed by those gospel rules; then, prayer at the water, and in the water, the following questions to be asked:
>
> Question: Dost thou believe that Jesus Christ is the Son of God, and that he has brought from heaven a saving gospel? Answer: Yea.
>
> Question: Dost thou willingly renounce Satan, with all his pernicious ways, and all the sinful pleasures of this world? Answer: Yea.
>
> Question: Dost thou covenant with God, in Christ Jesus, to be faithful until death? Answer: Yea.
>
> Upon this thy confession of faith, which thou hast made before God and these witnesses, thou shalt, for the remission of sins, be baptized in the name of the Father, and of the Son, and of the Holy Ghost. After baptism, while in the water, the administrator to lay his hands on the head of the candidate, and offer up a prayer to God in his behalf, and then the member is to be received, by hand and kiss into church-fellowship.[5]

Love Feast (The Ordinances of Feet-washing, the Lord's Supper, Communion, and the Salutation)

Feet washing

The Brethren loved their practices. They were less rote and more real than religious rites often are. This was partly because members had *chosen* the church. It was also because they enjoyed being together and the practices were *corporate* events. Love feast was very dear to the Brethren. It gathered in one celebration the most important strands of their life—the New Testament faith, their love for one another, the sacrament of Christ's body, order and discipline, and special practices common only to them.

The following account by H. R. Holsinger is of a love feast around 1850. I have edited it to make it fit this chapter.

> ... The members are all seated around long, immaculately white tables. .... the white caps of the sisters, framing pure and peaceful faces, ranged on either side of their separate tables, forms a picture which lingers long in the memory, in its unique and singular beauty. A narrow space along the walls of the church accommodates the audience, the outsiders, and thickly standing upon the benches which have been packed into this space, they gaze upon the scene before them with eager and unflagging interest, not seeming to be conscious of the long hours, nor of the fatigue attending their crowded and uncomfortable position. At a central table solemn and venerable men are conducting the service. A devout atmosphere pervades the house. The reverent voice of the officiating bishops arrests even the most careless ear, and all who are present feel that the place is holy, and that God himself is not very far away.
>
> The Tunker love-feast embraced a series of services, beginning usually on the forenoon of Saturday, and ending with a great assembly and a notable sermon on Sunday afternoon. If any other day was selected for the

The Lord's Supper

opening, substantially the same course was pursued. The
Saturday-forenoon service was followed by a dinner,
which was served to the whole congregation, having
been prepared in the kitchen apartment. The young people belonging to the Tunker families in the community
would assist in spreading the tables and waiting on the
people. It was not unusual for the dinner to continue until three o'clock in the afternoon, and from three to nine
hundred persons were fed. The menu varied somewhat,
according to the financial ability of the congregation. It
invariably consisted of the very best bread, good butter,
apple butter, pickles, and pies and coffee. If the church
could afford it, fresh beef was also supplied.

Illustrating the fact that the throng is often hungrier
for the loaves and fishes than for the spiritual gospel, it
was often necessary to appoint door-keepers to regulate
the crowd while the meal was in progress, and the
strongest men in the community were chosen for this office. The recess following this meal was enjoyed by the
members as a season of delightful social intercourse. In
later years, however this Saturday morning sermon and
dinner were abandoned by some congregations, and the
services began with the "examination" in the afternoon—a season of devout seriousness, a spiritual
preparation for the communion proper—which was
soon to follow.

1 Cor. 11:38 was read as a basis for one or more dis-
courses, after which the officiating elder would deliver
an exhortation to prayer, being careful to remark in conclusion that there would be perfect freedom to any one,
brother or sister, who might feel pressed to lead in open
prayer, and the season would close with the Lord's
Prayer. It was not unusual for three or four brethren to
exercise in prayer, but it was very unusual to hear a
sister pray on such or any other public occasion.

Then followed a short intermission after the announcement that the next service would be indicated by
singing, when the members who expected to participate
in the communion would take their seats on long

benches at the tables immediately on entering the house, so that the deacons might know whether sufficient table-room had been prepared.

The song having been completed, the thirteenth chapter of John was read to the end of the thirtieth verse. After reading the scripture, with suitable admonition, the washing of the feet began. . . . At this point those who had been appointed to lead would arise, two by two, lay aside their garments, gird each other with a white apron, pour water into a small vessel, and proceed, one to wash and the other to wipe the feet of such persons as might be prepared to receive the service. The first two would wash and wipe the feet of from six to ten or more persons, when they would be relieved by such other two persons as might volunteer. This was called the "double mode." By the "single mode" one person arose, commenced the service by laying aside his coat, girding himself, and washing and wiping the feet of the member seated next to him. Then he gave the towel to the person whom he had served, who would proceed in the same manner to number three. Thus the work continued to the last one on the bench at a table, who, in turn, served number one.

After having washed and wiped the feet, the members saluted each other with the holy kiss. . . .

Clear water and clean towels are supplied for cleansing of hands. Besides the esthetic purpose, this washing of the hands indicates the sacredness of the succeeding ordinances of the Lord's Supper and the Communion.

Feet-washing having now been concluded, the Lord's Supper was next placed on the table. Certain ones had prepared the food during former exercises. It consisted of bread, mutton or beef and soup made of meat broth. Thanks being offered, the meal was partaken of. After supper, during the singing of a hymn, the tables were cleared of everything except the cloths, which were turned. Then the Communion bread and wine were placed upon the table.

Then, usually, the nineteenth chapter of John was

read, followed by a dissertation on the sufferings of Christ, by some preacher of merit, and closed by the elder, with an admonition to love and other duties. During this exhortation the elder prepared the Communion bread by breaking the loaves into narrow slices indicated by slight indentures before baking. These were placed side by side and crossed until the process was complete, and was performed with much exactness, and observed by all within sight with as much solemnity as the ordinance itself.

Then the salutation was introduced, quoting I Cor. 16:20, "Greet ye one another with an holy kiss," or kindred passages. Then the elder would extend his right hand to and kiss the brother next to him. Thus the salutation would pass to the last brother at the last table, who would kiss the officiating elder, thus completing the circle. After having started the divine command with the brethren, the elder in charge extended the right hand of fellowship to one of the sisters occupying an end of the table, with instructions to pass the salutation among themselves, and he followed the line to see that it was properly observed.

The following remarks were then made by the elder in charge: "The apostle Paul says, 'I have received of the Lord that which also I delivered unto you, that the Lord Jesus the same night in which He was betrayed took bread, and when He had given thanks, He brake it.' So, in like manner, we will also return thanks for this bread." Than all arose, and thanks were given for and a blessing asked upon the bread. After all were again seated, he proceeded. "The apostle says, 'The bread which we break, is it not the communion of the body of Christ?' which is equivalent to affirming that it is. So I will say to my brother, Beloved brother, the bread which we break is the communion of the body of Christ," and while speaking these words, he breaks a small piece from the long slice and hands it to him. The larger piece, from which he had broken, is passed to number two, who repeats the same to brother number three, etc. One or

The Holy Kiss

The Holy Kiss

two sub-elders accompany the line with supplies of bread.

The leader then turns to the sister to whom he had extended the right hand of fellowship, saying, "Beloved sister, the bread which we break is the communion of the body of Christ," breaking a piece and handing it to her. This he repeats substantially to the next sister, breaking bread for and to every sister at the table.

Both circles having completed the breaking of the bread, the bishop remarks, "We have tarried one for another until all have been served, and we will now eat this bread, contemplating the sufferings of our Saviour." After all had eaten in silence, the white covering was removed from the wine, and two cups were filled. If several bottles were at hand, wine was poured from each one into each cup. This was done, we presume, to show that it was all alike. "After the same manner also He took the cup, when He had supped," is the bishop's next quotation, and he continues, "from which we conclude that as He had given thanks for the bread, He did also for the cup. Let us rise and give thanks for the cup."

When the members are seated again, he says, "Beloved brother, this cup of the New Testament is the communion of the blood of Christ," and hands a cup to whom he had broken bread; who, after taking a sip of wine, passes it to the next brother, and so on until the circle is complete, the leader partaking last of all. A sub-elder follows the line with a supply, replenishing the cup when required.

The same quotation is repeated to the sisters, as the bishop hands the cup to the first one. After taking a sip, she returns the cup to the bishop, who hands it to the next sister, and so on until all have been served. No matter how inconvenient it may be for the leader to give and have returned to him, the cup must be given to each sister by the officiating elder. . . .

During the passing of the cup the congregation

engages in singing, but during the breaking of bread
singing is not generally permitted.

The last quotation, to close the Communion, is now
repeated; "And they sang a hymn and went out." This is
followed by prayer and song, and the congregation may
consider itself dismissed.[6]

Love feast began with self-examination when each
member looked inward for any unrighted wrongs or un-
resolved grudges between himself and any other brother
or sister. If he found something he had to exclude
himself. Love feast was to be unstained by dissension.
Then John 13 was read to set the stage for the feet-
washing.

Peter Nead wrote, ". . . Feetwashing represents that
state of purification through which the believer must
pass, so as to be received at the coming of Christ. . . .[7] It
was also a symbol of the Christian's willingness to go
and help cleanse a brother or sister of trespasses by
humble admonishment, a task sometimes as difficult
and unpleasant as washing dirty feet. Feet washing
meant both cleansing from sin and service. Brethren in
1840 stressed the former; Brethren today stress the
latter.

Usually two of the oldest elders began the washing.
Most of the Brethren followed the "double mode" as
Holsinger describes it. However, the churches in Illinois,
Missouri, and Iowa used the "single mode." Known as
the "Far Western Brethren," they had lost contact with
the eastern part of the brotherhood for several decades
as they moved west. When they reemerged in the late
forties, the two groups discovered to their dismay that
they had dissimilarities. Feet washing was the most
critical issue in the debates that finally brought reconciliation in 1859. Those who washed saluted the
recipient with the holy kiss and the hand of fellowship.

THE ORDINANCES OF THE LORD

Then all washed their hands to be clean and fully prepared for the rites to come.

The Lord's Supper was an enjoyable affair with good food and fellowship. Brethren were counseled not to think only of feeding their bodies, but the food was not symbolic either. It was a common meal, the evening food, like the meal Jesus shared with his disciples in the upper room. Fellowship too was restrained for love feast was a solemn occasion, but brothers and sisters visited quietly. Unlike the communion of most churches, the Brethren love feast embraced the informal friendship of the members. The spirit of Christ lived not only in the seriousness of the bread and cup but in the good cheer of the partakers too. The supper reminded them of the great heavenly feast, "the marriage supper of the lamb, which the children of God shall celebrate in the evening of this world,"[8] when Christ returns. The New Testament is replete with banquet imagery. It seems God is not adverse to His people eating and has more feasting in store for the future. The Brethren recognized this and put it into practice. The meal was leisurely, for they took seriously the pleasant words from 1 Corinthians 11:33, "Wherefore, my brethren, when ye come together to eat, tarry one for another."

The meal was cleared away; the bread and wine were placed on the table. John 19, the chapter on Jesus' suffering and death, was read and amplified. All was prepared for communion, except for one event. The holy kiss and hand of fellowship were passed through the host with great deliberation—a marvelous act that bound the members together in body and affection in preparation for the final spiritual binding in holy communion. It is no wonder that the Brethren were as deeply knit as they were. One could not remain unmoved by this act.

The kiss and the hand (called together the salutation) were used often, sometimes informally, sometimes solemnly. Members greeted each other with it at meeting and elsewhere. At baptism those on the shore greeted the new members thus as he came up from the water. It was used when a deacon was installed, when a minister was elected or ordained, and after the feet-washing. Its most profound use was before the bread and cup. On this occasion the Brethren recalled the Christ's suffering and, not knowing when they might suffer likewise, they bound themselves together to be true to one another even in tribulation. It was based solidly in Scripture. Peter Nead wrote: ". . . I will venture to say that we have not, in the Bible or Testament, a plainer command of anything, than that of the observance of the Holy Kiss."[9] He also wrote: "The spiritual import of this performance is spiritual affection, and is intended to promote mutual love among the fraternity."[10] And that is what it did.

Finally the elder called everyone to rise, and gave thanks for the bread. Then he passed it to the brother next to him who broke off a piece and passed it on, each saying, as he did so, "Beloved brother, the bread which we break is the communion of the body of Christ." The cup of wine was passed in like manner, preceded by rising and giving thanks. After sipping it each brother passed it on with the words, "Beloved brother, this cup of the New Testament is the communion of the blood of Christ." The Brethren believed that men were head of the family and the church; women held no offices. Consequently the bishop or elder administered the bread and cup to each sister individually so that each would have received them from a man. It was a symbol of their supposed spiritual dependence upon men.

The service lasted four or five hours. After the com-

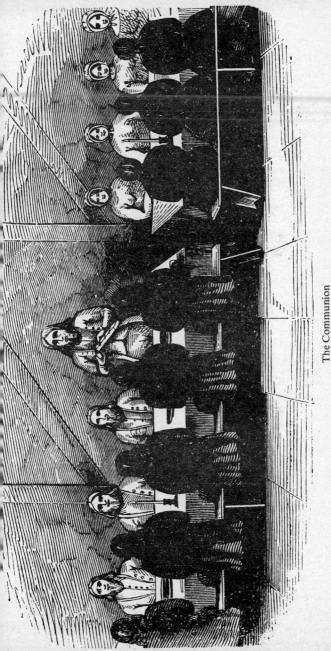

The Communion

munion, which was·the climax, it ended abruptly and
without fanfare. They took literally the Biblical description, "And they sang a hymn and went out." However,
sometimes they lingered on the benches though they had
been sitting for hours, still enjoying the rich fellowship
that was theirs.

The Laying On of Hands

Laying hands on a person enabled the holy spirit to
flow into him. Those whose hands were laid on did not
control the spirit; they provided the occasion for it
through their prayers and presence. This was a corporate act in which God's spirit was given to another
person through his brethren for a specific purpose. The
Brethren had three purposes for the rite. First, in baptism after the new Christian had been three times immersed, the elder placed his hands on the person's head
and prayed for him. The second occasion was at the ordination of an elder. Because the eldership was so important, ordination required a special act. So hands
were laid on, in this case by other elders only, and a
special blessing was asked. There was no mystical
transfer of power, but the Brethren did believe they were
setting the man apart for a special function. God's spirit
was called forth to seal that charge and to aid the new
elder. It was only after this that any man was fully em-
powered to exercise all offices of the ministry. The
Brethren sometimes called this "the laying on of hands
by the presbytery," a phrase taken from 1 Timothy 4:14,
the presbytery being the body of elders. (See Chapter
One, page 37 above).

The Brethren also laid hands on the sick. This was
usually at the request of the ill person or his family, and
was a special service different from either of the above.

Anointing

It was called the Anointing Service. They followed
James 5:14 to the letter. "Is any sick among you? let him
call for the elders of the church; and let them pray over
him, anointing him with oil in the name of the Lord"
(KJV). Two elders took oil (usually sweet oil) and put it
on the head of the sick person, after which they laid their
hands, one on top of the other, on his head and prayed
for healing and for the forgiveness of his sins.

The hands were laid on in baptism to bring cleansing
and faithfulness; in ordination to consecrate and
strengthen; in anointing to heal and make whole. All are
offices of the holy spirit, and in each case the church or
its representatives were the instrument. But the first two
were ordinances necessary to the church as well as the
individual. Anointing was instead a sort of privilege, a
gift to the individual Christian to lighten his suffering.
Peter Nead wrote: "Now, this is the privilege of the
afflicted sons and daughters of men; and if they do not
embrace this opportunity, it is their own fault." It is a
gift, however, that needs a receptive vessel. He added:
". . . they ought to make a complete surrender of
themselves into the hands of the Lord . . ." Anointing
was the one practice that was solely for the benefit of the
individual believer.

Commentary

The ordinances of the Brethren were corporate
experiences almost before they were anything. There
was little room for a lonely faith. A brother or sister did
not stand alone before God; he stood in the church with
Christ at its head. The closest he came to a private experience of God was in personal devotions and even
those were usually a family affair. Baptism was in the
presence and joy of all the members. Love feast was
deep in fellowship, each part binding the members

closer. Laying on the hands each time made the church or its officers the vehicle for God's activity. It was in the church and its ordinances that God was present. "For where two or three are gathered in my name, there am I in the midst of them" (Matt. 18:20 KJV). They were in it together. That is why among themselves they had no other name but *Brethren*.

CHAPTER 4

Chapter Four
The Fraternal Spirit of Worship

We have seen what the Brethren believed and some of their practices, but we have yet to know what they did when they came together for worship. A church is many things—faith to be sure, beliefs and moral injunctions to a greater or lesser degree, practices, fellowship, and even gossip. But somewhere near the heart of the member's experience with each other is common worship when everyone comes together—where the faith is reaffirmed, beliefs stated and defined, and fellowship enjoyed. If you wish to learn something about a church, look at its worship—which is what we will do in this chapter.

We have the good fortune of having two accounts of worship in or around 1850. The first is by H. R. Holsinger, born 1832, died 1905, who, being a minister with progressive ideas and an irrepressible if not contentious spirit, caused great turmoil in the brotherhood in the 1870s and who in 1882 was expelled from the church.

He, with several thousand others who left the church with him, formed a new group and called themselves the Brethren Church. He wrote and published in 1901 a history of his new denomination and of the other portions of the original Brethren fraternity.* In this book, *History of the Tunkers and the Brethren Church*, he sometimes looks back with fond nostalgia on his youth in the Fraternity of German Baptists. In this spirit he describes a typical worship service around the middle of the century in his home church. His affection for the church he left is undisguised, if not exaggerated into sentimentality. From him we get a cameo portrait of the Brethren.[1]

Julius Hermann Moritz Busch tells a different story. If Holsinger saw the special joy in being Brethren, Busch saw the peculiarities. Where Holsinger wrote with fond sentiment, Busch wrote with amused curiosity, liking the Brethren not less but seeing them as an interesting anomaly. Herr Busch was a German journalist who as a young man spent 1851 and 1852 in this country. Years later, after returning to Germany, J. H. M. Busch entered politics and before his death achieved sufficient distinction to go with his already imposing name by accompanying the German chancellor, Otto Von Bismarck, and chronicling much of his activity.

However, in 1851 he chronicled the activities of a group of persons of less eminence. He visited the Lower Stillwater church in southern Ohio and observed this congregation of Brethren at worship in a morning ser-

---

* In 1881 a group of several thousand withdrew from the Brotherhood and formed the Old German Baptist Brethren, still known by that name today and colloquially as the Old Order Brethren. These along with The German Baptist Brethren (now The Church of The Brethren), Holsinger's denomination (The Brethren Church), and several splinter groups, were included in this book.

vice and an evening love feast. Busch described this visit with the Brethren in a book entitled *Wanderungen Zwischen Hudson und Mississippi, 1851 and 1852 (Travels Between the Hudson and the Mississippi, 1851 and 1852)*, which he had published in Germany in 1854.[2] Following Holsinger's narrative is a portion of that account, translated into English by Dr. Donald F. Durnbaugh, professor at Bethany Theological Seminary.[3] The chief value of this account is of course in the detailed description of the Brethren at worship, but its charm lies in Busch's candor.

Holsinger's Account

Let us now take a look at the old meetinghouse and its surroundings. It usually stands in some stately grove of old oaks, but is not itself a stately or imposing edifice. It is generally a long, low building, capable of seating a large congregation, for the Brethren in old times worshipped in barns or private houses until they were sure that a house of worship would be permanently needed, and until they were well able to build large enough for the present and prospective population of the community. The old churches are all pretty much of the same style of architecture, and adapted to large congregations and communion purposes. On such occasions everybody attended, saints and gentiles. Neither inside nor outside was a dollar spent for any sort of ornamentation. The style of architecture was bare in its simplicity, and far removed from such vanities as spires, towers, stained windows, painted or cushioned pews, ornamental pulpits, or anything else which could not show the passport of indispensable utility.

Places for Meeting In 1850, less than half of the congregations had meetinghouses. The others met in homes, and sometimes in barns for love feast. In order to ac-

Movable partitions

Old Grove Church, Berlin, Pennsylvania. Home church of Holsinger. Site of Yearly Meeting, 1849.

commodate a large meeting in a home, the Brethren used a special construction. Partitions between rooms were made moveable so that the entire floor area could be opened up. Pages 98 and 99 show such moveable partitions. The picture is recent and the furnishings are therefore not what they would have been in the 1840s. Especially the carpets would not have been there, the Brethren believing that carpets contradicted their nonconformity and simplicity in living. The Brethren were sometimes reluctant to build meetinghouses, fearing that their worship would lose its intimacy and informality.

"Saints and Gentiles" The Brethren community was made up of more than the members. There were the young adults, sons and daughters of members, who had not yet joined the church, and who indulged in a somewhat "faster" lifestyle. There were relatives of members who had fondness for the church and often came to meetings but were unwilling to accept its full order. And there were frequently neighbors and townspeople who came around just to loiter or sometimes to have some fun at the expense of the mild Dunkers. Presumably by "gentiles" Holsinger meant persons of these three groups and by "saints" he meant the Brethren.

It included, also, a kitchen department, for the purpose of preparing the food part of the Lord's supper, as well as that of the common meals. . . . Many of the old houses also have a nursery, generally in the attic, and supplied with beds and cradles for the accommodation of sisters with young children and the aged and infirm.

Kitchens Kitchens were common in meetinghouses

because love feast required food preparation. They were uncommon in the church houses of other denominations.

Attics Meetinghouse attics were also used for accommodation for brethren or sisters who had come from too far away to return the same evening. This was especially true at love feast time when too many brethren to be kept in homes flocked to the meetinghouse. Long rows of beds were placed in the attic with a partition down the middle to separate men from women. Note this partition on the left side of the picture. With bare rafters, wood floors, and no heat, the attic was hardly first class accommodation. But what they lacked in comfort the Brethren from afar made up for in fellowship.

Let us stand among the grand old oaks, and witness the gathering of the faithful. Evidences of rural prosperity abound on every hand. The sleek, gentle horses bear testimony that "the righteous man regardeth the life of his beast." Blessed is the horse whose lot was cast with a good Tunker farmer. Think you not that he came to reflect the peaceful, unworldly, unambitious, and contented temper of his master? Their very looks and actions were in harmony with their belonging. I have seen a hundred horses lining the fences or standing by the great trees, and heard the joyous neigh of recognition ringing through the quiet Sabbath morn. There was no discord in the sound. There was rather the harmony and sympathy of friendship and joy, almost human in its intelligence, and none the less in its sincerity. The very horses entered into the fraternal spirit of the worshipers.

The Brotherhood of the Horses Even the Brethren horses liked to visit. Brother Holsinger is exaggerating a bit.

Interior of Blooming Grove Meetinghouse, six or seven miles north of Williamsport, Pa.

Meetinghouse kitchen. The faucet is a recent addition.

Meetinghouse attic.

However, the peacefulness of a master is reflected in the demeanor of his animals. Holsinger is coyly touching a theme he will return to frequently in this account. The Brethren valued brotherhood so highly that harmony and love were evident throughout their lives—even in their horses. Perhaps to an objective observer their horses were as contentious as anyone else's horses, but the owners were not, and that is really Holsinger's point.

The members, having alighted from their plain, almost crude vehicles, are greeting one another with the holy kiss. They linger around the church doors in quiet converse. It yet lacks ten minutes of the appointed hour for worship, but the worshipers have all arrived. There is an unwritten law against the late comer which no discreet Tunker will violate.

Our description concerns a typical Tunker congregation, such as could be seen anywhere in the fraternity about the middle of the nineteenth century. Meeting day, which was usually only once a month at the old church, was the great Sabbath of the month. All who were physically able to be out, were sure to be there. Tunker houses were closed that day, the whole family and the help at church. They never were and never will be more diligent in this respect than during the period mentioned. Duty called them to the house of God, but another and still louder call urged them. It was the call of love. They loved one another, and they loved to meet and greet each other at the doors of the sanctuary. They loved the plain gospel, full of consolation and rest. They loved the glorious congregational singing, which swelled triumphantly in the great church, and rolled its billows of sublime harmony out through windows and doors, and up through the solemn oaks toward heaven. They loved the preacher, who earnestly and honestly, and in their own language, spake

to them the Lord's message. He might not be able and
eloquent, but they cared little for these things. His honest
out-giving, the tones of his voice, his very looks, rested and
fed their souls. The polish and accomplishments of the
schools would have separated him from them. Rhetorical
language and flowery periods would have estranged them
from each other. The "manner of man" he was, became to
them eloquence and power.

Peace is written in the faces of young and old, in the
mild looks, the quiet kindness in every eye, the modulated
tones of brotherly love in every salutation. It is the con-
tagion of the place, and broods over all, so that one feels
himself immersed in an atmosphere of peace. The world
seems far away. Toil and care and worry are forgotten,
and you rest in the motherly arms of peace, as one that is
weary hastens to the enfolding of maternal love.

Meeting Once a Month It may come as a surprise that
the Brethren did not go to church every Sunday.
Congregations were spread over large areas; horse and
wagon travel was slow. Distances were simply too great
to travel every weekend. Frequently, there were several
preaching points, and "appointments" were made to
have ministers hold meetings there on a rotating basis.
Depending on the size of the congregation, a preaching
point near one's home came around every two to four
weeks. A congregation might have four preaching
points—two meetinghouses and two homes.

Sunday Schools The Brethren did not have Sunday
schools. They believed that the home was the place to
read the Bible and learn the faith and the parent the one
with the responsibility to teach. Nowhere did the Scripture designate Sunday schools.

"Having alighted from their plain, almost rude vehicles…"

Duty and Love Brethren did not go to meetings only out of duty. They genuinely enjoyed it. Holsinger is accurate when he says, "They loved to meet and greet each other at the doors of the sanctuary." And beyond that they did enjoy the preaching even though it was interminably long and often repetitious and unschooled. It was not uncommon for one preacher to preach an hour and for the whole preaching to last several hours. People in the last century appreciated the spoken word more than we do. We are constantly bombarded by words—from TV, radio, teachers, or the many persons we encounter in our crowded society. Not so in the sparsely settled rural areas where gatherings were infrequent, school seldom held, and of course no radio or TV. A speaker today needs to be skillful to retain our jaded attention, where he could in the 1840s simply say what was on his mind, even stumbling or repeating himself, and still keep his hearer's ear. Beyond that, plainness of delivery was appropriately not conforming to the world.

The congregation is in its place. Behind the long, unpainted table, instead of a pulpit, the long plain bench is filled with the elders and preachers. There are no upholstered chairs for this unpretentious clergy. They allow themselves no luxury denied to the people.

Ministers' Seating Arrangement There were sometimes as many as four or five ministers in a congregation, if it was large. They would all sit on a bench at a table in the front of the meetinghouse. The elder-in-charge, or overseer, would occupy the leading position. The deacons sat on the other side of the table facing the ministers and with their backs to the congregation or else on the front bench, called the deacon's bench.

A steady, strong, musical voice on the deacon's bench raises the tune, and soon the whole congregation join in the hearty singing. This was always the most attractive part of the old-time Tunker service. No congregation ever sang better. It was a beautiful, spiritual, refreshing worship, and the sound of an instrument in one of those old-time Tunker congregations, where every voice made "melody unto the Lord," would have seemed a discord and a profanation.

But the hymn, lined out in a rather unnatural and sanctimonious style, is finished. Every verse was sung. The Sabbath is before them. No conventional hour shall limit the heavenly feast. The echoes of the last notes having died away, the preacher prepares to further enforce the sentiment of the hymn, and gradually prepare the minds of the people for prayer. His remarks are a prosy repetition of the sentiment of the lines, but they do not seem to be superfluous, or out of place. There must be no hurry on the threshold of the mercy-seat. Plainly, simply, unostentatiously, he talks for five, ten, even fifteen minutes. An increasing weight of solemnity comes down upon the congregation. They are about to appear before God, and to speak with Him, as friend to friend. The very place is holy, and profound seriousness is marked upon every countenance.[3]

Singing a Hymn This might be sung in either German or English. By 1850 German was sharing its place equally with English. By the end of the century German was hardly used at all. The singing proceeded by a peculiar method called *lining*. A deacon (called the "Vorsinger") would set the tune and the pitch. Then he (or a minister) would speak the first two lines of the hymn. The congregation would follow, singing those lines, then stop

A

CHOICE SELECTION

OF

HYMNS,

FROM VARIOUS AUTHORS,

RECOMMENDED FOR THE

WORSHIP OF GOD.

"Sing unto the Lord a new Song, and his praise in
the congregation of saints."—Ps. cxlix.

STEREOTYPE EDITION.

PUBLISHED BY HENRY KURTZ,
POLAND, MAHONING CO., O.
James & Co., Stereotypers.
1852.

The first edition of this hymnbook was published by Elder Henry
Kurtz in 1830. There were 13 editions in all.

completely. The deacon would speak two more lines; then the singing would begin again. The process continued until the end of the hymn. The Brethren always *lined* their hymns; there was no deviation from this. The reason was custom and the fact that not every member owned a hymn book. The congregation did not purchase books for the meetinghouse as we do today.

Those who did have hymn books owned one of two: *Die Kleine Lieder Sammlung, oder Auszug aus dem Psalterspiel der Kinder Zions (The Little Hymn Collection, or An Abridgement of the Psalter of the Children of Zion)* for singing German hymns; or *A Choice Selection of Hymns, From Various Authors, Recommended for the Worship of God* for singing English hymns. These two were sometimes bound together into one volume. The hymn books did not have any musical notation, only words. There were a number of different tunes that the Brethren might use. The deacon chose one that had the right meter to fit the words and started it. It was not uncommon to use the same tune for different hymns or to sing the same hymn to different tunes. Since musical notation was added to our hymn books, we no longer practice that flexibility.

There were no musical instruments in the meeting, no piano or organ. The Brethren were unalterably opposed to instruments in worship and remained so in some congregations well into the twentieth century. They believed worship should be plain and unadorned.

The preacher calls to prayer. Immediately a great rustling is heard throughout the church. Every man and woman is on bended knees. No resting of foreheads on hands of bench backs will suffice to express the reverent spirit of the congregation. The leader in prayer tarries long at the mercy-seat. He may not be gifted, though

many of the old brethren were gifted in this grace. They spake not the eloquence of the schools, but the eloquence of the heart, which, after all, is the truest eloquence. The seeming formality of the prayer is lightened by the evident sincerity of the man. Some prayed almost the same prayer for years, without becoming wearisome or disappointing. Like a chapter in the Bible, it never grows old.

Exhortation to Prayer One of the ministers would call the people to worship and prepare them for prayer. Henry Kurtz called this exhortation "to humbly worship God in spirit and in truth".[4] This was a part of the service a deacon was permitted to lead, if requested to do so by a minister or the elder.

Prayer The worshipers considered kneeling indispensable to proper prayer. Apparently later in the century half-kneeling was sometimes practiced by leaning forward against the back of the bench in front or by bowing one's head and resting it on one's hand. That is what Holsinger has reference to. But in the 1840s, the Brethren always knelt. Frequently, this prayer was ended with the Lord's Prayer.

The initial season of devotion having closed, the oldest bishop extends "the liberty" to his associates, who, in turn, offer it to each other. This interchange of courtesies occupies a minute or more, the congregation meanwhile looking on, and wondering who would deliver the sermon, a point that in few congregations was settled before the time had actually arrived. If there happens to be a visiting brother on the bench, he usually finds it impossible to decline the "liberty." If there are none, one of the home ministers yields, with apparent reluctance to the importunities of the brethren, and arises to sound forth the Word.

A sister kneeling in prayer.

Giving the "Liberty" The overseer or housekeeper, who was also usually the oldest elder, had the first privilege to speak. Not infrequently, he extended the liberty to speak to the minister next in seniority and next on the bench, choosing not to exercise the privilege himself. That minister then had the choice to preach or to give the "liberty" to the next brother on the bench and so on down the line. Often several ministers spoke, in which case the man with the liberty passed it on after completing his remarks. If there was a visiting minister, the liberty was passed to him almost immediately, for the Brethren loved to hear a new minister and to extend courtesy and welcome to a ministering brother from afar.

There was an event that occurred in the Antietam Congregation in southern Pennsylvania somewhat later than 1850 but close enough to illustrate this process. The church was well filled for the Sunday morning service, and the preacher's bench held many "brethren-at-the-word." After the opening hymn and prayer, the bishop spoke to the ministers next to him, "Now Brethren, take up the subject," and since on that day special courtesy prevailed, the brother extended the liberty to the next minister and he to the next on down until it came to the last man who was the youngest minister present and a stranger. Having no one further to whom to give the liberty, he looked up to the elder for his consent. The old elder was somewhat annoyed that this young man should lead out, even though custom was to extend the liberty to a strange minister. Hoping to relieve matters gently, he said in Pennsylvania Dutch (a Dutch dialect among German-Americans), "Canst du Deutsche sprechen?" He was thinking that the young man did not know German, and that the way would be clear to pass the liberty to an older, more experienced minister who did. "O yaw," came the young brother's reply. The elder could only say, "All recht," and the young minister arose and preached in clear German the finest German sermon heard in that congregation for many years. This brought appreciative comments from the people.[5]

Lifting the big Bible from the stand, the preacher of the day, while looking for his text, or perhaps while trying to decide what text he would take, requests the congregation to sing either one or the other of two well-known hymns:

"Father, I stretch my hands to thee,
   No other help I know;
If thou withdraw Thyself from me,
   Ah, whither shall I go?"

or,

"A charge to keep I have."

One who never heard a congregation of Tunkers sing one of these hymns just before the sermon would find it difficult to form any adequate idea of the quiet, deep fervency and solemn earnestness with which they were rendered. Deep feelings, not the kind which take emotional forms, for the Tunkers are not and never were an emotional people, but the kind which springs from profound sincerity, inward truth, marks the singing of this hymn, and the preacher arises to his task with every spiritual support. . . .

Many a time, but not every time, we have heard a long, rambling, illogical, ungrammatical, confused, vehement discourse, which would scatter any other but a Tunker congregation to the four winds. Some signs of disappointment and weariness might be observed here and there, but the great majority of the members followed the preacher through all his devious and obscure wanderings, apparent-

ly with unflagging interest. He fed their souls, and that
was all they were looking for. He ministered to their
spiritual life, whether that was strong or weak, and beyond
this they had no consciousness of comparatively unimport-
ant defects. The only eloquence that was eloquent to them
was the purely spiritual, and the dull apostle, if his heart
and life were right, if the spirit rested upon him, imparted
as much grace as the brilliant one, and in so vital a con-
nection mere talent, oratory, phrase-making, exegetical
skill was not to be mentioned at all. . . .

The sermon finally concluded, a word of testimony is
borne by one of the associate preachers, and this is followed by the concluding prayer and hymn. Then with the
usual announcements, the congregation is dismissed
without the benediction, to return to the beautiful farms
and fragrant orchards, the better benediction of God's
peace resting upon each one as he carries with him the consciousness of duty done, the sanctified memories of a holy
place, and the sweet echoes of melody and song.

Reading the Scripture This might be done by a minister
other than the speaker at his or the elder's request or
even in some cases by a deacon.

The Sermon or Sermons There has been an impression
among some of our historians that the Brethren between
the Revolutionary War and the Civil War were un-
educated and uncultured and were therefore country
bumpkins that we can remember fondly for their in-
dustriousness and faithfulness but with embarrassment
for their lack of polish. It is true they were uneducated
and unpolished; their faith precluded both education
and culture as it was defined by the world. They were
isolated from the centers of communication and commerce. But they were not bumpkins; nor were they

ancestors we can smile at with condescending appreciation for their simple virtues while believing ourselves better for our progressiveness and education. There were among the Brethren competent and masterful men in no less numbers than there are today. They were unschooled but not dumb; and some were self-read and well-educated after a peculiar individualistic fashion. There were men of character with strong leadership.

However, it appears that the lack of education was sorely felt in the preaching. There are enough accounts of monotonous, unschooled preaching to suggest that if you went to a Brethren meetinghouse you would find a delightfully straightforward minister with quiet dignity who couldn't preach. There were some excellent preachers, with well-organized delivery, good examples, and clear thoughts. But apparently for every such preacher, there were two whose notion of homiletics was to make a point and then repeat it. The Brethren tolerated this, sometimes enjoyed it, and garnered some enrichment, but strangers to the brotherhood frequently reported only boredom.

Testimony (or Exhortation) After the sermon or sermons, there was still more speaking of a kind—it was called "bearing testimony," and was undertaken by one of the other ministers (perhaps of lesser degree than the speaker) or by a deacon. This was one of the parts of worship permitted to the office of deacon. Whether a deacon or minister depended on the size of the congregation and the number of ministers. A word of testimony was a further elaboration on the theme of the speaker, which by this time probably had been sufficiently made.

A Final Hymn This came before or after the testimony.

Prayer A simple prayer closed the service. The Brethren were against using a benediction. A query to Yearly Meeting in 1849 asked, "Is it in accordance with the gospel for a brother to call the meeting to rise upon their feet, after worship is concluded with singing and prayer, and then with uplifted hands, pronounce a blessing over them?" The answer was: "Concluded, that it should not be."[6] The benediction smacked of a formality the Brethren wished to avoid.

Prosperity Holsinger also notes that the Brethren were prosperous.

Busch's Narrative

About six miles from Dayton, a few hundred steps off the road to Salem in a clearing in the endless woods stands a long, low brick house covered with shingles, which is enclosed by a typical worm fence with a circumference of about one American acre. In front of it is found a spring under some trees, next to which has been built a rough bench. It is a meetinghouse of the Dunkers, who settled in great numbers in this area, as is true for the entire valley through which the Mad River and both Miamis run.

It was on October 7 [1851] that I attended there one of their meetings, to which they often come from many miles distance in order to hear the Gospel preached and to hold the Lord's Supper with feet-washing. The loveliness of the morning persuaded me to set off on my journey by foot. Soon I had gone from my place of residence in the suburb Macpherson Town, past the huge sycamores (Author's note: A kind of plane-tree in America is called "sycamore" which often grows in moist places.) which shadow the bank of the Miami at the Covington bridge, and had reached the crest of the hill and the board shack which bore the grand name "Montgomery Starch

Manufactory" on its forehead. From there a perfectly straight road led completely out of the valley to the wooded heights. Huge red-painted barns behind elegant homes told here a story of the prosperity of those whose good star had led them to settle along this stretch. Mounted shepherds in light blue great coats and brown Buena Vista hats, belonging to the guild of the "divine Eumaos," ponderous carts pulled by two or three oxen teams, and neat little "buggy wagons" from which waved the inevitable green veils of the local small town girls and farmer's daughters, bluebirds, butterflies, and hordes of grasshoppers enlivened the road, upon which as I neared my destination came into sight also a few Dunkers in white coats on fine ponies, with wife and children in the wagon next to them.

White Coats There is only one other place that I know of where it is suggested that a brother wore a white or light-colored coat.[7] Almost all descriptions and all photos indicate dark or black coats. It is possible that a few brethren might have been wearing coats made of nearly white cloth. While plain dress was expected of all members, the exact form was not yet specified in the 1840s. It is also possible, however, that the author was mistaken. The person he saw may have been a young man not yet in the church.

It must have been nine o'clock when I arrived at the meetinghouse. In the woods in front of the fence a peddler had set up a bar, and in his vicinity were found under the trees many coaches and horses, belonging to people, who, like myself, had come without belonging to the brotherhood. Among them the genus "Loafers" (here, as in every other place in Uncle Sam's land composing at least a fourth of the male youth) was present in numbers.

"Loafers"

Inside the fence, however, there teemed the long-bearded figures and beaver-tailed coats of the "Brethren," whose numbers increased by the minute. They walked about hand in hand, and all newcomers gave and received the "brotherly right hand" and the "holy kiss." It must be said that the latter ceremony was practiced only between brother and brother, or sister and sister.

Peddler's Bar We will presume that the peddler's whiskey was for the "loafers" and visitors. The Brethren in the 1840s did not have quite the same view of alcoholic beverages as many Brethren do today, but they valued sobriety very highly. It is safe to conclude that a brother would not enter the meetinghouse with whiskey in his belly.

Nonmembers and "Loafers" This was a morning service preceding a love feast in the evening. On these occasions many persons came just to observe or to have a good time. In rural areas, large public gatherings were infrequent, so people would go to a Brethren love feast just to be with a crowd and to see people from the other side of the country and to observe the love feast, which many thought strange.

Along the fence behind the house a square of buggies, market carts, and riding horses was formed, which had brought the believers of both sexes. From one door of the meetinghouse, which opened onto a small veranda, flamed an open fire around huge pots and kettles, attended by women in white caps and aprons, and a blue pillar of smoke spiraled from the chimney. On a stone near the spring was placed a metal cup with which those who had no interest in refreshing themselves from the peddler's barrel of whiskey could slake their thirst.

"Roughly-hewn timbers"

Suddenly all moved toward the entrances, and in a short time the house was so filled with Dunkers and onlookers that several latecomers had to stand beside the door, which was almost completely taken up by a colossal deacon with a long brown beard, the largest and most handsome male figure which I encountered in America. The room was a rectangle, with nine windows and three doors. Its low board ceiling was supported by four roughly-hewn timbers as pillars, and it probably contained at this time between three and four hundred persons. Neither choir nor chancel, organ nor altar, nor burning candles were to be seen in it, and therefore the room was more to be compared with a large farmhouse room (Bauernstube) than to a German church. . . .

In the middle of the room was a whitedraped table made of two trestles with rough boards laid on them, at which sat about twenty, mostly elderly men in the sectarian garb and adorned with long Noah-beards. These were the preachers and bishops. Around them on both sides of the passage which divided the room the long way into two equal parts, were lined up the closely-packed-together sisters on the right side where the kitchen was located, in their white caps and aprons, on the left with their hats on their knees, the bearded and long-haired brethren. My good fortune had brought me a place directly opposite from the preacher's table, and thus nothing of this peculiar ceremony escaped my attention.

The worship service began with an English hymn. Following this anything but pleasant-sounding singing was a prayer in German by a preacher with a whining voice. During this the profane fire crackled in an unmannerly fashion through the open kitchen door and was also accompanied—a not unusual occurrence in American churches—by the unashamed and frightful crying of one of the infants which had been brought along. After the one

Die kleine

Lieder-Sammlung

oder

Auszug aus dem

Psalterspiel der Kinder Zions,

zum Dienste inniger, heilsuchender Seelen,

und insonderheit

zum Gebrauch in den Gemeinden der Brüder,

zusammengetragen in gegenwärtige kleine Form
und mit einem dreifachen Register versehen.

"Ich will den Herrn loben, so lange ich lebe,
und meinem Gott lobsingen, weil ich hie bin."
Psalm 146, 2.

Stereotyp-Auflage.

Poland, Mahoning County, Ohio.

Zu haben bei Heinrich Kurtz.

1850.

Front page of the German hymnbook probably used by the Brethren at this time. First published in 1826. This is an 1850 reprint by Henry Kurtz. This book and the English hymnbook were very small, only 3 by 4½ inches.

praying pronounced the Amen, one of the bishops read a
chapter from Jeremiah, and that from an English Bible,
whereupon several German verses were sung. These were
read line for line by a preacher for the congregation, a circumstance which is possibly based on the fact that only a
few of those present still owned a songbook in their mother
tongue. It also happened that more parts had been sung to
the English hymn, and from this one does not seem to go
far wrong in assuming that the transition process which all
German settlers undergo who leave Pennsylvania is
already more than two-thirds completed among the
Dunkers in the west.

Transition to English A Brethren congregation in Pennsylvania was more likely to use German predominantly
than one in Ohio or Indiana. The older eastern churches
retained the German longer than the newer pioneer
churches.

After the singing an old German preacher rose in order
to treat in English the third chapter of Acts, which had
been read by another in Luther's German translation. His
exposition of the text consisted of a quite respectable com-
parison of the lame before the door of the temple with the
sinner who may not enter the kingdom of God, until he is
told in the name of Jesus to walk therein. Unfortunately,
this good image was trampled so broadly in innumerable
repetitions into a boring soup that only those used to such
rustic fare could swallow it. During this the speaker, as he
became warm, without finding it inappropriate, shed his
coat and hung it on a latch stretched overhead between two
pillars, on which many other vestments already balanced.

Boring Soup Here Mr. Busch corroborates Mr.
Holsinger. It seems that much preaching was rather dull.

We also see here, however, the informality of the minister—taking his coat off and hanging it on a latch. The Brethren meeting house was homelike, and the members were relaxed about noise, children, and over-heated preachers.

He must have spoken about a half-hour in this fashion, when his sermon took a characteristic turn as he suddenly abandoned the lame in the temple at Jerusalem, forgot his English, and in the purest Pennsylvania Dutch complained about the pains in his lungs: "I could talk much longer on this text, but my lungs won't stand it. Oh, my lungs!" (Mer konnt noch viel schwatze uber diesen Text, aber meine Lungs wolln's net stande. Ach, meine Lungs!) "But, however" (English in original) and then the flow of words poured forth well over another quarter of an hour without period or pause, in its rise and fall similar to that in which we sing the collect. If this example of Dunkard eloquence, as was to be expected, was hardly a perfect sermon, yet it seemed to please the congregation and it was in any case better and more substantial than the one his neighbor at the table held in German upon the same theme, which was nothing other than a poor translation of the first.

Quite a different impression was made by the following sermon of a preacher who came to the meeting from Southern Ohio. He had a long lean figure with noble, prophet-like features. His pale face was encircled by black hair, and his eyes glittered with that special fire and his otherwise strong voice was that hollow tone which we associate with consumption. The apt development of the sermon which he presented in excellent English could have been heard with success by a congregation of intellectuals. After he closed, a prayer followed whereupon the entire congregation knelt; the one who prayed, however, remained seated at the table with his head supported by his right arm and with his eyes closed.

Successful Sermon Apparently, this was one of the gifted preachers. It was not uncommon for a speaker to close his sermon with a prayer.

Then followed several more preachers who spoke with more or less talent, mostly in English, some in German, almost all disturbed by the screaming of infants and the noise of the fire which cooked their noonday meal and, therefore, seemed to have the right to speak along with them. All of them concluded their remarks with the naive sentence that if they had not brought anything to the benefit and edification of the brotherhood, they at least hoped that they had not said anything harmful.

Not Saying Anything Harmful This sentence seemed naive to the sophisticated Mr. Busch, and it may seem charming to us. It probably was a customary disclaimer, to which the speaker gave little thought. It embodies, however, an important concern. The unity of the brotherhood was so valued that most members genuinely wished to avoid saying something that would disturb it.

It was then three o'clock, and perhaps nine or ten speakers had appeared, when the presiding bishop ended further oratory as he directed those present to leave the house. It was time for the midday meal and the room had to be prepared for that. Since there was not enough space for all to be fed at once, as soon as it was ready the elderly and the women should eat first. The others, with which he also intended to mean those not belonging to the brotherhood, would find their portion at the second course. Finally, provision had also been made for the horses, and each one could obtain the necessary items from the deacons. This took place, and soon one saw brethren and strangers with handkerchiefs full of oats in their hands and ears of corn under their arms going from the kitchen to their horses.

"It Was Then Three O'clock." This service was unusually long (6 hours) because it proceeded a love-feast. People who came from far away wished to hear as many of the ministers as possible, knowing that some they may not hear until next love feast time. Normally two or three would speak rather than nine or ten.

The Midday Meal The Brethren fed anyone who wished food, including the "loafers," and of course the horses, who, having concluded their own morning fellowship, were hungry as well.

Commentary

We may take the accounts of Brother Holsinger and Herr Busch to be accurate because they so closely correspond. We may assume that if two so different observers report the same events in different parts of the brotherhood, the practices across the country must have been similar. Their accounts are further supported by Elder Henry Kurtz's description of the order of worship in the *Brethren's Encyclopedia.*[8]

We already know that the Brethren were decidedly New Testament centered. Their worship confirms this. The heart of the worship was the speaking, and this was always based solidly on a Scripture text. The only elaboration on the text permitted was whatever native wit or limited reading the minister might bring to it. It was neither enhanced nor encumbered by theological speculation nor by schooled interpretation. The

minister's task was to stay close to his text and to avoid
sophisticated thinking. He was to be simple and
straightforward.

The service as a whole was that way. It lacked the
liturgical mastery that Herr Busch's Lutheran service
would have had, but it also avoided the emptiness that
sometimes characterize oft-repeated liturgies. There was
no risk that a liturgical form or a credal statement might
get to have a life of its own and draw the attention of the
Brethren away from the New Testament.

The service was informal in its lack of set liturgy and
in the brethren and sister's genial toleration of crying
children, crackling fires, and shirt-sleeved preachers.
But it was orderly in its movement and the parts were
dictated by custom. While simple and informal, it was
not formless. The Brethren were reluctant to permit
even so small a change as the introduction of a benediction to close the service. In this sense they were no less
formal and ordered than a liturgical church.

Close to the heart of the service was the fellowship (or
fraternity) it created. Persons who are capable and willing to sit together on hard, backless benches for three to
six hours cannot help but have their sense of
togetherness increased, simply through having shared
such a lengthy experience. The compactness of the
meetinghouse, the congregational singing, the common
act of kneeling drew the worshippers into a body. The
service tended to play down personal individuality—in
music by forbidding anyone to play an instrument, in
preaching by centering the speaker on the Bible instead
of his own interpretation, and in the leadership by
spreading it among three or more ministers and/or
deacons and by having these men sitting on the same
level as the people. No one man (minister) or group of
persons (choir) dominated the service. Only the elder
had this opportunity, and he usually deferred and gave

the liberty to another. The words *fraternity, Brethren,* and *brotherhood* have always been first on the lips when our people have needed to name or describe our group. The worship service in subtle and not so subtle ways played down individuality and deepened brotherhood. It was in this fraternal spirit more than in the words one man might utter that God's presence was known by the Brethren.

CHAPTER 5

Chapter Five
The Ancient Order of the Brethren

The word *order* is an immensely important word for understanding the Brethren of the 1840s. Quite apart from the Brethren, it is extraordinarily rich in meanings—no less than twenty-four in Webster's New International Dictionary. The word has depth that we in our day overlook. Visions of knighthood and monastic orders and God himself ordaining the events of His world come off the dictionary pages. The Brethren were not interested in knights or monks, but they were interested in God and what He had in mind for their church. The conclusions they reached they called "the ancient order of the Brethren"—a magnificent term. It hardly seems likely that God did not have at least something to do with a thing as imposing as that. The Brethren at any rate believed He did and that what they were in their church was what God wanted them to be.

Annual Meeting, 1881

By order they meant in the first place those things
which God had already established by his word—such
as the ordinances of the church or the officers of the
church. Scripture, especially the New Testament, clearly
showed what God had in mind. This "ancient order"
was ordained by God to direct properly the practice of
the church and the conduct of the Christian. This is the
foremost and deepest meaning the word had.

The Brethren were known by outsiders to live orderly
lives. They believed that God expected them to live this
way, or at least that the other members expected it.
Their homes were neat, clean, and well organized. Their
business affairs were generally straightforward, uncomplicated, and above reproach—no guile, no "deals,"
no hazy promises. "The word of a Dunkard was as good
as his bond." They were sober. Their church services
were simple and without excessive emotion. They did
not like high-pitched revival meetings or the "mourners
bench" filled with wailing sinners, neither of which were
uncommon in other denominations. Persons viewing the
Brethren were struck by their simplicity and orderliness.
This is the second and less profound meaning that order
had for the Brethren.

There were some aspects of Brethren life that were not
clearly ordained; yet they were not altogether a matter
of common orderliness. Whether to build
meetinghouses, whether and how to use alcoholic
beverages, whether to have photos taken, or the exact
form of plain dress are examples. The right practice did
not seem to be established clearly, but it did seem that
God might have some wishes on the matter. These gray
areas caused endless debate, as the minutes of Yearly
Meeting testify.

This chapter does not deal with all aspects of the
order of the Brethren. Chapter Three already contains a

discussion of the ordinances of the church—clearly of the former sort of order. Chapters Six through Twelve will have many glimpses of everyday lifestyle—order in the second sense. This chapter does, however, deal with those parts of the order (in both senses) which served to uphold and enforce the whole order of the church. Therefore, I have felt justified in preempting this magnificent phrase and entitling the chapter "The Ancient Order of the Brethren."

The Yearly Meeting

In the 1840s there were two units of authority and organization—the Yearly Meeting and the congregational council meeting. Of these two the Yearly Meeting (also called Annual Meeting or Big Meeting) had final authority; here the order of the Brethren was established or changed. Questions, requests for guidance, even suggestions for change could originate in a council meeting, but they were sent to the Yearly Meeting for final decision. The word of the Big Meeting was binding. Article 28 from the Yearly Meeting minutes of 1850 makes this clear:

> How is it considered, when a district* or church do not observe the ancient order of the brethren and have new orders among them?
>
> Concluded, that no district church has any right to make changes in any thing whatsoever, contrary to the ancient order, without proper investigation before, and the general consent of, the Annual Meeting.[1]

---

* At this time congregations had geographical boundaries and were sometimes called *districts*. Today, in the Church of the Brethren, the word *districts* refers to a large number of congregations occupying a particular geographical area.

Place of Yearly Meeting, 1848. Farm of Jacob Kurtz, Chippewa Congregation, Wayne County, Ohio.

That Yearly Meeting spoke with authority is not hard to see from the foregoing. However, the Brethren did recognize instances where a binding decision could not be made, in which case Yearly Meeting gave advice, and further situations where complete discretionary powers were granted the congregation. The Brethren were somewhat careful to distinguish when they were doing which. For instance, Yearly Meeting, 1844, Article 6 is an example of a binding decision.

Whether it be allowable for Brethren to collect debts by force of law.

Considered that no brother has any right in the gospel to sue at law. Luke 3:14, Matt. 5:38, 6:12[2]

Yearly Meeting, 1850, Article 7, a gray area where advice was given.

Is a brother, being a full member in the church, allowed to purchase cattle, and other animals, and follow butchering, hire, or rent a stall in a markethouse, and attend market, as a butcher, every market morning.

Considered, that a brother engaged in butchering in the manner stated in the questions is surrounded with many difficulties and temptations, and that we would advise brethren not to do so.[3]

Yearly Meeting, 1849, Article 41, a decision allowing the congregation to exercise entirely its own discretion:

Concerning the propriety or necessity of giving meals to the congregation, at common meetings.

Considered, that we leave this matter altogether discretionary to every individual church or family.[4]

The Big Meeting was a very special event. It was the great council meeting, the arbiter of the church. But it was a good deal more than that. Brethren from the far reaches of the fraternity gathered together to visit. These were pioneering days when families and friends were often separated. Brothers, sons, and neighbors had taken their wives and children and moved west through the Allegheny passes into Ohio, Indiana, Kentucky, and Illinois or south into Virginia. Transportation was slow or non-existent, and there were no telephones. Brethren and sisters did not see loved ones for many months, nor did they have the pleasure of fellowship with those who shared their love for the faith and practice of the church. At Yearly Meeting the Brethren renewed these deep bonds of love, exchanged news, and delighted in being together. There was at least as much visiting as business, and if the business upheld the order of the church, the visiting upheld the hearts of the members. It is safe to say that visiting remains if not one of the Brethren virtues at least one of our cherished eccentricities.

There was, of course, a third reason for Yearly Meeting's place of favor and affection. The Brethren gathered together to renew their common faith and practice. There were great preaching services when as many as twenty elders and speakers preached. There was singing, and of course there was a love feast service. The beloved New Testament faith was reaffirmed with solemn rejoicing. No other service or organization or meeting combined as completely these three important elements—upholding the order, visiting, and renewing the faith.

> . . . it has pleased God to spare our lives, and to count us worthy once more to assemble at this yearly meeting, the design of which is to promote our union in love and concord of the spirit, to encourage one another to faithfulness and watchfulness in these last critical times, and to strengthen us mutually in the faith and obedience of the gospel, to warn of dangers, and to resist with

united efforts every evil which threatens to break in, and
especially in difficulties that may arise, on the request of
our beloved brethren, to give our simple advice.[5]

The procedure for Yearly Meeting changed several
times in the 1840s. The steps it went through are too
long a story for this book. What follows is a description
of Yearly Meeting as it operated in 1850.

The Brethren gathered together on the Saturday
before the first day of Whitsuntide (Pentecost Sunday).
Public preaching and worship services were held
through Sunday, either Saturday or Sunday evening (at
the option of the host church) being set aside for love
feast. On Monday, the business session (sometimes called council meeting) began, continuing until all the
business was transacted. Each congregation was requested to send not more than two delegates. The voting
body was made up of these delegates plus all elders who
were in attendance. A general committee of five or seven
elders was appointed by the elders of the host church to
receive the written queries (questions from the
churches), to examine them, and to present them to the
voting body. Great power rested with this committee to
influence the decisions. It was called the Standing Committee and remains to this day the steering committee of
Annual Conference. Where the name originated no one
knows, but one apocryphal story has it that the committee had been accustomed to read the Yearly Meeting
decisions while standing on the porch of the house
where the deliberation took place. Queries were farmed
out among designated working committees of delegates
to prepare them for discussion. Queries were generally
sent only by congregations, but individual members did
have the privilege of addressing the meeting with a
query.

Verhandlungen

der

Jahrs-Versammlung, 1846.

Am 29sten Tag des Monats May im Jahr des HErrn 1846, kamen
die Brüder zusammen in jährlicher Versammlung am Hause von Bruder
Johannes Royer an der Fore-Bay-Kreek in Lancaster County, Pa.
und nachdem die Versammlung eröffnet war mit Gesang, Ermahnung und
Gebet, wurde es beschlossen, daß alle bestätigte Brüder gegenwärtig sich als
eine Committee zurückziehen sollten, um alle die Sachen einzunehmen, welche
vor die Jährliche Versammlung gelegt werden sollen; — und diese waren wie
folgt:

1. Was die Art und Weise anbetrifft, Jährliche Versammlungen zu halten, so daß mehr Ordnung, Bequemlichkeit und Vergnügen dabei zu genießen wäre, wurde es angesehen in der Furcht des HErrn, daß die Rath der J.
Vers. vom Jahr 1837, in dieser Sache schicklich und zweckmäßig war, im
Fall er beobachtet würde, und daß der beste Plan die Sache nicht bessern
wird, wenn er ausgeführt bleibt. Verschiedene Pläne wurden vorgelegt,
und nach einer langen Unterredung und ernstlicher Ueberlegung wurde beschlossen, keine wesentliche Veränderung zu machen als diese, daß unsre westlichen Brüder jedes andere Jahr das Recht haben sollten, die Jährl. Vers. zu
nehmen, wenn sie es begehren, und daß unsere östlichen Brüder nicht fehlen
sollten, denselben beizuwohnen; — daß es ausdrücklich verstanden und ausgegeben werden sollte, wie am Freytag und Samstag nur private Raths-Versammlung sey, wobei alle bestätigte Aeltesten die Committee bilden sollen
die Sachen einzunehmen und vor die Versammlung zu bringen. Die öffentliche Versammlung sollte am Sonntag, und wo möglich nicht an nemlichen
Platz seyn, wo die Rathsversammlung gehalten wird.

2. Mag einiges einzelne Mitglied ein Recht haben, Fragen vor die Jährlich
Versammlung zu bringen, ehe sie durch den Rath der Gemeinschaft gegangen
sind? Angesehen, daß es schicklich ist, alle Fragen mit dem Rath der Gemeinschaft einzubringen.

3. Wegen dem Auflegen der Hände auf die Diener, (Besuchbrüder).—
Ueber diese viel und lang bewegte Frage wurde es schließlich niedergelegt als
der sicherste Weg, fortzufahren wie bisher. Die Einwendung, daß es doch
eine apostolische Ordnung war, die beobachtet werden sollte, wurde damit beantwortet, daß (angenommen, daß die Apostel den Sieben wirklich die Hände auf das Haupt gelegt hätten, welches unsers Wissens keineswegs bewiesen
werden kann,) so wenig als ein einziger Gang etlicher Menschen durch eine
Wildniß einen Weg oder gebahnte Straße machen, eben so wenig eine Sache
einmal gethan eine Ordnung machen kann, und daß wenn das Exempel, daß

Yearly Meeting Minutes of 1846 printed in German by Henry Kurtz

While only the delegate body could vote, any member could speak and frequently did. When a matter was put to a vote, the Brethren always preferred unanimity, but were willing to pass something if at least a two-thirds majority voted "yea." Yearly Meeting always had the option of deferring a matter to a later meeting and often did in cases where not only the desired unanimity was lacking but an outspoken or more than one-third minority existed. The Brethren during this decade were very reluctant to push through a measure that would cause division and controversy. They were willing to give such matters plenty of time either to gain support or to whither away. So great was the respect for the ancient order, that it was changed only with care and prayerful deliberation.

The Church Council Meeting

The second unit of authority and organization was the church council. If Yearly Meeting had the role of establishing and clarifying the order, council meeting had the responsibility of enforcing it. Beyond that, the Brethren performed in council the tasks necessary to keep the church functioning as an organization. Some of these tasks were routine and had little or nothing to do with scripturally established order; others were indispensible to the order. Council meeting, like Yearly Meeting closely interrelated everyday business matters with the faith and practice of the church. Council was called as often as it was needed, usually after a regular meeting for worship, was made up of all members, male and female, each of whom had one vote on any issue, and was presided over by the elder. Five important functions were performed.

(1) **Election of Officers** A unique method was used, unlike the methods we use today. An election became

t an Election held at the House of Brother John Mumma
the 26th day of May AD 1847. By the members of
Church at Big Canawago in Adams County. to elect
Brother to the Ward in Said Church. the following
s were given

. Adam Brown	⳾⳾⳾⳾ ⳾⳾⳾⳾ ⳾⳾⳾⳾ ⳾⳾⳾⳾ ⳾⳾⳾⳾ ⳾⳾⳾⳾ ⳾⳾⳾		33
. Joseph Myers	1		1
Daniel Longenecker	⳾⳾⳾⳾		5
Jacob Sower	⳾⳾⳾⳾ ⳾⳾		7

the undernamed Brethren do certify that the botes
the Stand above were given for the above named
thren. and appears that Adam Brown was
cted to the ward May 26th AD 1847
he Election held by us

David Routz
Samuel Miller
Andrew Milbr
William turner
Jacob Brown
Andrew ND us dorff
Peter derdorff

Teller's sheet from an election held in the Big Conewago congregation
in Adams County, Pennsylvania, May 26, 1847

necessary whenever a congregation needed another
deacon or minister when a minister was ready to be "advanced." An election board of one or two men, usually
elders or deacons, retired to a private room—the kitchen
or attic of the home or meetinghouse. Each member of
the congregation filed into the room and gave the name
of his preference for the office. The person receiving the
most votes was elected. There were no nominations and
no discussion of who might be qualified. It was believed
that the call to an office of the church was made by God
through the vote of the members. All members voted
and their task was to consider prayerfully their fellow
members and allow God's will to influence their judgment.

It may seem surprising to use what appears to be a
rather random method, where several persons could
split the vote and no one got a majority. That usually
did not happen. In cases where two men were tied or had
close to the same number of votes, both were sometimes
installed. Other times another election was held. The
election was not blind or random but was guided by unofficial preferences already in the congregation. The
Brethren believed God's will guided the election and
they sometimes prayed and fasted in preparation for it.

Election was used with slight variations to place men
in four different offices—speaker or teacher (minister in
the first degree), minister in the second degree, elder or
bishop, and deacon. Only men were eligible; women
held no offices in the 1840s.

(2) Installation of Officers Once elected, the officers
were installed by special procedures and with a commission unique to each office. This was always done at
council-meeting by an elder.

(3) Examining Applicants for Membership The first
step in entering the church was to apply to the congrega-

tion for membership. The application was expected to be on the initiative of the applicant. The Brethren did not pressure persons into the fellowship by soliciting their application too quickly or aggressively. That is why they disliked the high emotions of "protracted meeting" (the term used for a series of revival meetings). The brotherhood needed earnest members who had considered their decision soberly and at length. The application was usually made to the elder who carried it to the council. Then the prospective member was called before the council and asked if he understood and ascribed to the faith and practice of the church and if he was willing to live by the principles of nonconformity, nonswearing, and nonresistance. If his answers were yes, the council would vote whether or not to receive him. If their answer was yes, then he would be baptized. (See Chapter Three on baptism.)

(4) **Enforcing the Order of the Church** If a member transgressed against one of the orders of the church, his transgression was brought to the attention of the council, and a trial was held to determine his guilt or innocence. Testimony was given by witnesses, and he was given opportunity to defend himself. Only testimony given by members was acceptable. If testimony against him arose among non-members it was the duty of the church to have members (usually ministers and deacons) investigate before it was brought to council. If he was found guilty, he was expected to acknowledge his transgression before the whole church and ask forgiveness. If he refused, he was put into "avoidance" (excommunicated).

Trials were obviously very important for maintaining the order. Order is meaningless if it is not enforced. However, sometimes order was upheld at the expense of unity and love. Enmity and division as well as healing

and reconciliation resulted from council meeting
judgments. Council meeting was a two-edged sword.
One the one hand it gently admonished and lovingly
recalled transgressors; on the other it judged and weeded
out recalcitrant wrongdoers. Both can be done in love,
but sometimes the latter was not. On these occasions,
the Brethren distinguished themselves not by
forbearance, but by self-righteousness. The Brethren in
the 1840s were more likely to have forbearance than to
make peremptory judgments.

(5) **Directing the Business of the Congregation** The
council meeting decided if and when to build a
meetinghouse, when the church territory needed to be
divided, and where the boundary line with another congregation was. Most of the day-to-day affairs were in the
hands of the officers, but it was not uncommon for the
elder to request the guidance of the council.

Business and organization matters were always ruled
by matters of faith and practice. Everything the council
did was disciplined around its central function to
strengthen the community of faith. Elder Henry Kurtz
described that task this way:

> These our common council-meetings I had learned to
> consider as practical schools of Christian morality
> where the general principles of the gospel were applied
> to individual cases; where every Christian virtue, such as
> love, humility, patience, forbearance, etc., was called
> into exercise and where every moral evil was to be set in
> its true light in order to remove it.[6]

Officers of the Church

The Brethren believed that the offices of the church
had a Scriptural basis, but they had practical reasons for
them as well. The ministry had three levels because it
recognized that a man grew and matured in his ministry.

A minister in the first degree was in a trial period where he could gain training and experience before assuming heavier responsibilities. He was called "speaker" because his only real function was to preach. He had the following authority:

(1) To preach, but only when the elder or older ministers "gave him liberty" to do so

(2) To conduct a meeting if none of the "older ministering brethren" were available

(3) To preach at funerals.

He did not have authority to make or announce his own preaching appointments. Each congregation had several preaching points and the ministers made appointments to preach there on certain dates. The elder made the appointments for a speaker. While speaking was his only function, it did not cease to be the main function when he was advanced. Ministers in all three levels were sometimes referred to as "Brothers at the Word."

If a man proved competent as a speaker and mature in the faith, he was advanced to the second degree. Here his responsibilities increased as well as his prerogatives. He had authority to do all that he did in the first degree and:

(1) To make his own appointments

(2) To administer baptism

(3) To take the counsel of the church on the admission of an applicant for baptism (if the elder was absent)

(4) To serve communion (if the elder was absent or at his request if present)

(5) To perform marriages

A minister in the second degree was authorized to perform all the functions needed to be a pastor to the congregation. There were yet several prerogatives of church leadership and administration that only an elder could perform. An important injunction was placed on the men in the first and second degrees—"Ye younger, submit yourselves unto the elder" (1 Peter 5:5). They were at all times to defer to the wishes of the elder or elders.

The eldership was the most highly regarded and powerful position in the church. The elder was the respected patriarch, whose guidance was sought and whose judgments were sometimes feared. He was also the chief administrator whose task it was to keep order and harmony. Sometimes called "housekeeper" or "overseer," he was judged not only by how well he preached or how exemplary his life was, but by how well he "kept his house" (the church) in order.

There were in some congregations two or even three elders, in which case the oldest was the "housekeeper" or elder in charge. The others had the same prerogatives, the only difference being that they had to defer to his seniority. An elder was *ordained* by a special service conducted by at least one other elder. This followed two events: a vote by the congregation to decide whether to advance him (if the vote was not unanimous, the church was reluctant to ordain him); and an examination by a board of elders (often from other congregations and called "impartial" or "strange brethren"). Having been duly elected and examined, he was charged with his new responsibilities and asked to kneel. The officiating elders laid their hands on his head and made a solemn prayer for blessings upon his work. Then he was given the hand of fellowship and the kiss of each member (the women gave him only the hand). Only the elder was ordained by the sacred ceremony of the laying on of hands, and only the elder was asked to kneel. Ministers in the other degrees received an installation charge while remaining seated or standing and then were given the hand and the kiss. It is fitting that a man who was to be entrusted with great responsibility was asked to humble himself in a kneeling position.

Elders were sometimes called bishops and had authority to exercise the prerogatives of the first and second degrees and:

(1) To preside at any council meeting either in the home congregation or in another

(2) To give the charge to ministers and deacons and to install them

(3) To serve on the Standing Committee of Yearly Meeting

(4) To ordain other elders

(5) To be held equal with all other elders, except where appropriate to defer to an elder with seniority.

An elder had great power, both spiritual and administrative. However, his office did not convey upon him a superior spiritual position, nor did it establish him as the channel of God's communication. He was not a hotline from God. He was the elder brother whose task it was to help his brethren and sisters. He was the servant of his brethren, not the assistant to the Father. He was raised up and designated by God only through his brethren and not directly. The Brethren believed that God speaks through his people, the church, and not through the words or actions of one man. The most any one member could do, even an elder, was to uphold and nourish that church. Never in any way was he a lord in the church. He was not a priest; he was an elder. God called him through the will of the congregation and he remained accountable to that. He was reminded sternly of this in the charge placed on him. The following is part of the charge as it was used in the 1880s. We have no record of the charge used in the forties but we may presume that it was in the same spirit.

> . . . should you manifest an arbitrary, self-willed, and domineering spirit, the church will hold you subject to her council, and suspend you, and again reduce you to the layity, or even expel you from membership if necessary.[7]

In practice, the elder was powerful and respected, but congregations could and sometimes did remove him if he abused his power or violated the order of the church.

The fourth officer of the church was less visible but no less valuable. He was the deacon, sometimes called "visiting brother," whose ancient office was established by scripture and indispensible to the church. His was an office not so much of prerogatives as of responsibilities.

(1) He cared for the poor, seeing that the congregation adequately provided for them

(2) He made an annual "visit"—a house-to-house circuit of the congregation once a year before love feast—to admonish the members to faithfulness, to point out and hear reports of irregularities, to announce the date of love feast, and to receive contributions toward the expense of the church

(3) He accompanied the ministers in investigating problems or did so alone when requested

(4) He assisted in the meeting when requested by the minister by reading scripture, leading singing, prayer, bearing testimony to what the ministers said, and exhorting members in the faith. When no minister was present, he took charge of the meeting and did all of the above. He did not preach

(5) He took charge of all the preparations for love feast. None of the officers of the church was paid for his services. The Brethren had a "free ministry" made up of dedicated men who made their own living and performed their ministry in their non-working hours. They believed this was the Biblical way and looked with disapproval on ministers who accepted pay for doing God's work.

Avoidance

When a person joined with the Brethren, he was expected to follow the order of the church in all its particulars. If he did not, an elder or minister visited him, laid before him his behavior, and admonished him to desist. If he refused, or if the offense was serious, he was brought before the council. If the council found him guilty, he was "placed in avoidance." There were two levels of avoidance. On the first level, three privileges of membership were withdrawn—breaking of bread (communion); the salutation of the kiss (and the hand of fellowship that went with it); and participation in the church council. The person became like a nonmember. The basis for this was Matthew 18:17: "Let him be unto thee as a heathen man and a publican." The same courtesy and friendship were still due him that were due a neighbor who was a nonmember, but the special intimacy of membership was withdrawn. This was used against a brother or sister who committed an offense against a fellow member, in which case acknowledging the offense and asking forgiveness restored the person to full membership. Or it was used when a member was accused of a very serious offense, prior to and during the investigation and trial. Because the Brethren wanted to risk no impurities in the fellowship, they would place him in avoidance until he was found guilty or innocent. The second level was used when a member committed an offense "against God and the truth." All relationship of any kind was withdrawn. The Brethren were not even to eat a common meal with the offender. 1 Corinthians 5:11 states: "But I have written unto you not to keep company . . . with such a one, no, not to eat." The only thing permitted to "such a one" was charity. If he were starving, the Brethren were of course obligated by gospel to take him food.

The Brethren did not spell out clearly what offenses merited such avoidance. An example of the first kind of offense might be chiseling a fellow member in a business transaction, slandering a fellow member, or being disruptive in church council. The second would be a more profound violation of Brethren order—marrying a divorced person, disputing the form of baptism, or joining the military.

That avoidance was practiced there can be no doubt. How widely it was practiced we do not know. We do know that complaints were made in Annual Meeting about churches that were not using it. Probably the milder form was used mostly, because there are rather few reports where a person was totally shunned. That it was, however, a powerful instrument for enforcing church order there also can be no doubt.

CHAPTER
6

Chapter Six
Two Brethren from Ohio

Our Little German Brothers

Henry Kurtz was uncommon. In the first place, he was German-born. He came to this country in 1817 at the age of twenty-one from the duchy of Wurttemberg in Germany where he was born on July 22, 1796, in the town of Bonnigheim, and where he received a good classical education. In the eighteenth century, it would not have been uncommon to find many German immigrant Brethren, but by the mid-nineteenth century, while still German in culture and partly in language, the Brethren were mostly American by birth. Henry was an exception.

He was also unusual because he was ordained to the ministry in another denomination. Some time after arriving in this country, he decided to put aside what he called his "folly and godlessness"[1] and become a Christian. He decided to enter the Lutheran ministry and in 1819 was called to be the pastor of the Plainfield Lutheran Congregation in Northhampton County,

Pennsylvania. He served this congregation for four
years; he did a good job and they liked him.

He was then called to be the pastor of the German
United Evangelical Church in Pittsburgh, Pennsylvania,
an ecumenical Lutheran and Reformed congregation.
Pittsburgh was a frontier town and Henry must have
looked forward to its challenge. He was installed on July
21, 1823, and his service there was turbulent. The
Lutheran and Reformed members did not get along with
each other; church discipline was poor; the church was
badly in debt; and ministers were coming and going in
good succession. In the first year Henry retired the debt,
for which he was well praised. But when he sought to
reform the church discipline, he got into trouble. The
members at first agreed to his proposal, which spelled
out the duties and rights of laymen and pastor, but when
he tried to enforce it he met with resistance. That increased considerably in the fall of 1825 when he began to
urge his parishioners to sell their possessions and join
under his leadership a Christian Communitarian colony
like the early Christians. The congregation split into fac-
tions for and against Henry and the controversy continued through the fall of 1826 when he resigned to pre-
vent a permanent schism. The church was to blame, but
so was Henry. He admitted later (in 1827) that his:

> . . . violent encroachment, unsympathetic severity, pride
> in [my] own strength, and trust in [my] influence upon
> the emotions created anger, irritated the passions, in-
> jured love, . . . and thus I myself helped to overthrow the
> edifice.[2]

At the age of thirty the promising young man was a dis-
mal failure.

Meanwhile Henry had become interested in com-

The church and parsonage in Pittsburg

munitarianism and Christian socialism. In fact, this interest partly brought his resignation, for it was his
preaching for a Christian community of shared goods
that finally pushed the matter past reconciliation. He
came under the influence of Robert Owen, well known
Scottish socialist, whom he met and whose ideas he
borrowed. But Owen was not a Christian so this interest
turned to George Rapp, founder of a Christian colony
called the Harmony Society. He visited the society at its
site called Economy, near Pittsburgh. In 1825 he decided
to try a similar venture and in August of that year he
and several others issued a proposal for establishing a
"German Christian Industrial Community," which they
later called Concordia. In September, Kurtz began to
publish a periodical to support the idea. He called it *Das
Wiedergefundere Paradies*, which translated means
Paradise Regained.

Between the fall of 1825 and the end of 1827, Concordia grew till nearly fifty families were pledged to join,
then diminished and died out. Henry worked hard to
make it succeed. In late 1826 or early 1827, he moved his
family to Stark County, Ohio, near Concordia's anticipated site. He published another periodical called
*Der Friedensbote von Concordia (The Peace Messenger of
Concordia)*. But all this came to nothing. Henry's project
was stillborn, his career in shambles, and he was stuck in
sparsely settled Ohio.

Why Concordia failed we can only speculate. Such
communities often had a short life but others at least got
started. Perhaps Henry could not get along with the
other organizers. Maybe he had some lingering doubts
that undermined his efforts. We do know that he did not
lose his fundamental concern for Christian discipline.

Sometime between then and April, 1828, Henry met
the Ohio Brethren. Here he found finally people who

Das
Wiedergefundene Paradies;

kein Gedicht.

Eine Zeitschrift,

Für Christen von allen Benennungen.

Herausgegeben

Von einer Christlichen Gesellschaft,

In monatlichen Heften.

Erster Band.

Zweyte Auflage.

Die Aufsicht über den Druck, und die Versendung
dieses Werkchens, so wie die darauf Bezug habende
Correspondenz, wird besorgt von Heinrich Kurtz,
Prediger zu Pittsburg.

Gedruckt bey J. J. Cope u. Co.
1825.

Paradise Regained

practiced what they preached and believed in church discipline. We do not know much about his conversion or his early years among the Brethren, but we know he must have found something he had not found in Pittsburgh or in Concordia, for not only did he stay with the Brethren until his death, but he became one of the century's most important elders. The brotherhood would have survived without Henry, but its Annual Meetings, hymnbooks, and publications would have been different. The Lutheran's loss was the Brethren's gain.

Elder George Hoke baptized him on April 6, 1828, on the Old Royer farm in Osnaburg Township, under a large maple tree. Legend has it that Henry wore his Lutheran pastoral robe, which as he came up from the water he slipped from his shoulders. He thereby renounced his previous ordination but not the ministry itself, for two years later the Brethren elected him to their ministry. He was soon advanced to the second degree and in 1844 he was ordained an elder. Each of these events were presided over by Elder George Hoke, who became Henry's longtime friend.

In 1841, the Brethren of Northeastern Ohio made Henry Kurtz overseer of the Mill Creek church (renamed the Mahoning church) in neighboring Mahoning County. On the surface this was not unusual. Often elders would oversee a church many miles distant if that congregation did not have an elder. We can only speculate that leadership was lacking in the Mill Creek congregation and in short supply elsewhere. Henry's experiences and qualifications were obvious. However, it was very unusual to make a man an overseer before he was ordained. For a year he made the forty-mile horseback ride once a month, finally moving into the congregation onto a farm five miles south of Poland in

Artist's drawing of Henry Kurtz's springhouse

Springfield Township. Here he lived until 1857 when he moved to a small town, Columbiana, not far away, where he lived until his death.

Born in Germany, former Lutheran pastor, well-educated, communitarian thinker, in charge of a church before his ordination—few in the brotherhood would have had even one of these peculiarities. Beyond this, he continued the publishing he had begun at Pittsburgh and set up his own print shop. Along with farming, printing became his occupation. He himself noted that the Brethren did not "feel much inclined to book-making and publishing."[3] Yet printing more than anything else made him valuable to the Brethren. He printed three different hymnbooks, Luther's German translation of the New Testament, the first Brethren periodical, the *Brethren's Encyclopedia*, and the Yearly Meeting minutes, plus many other non-Brethren materials.

The Brotherhood began to use Henry's trade in 1837 when they authorized him to publish the minutes. This he continued for many years, and it was probably what brought him into prominence, for he became clerk of the Yearly Meeting and therefore an adjunct to the Standing Committee. And all this long before he was ordained! Another extraordinary circumstance! Those privy to the councils of the Standing Committee were usually ordained elders only. Henry served either as clerk or as a committee member or both nineteen times.

Henry had one peculiarity he considered a shortcoming. H. R. Holsinger gives us this priceless description:

There was one German habit that Brother Kurtz had contracted which was a painful thorn in his flesh in his declining years. It was the tobacco habit. According to the flesh, he dearly loved his pipe, but he groaned in spirit to be relieved of the slavish bonds it had woven into his nature. And his experience furnished me with my strongest anti-tobacco sentiment. Poor old man! I would gladly have granted him full absolution, but his conscience would not. It was sad, and yet it was amusing to witness the pranks resorted to by this good man of mighty intellect and finished education. After dissipating with his pipe until dyspepsia and conscience came to his rescue, he would take the instrument of his torture to his wife, with the instruction, "Now, gib mir sie nimmermehr." (Never give it to me again.) From the tone of her reply I'm very certain that she received the same instructions before. Her reply was, "Es Doart nicht lang," (That will not do any good.) and she knew what she was saying. Perhaps he held out faithfully for a whole week, and sometimes possibly longer. The first time he went to the kitchen, he feigned sociability and business, and returned to his room without any farther advancement, to continue the warfare with the giant habit. After battling a day or two longer, he went again, ostensibly upon marital duties, but, in fact, with a view to the gratification of the baser passion. The mistake which he would invariably make before he was overcome would be in overdoing himself by unnatural smiles and courtesy. In this case he was told where he could find his old pipe, and he went his way rejoicing, although defeated and humbled.[4]

Henry also owned an organ, as if he needed still another peculiarity. He could and did play it and sang as well. Maybe it was his love of music that prompted him to publish those hymn books and in his old age to help compile still another one. However, the use made of his musicianship stopped there. We already know the Brethren did not allow musical instruments in their meetinghouses and frowned on them in the home. It is surprising that his organ never became an issue, for it was most unusual. Holsinger, who was Kurtz's apprentice for about six months in 1856-57, writes:

> Brother Kurtz was quite a musician, vocal and instrumental, and had an organ in the house, but rarely used it. I shall long remember one occasion on which I heard him perform and sing one of his favorites. I went to the house, where the editorial sanctum was, on business connected with the office. After entering the hall, I heard music, and finding the door ajar, I stopped and listened till the hymn was completed, much delighted with the strains. When I complimented him on his success, he explained that he had been tired of reading and writing, and had sought recreation and solace in the music.[5]

The most important venture Kurtz undertook was *The Gospel-Visiter.* Despite name changes, mergers with other periodicals, and several different places of publication, it is still issued and is the official Brethren periodical, *Messenger.* It is one of the oldest American denominational journals and was the first published for the Brethren.

Henry knew that his paper would meet resistance, for the Brethren were slow to embrace innovation. He knew he would need two things: the endorsement or at least acquiescence of Yearly Meeting and the interest of the people. The latter he needed because *The Gospel-Visitor* was a private venture; it had to sell so he could make his living. In 1849 he sent an explanation of his idea and a request for subscriptions to many congregations. He also planned to issue trial copies before the 1850 Yearly Meeting and submit them for a decision. Illness in his family prevented him from doing that, but he sent a query anyway:

GOSPEL - VISITER,

A MONTHLY PUBLICATION

DEVOTED

To The Exhibition of GOSPEL-PRINCIPLES & GOSPEL-PRACTICE
IN THEIR PRIMITIVE PURITY & SIMPLICITY, IN ORDER TO PROMOTE
CHRISTIAN UNION, BROTHERLY LOVE &
UNIVERSAL CHARITY.

"For I am not ashamed of the Gospel of Christ, for it is the power of God unto salvation to every one that believeth, to the Jew first, and also to the Greek." Rom. i. 16.

VOL. I.
1851-2.

PRINTED & PUBLISHED NEAR POLAND, OHIO,
BY HENRY KURTZ.

Title page *The Gospel-Visiter,* Vol. I, 1851–52

"Whether there is any danger to be apprehended from
publishing a paper among us. This subject to lay over till
next Annual Meeting." (Article 21, 1850)[6] The elders
tabled the query.

By early 1851, the better part of two years had passed.
He had sent the letter of inquiry and tested Yearly
Meeting. Henry must have become impatient. He decided to hazard the venture without the blessing of Yearly
Meeting and give the Brethren something real to discuss
at the meeting in 1851. Accordingly, in April in the loft
of his springhouse where he had his print shop, he
published the first issue of the first Brethren paper. It
was undistinguished in design and content, but its birth
was more important than anyone could see. The Old
Order Brethren were later to trace the falling away from
the old ways to publishing. For the rest of the century,
publishing was related to foreign missions, higher
education, and cultural changes in the church. Henry's
little paper was the beginning.

He went to the Meeting in 1851 with anxiety. He
wrote that he labored under uncertainty.

. . . . whether the *Visiter* would be permitted to live and
go on his way rejoicing, or whether he would have to be
sacrificed on the altar of brotherly love as a peace
offering.[7]

Years later, old brother John Leedy in Virginia recalled that meeting:

. . . I was but young then, in 1851. I remember well the
old Brethren that were present from different
states—Henry Tracy, of Ohio; D. P. Saylor, of
Maryland; Daniel Brower, of Ohio; and a host of
Virginians, John Kline, Jacob Brower, Benjamin Bow-

man, Daniel Yount, and John Harshbarger. I think
Brother B. F. Moomaw and some of the Niningers were
also present.

I stood near by, and well remember our little German
brother pleading that the church grant him the right to
publish a paper, called *The Gospel-Visiter.* Some of the
old Brethren opposed him, thinking there might be
danger in the paper. Others thought it might be well to
let him have a trial.[8]

After considerable discussion, the latter opinion prevailed.

Considered, at this council, that we will not forbid
Brother Henry Kurtz to go on with his paper for one
year; and that all the Brethren or churches will impar-
tially examine the "Gospel Visiter," and if found wrong
or injurious, let them send in their objection at the next
Annual Meeting. (Article 8, 1851)[9]

Henry was past his first hurdle. He had before him a
whole year to endear his paper to the Brethren.

By the Yearly Meeting of 1852, thirteen issues and
one number in German were in the hands of the
Brethren. Henry awaited their judgment with curious
faith. He wrote in March:

Though we are fully apprised of a coming storm at the
Yearly Meeting which threatens to sweep the *Visiter*
from the face of the earth, we fear not, in as much as we
believe, that Jesus is with us in the ship, who is yet able
to speak effectually to the storm, 'Be Still!'[10]

Maybe he had assessed the situation as well as a correspondent from Maryland who wrote:

Methinks the brethren in Yearly Meeting . . . will give

the advice of Gamaliel, "To let this matter alone, for it be not of God, it will fail; but if it should be of God, beware, lest haply ye be found even to fight against God."[11]

The Meeting took Gamaliel's advice and concluded

... inasmuch as there is a diversity of opinion upon the subject—we cannot forbid its publication at this time, and hope those brethren opposed to it will exercise forbearance, and let it stand or fall, on its own merits. (Article 4, 1852)[12]

Henry was over the second biggest hurdle. The church had examined a full year and the Yearly Meeting had allowed it to live.

Another year had to pass before the matter was laid finally to rest. The Meeting in 1853 concluded:

Inasmuch as the "Visiter" is a private undertaking of its editor, we unanimously conclude that this meeting should not any further interfere with it. (Article 3, 1853)[13]

Henry wrote with more jubilation than his German temperament usually admitted:

... thanks be to God, the cloud has been lifted up ... and The *Gospel-Visiter* may continue his course, if not rejoicing, at least unmolested, yet with fear and trembling.[14]

It is extraordinary that a man so un-Brethren in background could persuade the Brethren to accept a church paper. The impatient young man who left Pittsburgh in discord had learned forbearance. He wrote in the second issue, ". . . our full determination is, to preserve a conciliatory spirit in the paper"[15] and he did.

Kurtz's prime years spanned more than the 1840s. The fifties and early sixties were his years of greatest achievement. Yet 1844 brought his ordination; 1841 the beginning of his long eldership in Mahoning County; 1849 the beginning of his *Visiter* venture; and April, 1851, just four months out of the decade, the first issue. He signed the Yearly Meeting minutes every year except 1850, his name appearing at the end as clerk until 1844, when his ordination placed his name up among the elders. There was only one other man whose name appeared as often during the decade, his friend Elder George Hoke. Henry Kurtz was an important and visible leader in the 1840s.

The number of Henry's peculiarities is astonishing. Yet he caused little trouble. That is startling, for there have been men less unique who have upset the Brethren far more. His former apprentice, H. R. Holsinger, was not nearly so singular, yet the Brethren eventually threw him out of the church. Why Holsinger and not Kurtz? Both were printers; both used their press to advance new ideas. The answer lies partly in the Brethren and the rest in Henry's understanding of them.

The Brethren were open-minded in a peculiar way. They were willing to consider a new idea, if it was advanced with respect for the order and for the church's right to decide. They were reluctant to consider an idea if bludgeoned with it. Henry did not push too quickly. He gave people time to consider and the opportunity to object. He loved the Brethren and acknowledged the discipline of the church. If Yearly Meeting had forbidden him to continue the *Visiter*, he would have stopped.

That was the difference between Holsinger and Kurtz. The former was impatient and aggressive; the latter was

cautious and excessively deferential. The Brethren
favored the latter qualities and Henry knew that. He
could have been a "sore thumb" and instead became a
beloved brother.

Old Brother Hoke

There is no elder who did more and about whom we
know less than George Hoke. He was born in Pennsylvania on July 1, 1783, and like so many other
Brethren moved west. He was in northeastern Ohio
sometime before his marriage in 1805 to Christina
Mellinger, and that is where he stayed all his life. He was
called to the ministry in the Mill Creek church, where
Henry Kurtz was later to be elder, and was ordained
sometime before 1820, possibly in 1812. In 1826, he
moved to the Canton church some forty miles west of
where he lived until 1844 when he moved into the nearby
Nimishillen congregation. After leaving Mill Creek he
remained elder in charge there until Henry Kurtz was
appointed to that position in 1841. He was the overseer
of the Canton and Nimishillen congregations from 1826
until 1852, when he moved some forty miles further west
into the Ashland congregation where his son-in-law
Elder Elias P. Dickey was in charge. Here he died on
June 23, 1861, aged seventy-seven years, of a "stroke of
palsy"[16] which had rendered him partially paralyzed and
speechless two and one half years before.

Elder Hoke was on Standing Committee twenty times
and served as moderator of Yearly Meeting eleven times
running (1848 through 1858) more often than anyone
else save Elder H. D. Davy who served twelve times
(1865-1876) and about whom we also know little. He
was on Standing Committee nine times in the 1840s.
"Our beloved old brother George Hoke" was a title of
respect throughout the brotherhood.

In April of 1828, Hoke baptized Henry Kurtz. Tradition has it that he also converted him. This was the beginning of a long association between the two men. Hoke also presided at Henry's election to the ministry and his ordination. It must have been George Hoke who persuaded Henry to be the overseer at the church in Mahoning County, where Elder Hoke himself had been the nonresident elder for years. Hoke was on Standing Committee the year Henry was first asked to be clerk, and maybe it was George who introduced Henry. Finally, we know that he was the moderator at Yearly Meeting during all the years *The Gospel-Visiter* was discussed—1850 through 1853. We must presume that Henry had George's support. Hoke was so well respected that it seems impossible for the *Visiter* to have succeeded against his opposition or that he and Kurtz could have had an ongoing relationship if he had opposed printing. However, we do not know any of this for sure except that he did preside over nearly all the important events in Kurtz's church life.

Those few bare bones make for tantalizing speculation. If we knew more about George Hoke and his friendship with Henry Kurtz, we would know a lot about the inner workings of the brotherhood in the 1840s and 1850s. It is safe to say that George Hoke was the strongest and most prominent elder in the 1840s.[17]

We know four unrelated facts about Elder Hoke. He wrote down some of his thoughts on doctrinal issues which his widow published in *The Gospel-Visiter* after his death. He once had a lengthy correspondence with a man on slavery and persuaded him it was wrong. He was an agent for the sale of the *Martyr's Mirror*, a large book published by the Mennonites with stories of all the Christian martyrs. And in 1856, he got sick from the bad weather at the Yearly Meeting at Waddam's Grove,

Illinois, and missed the first session. That is all we know about his leadership.

Otho Winger gives this terse description of him:

> He was a strong leader, very kind but very decisive. He could call brethren to order in a very kind way. His voice was clear, strong, and musical. He was short in stature, but rather stoutly built. He had a pleasant countenance, a dignified and courteous manner. He had a good command of both English and German. He was an able minister, a clear thinker, a profound and logical reasoner.[18]

When he died, Henry Kurtz had only this to say about him: "A useful man, a servant of God, a loving member of a meeting for many years. Peace be to his ashes."[19] A good man passed and took with him all trace of himself. Those who knew him remained curiously mum and Brethren history is blank on its old Brother Hoke.

Commentary

We know so little about the Brotherhood in the 1840s that conclusions about its leadership are risky. Elders Hoke and Kurtz were the most visible leaders, if the signatures on the Yearly Meeting minutes are a trustworthy gauge. But visible leaders are not always the most powerful. Peter Nead of Ohio, David P. Foutz of Pennsylvania, James H. Tracy of Indiana, John Price, John H. Umstad and Andrew Spanogle of Pennsylvania, Benjamin Bowman of Virginia, Christian Long of Illinois, and others were also frequent members of Standing Committee. Who is to say what role they played? Unless there are documents or first person accounts, which there aren't, no one can know who influenced decisions.

Yearly Meeting set policy, but local congregations were pretty much on their own to enforce it. There were elders who had great influence in their congregation or region who may seldom have attended Yearly Meeting. Neither the meeting nor the brotherhood was ever dominated by one or two men only.

The Brethren were busy in the 1840s *being* the church and hardly interested at all in recording it. They probably felt that anything more than the laconic Yearly Meeting minutes was vain. They were a circumspect people and their rich qualities are partly lost to us. We must be content to conclude that these two brethren from Ohio were what they appear to be—the prominent leaders. If they were not, there are some gifted old elders who will remain unsung.

CHAPTER 7

Chapter Seven
A Bold and Masterful Elder

It was fortunate that Elder George Wolfe lived in Illinois. He would have been strong meat for the eastern Brethren. Either they would have shackled his splendid spirit or he would have disturbed their equanimity. For George Wolfe was a masterful man. He was not cautious like Henry Kurtz, yet he was not headstrong and defiant either. He was simply master of himself and his situation—sure-footed and dauntless, a man who moved only when he wished to. Yet he could be moved—by reason, truth, or need. He was strong and kind, stern yet with the gift of tears. He had a rare quality sometimes found in big men to forebear his power and be gentle in the extreme.

Back in the east the Brethren had strong leaders, but they were seldom masterful. Where there were many Brethren and many elders, the power of the church tended to blunt the sharp edge of brilliant leadership. Out on the frontier where the nearest congregation was far away, George Wolfe could follow his own ways, and he did. The Brethren were more comfortable with forbearance than mastery, and while George Wolfe had both, he had more of the latter than the eastern Brethren would have cared to have.

His sphere was wider too. He was active in civic affairs, widely respected outside of the Brethren, friendly to politicians and to clergymen of other denominations—far more a man of affairs than the eastern elders who stayed clear of secular matters.

Yet this masterful man was mastered by the church and gave it his untiring service for over fifty years. Despite his bold spirit, he put himself under the church's discipline as he understood it, never defying his Illinois Brethren or getting into serious dispute with them. And in his old age when contact was reestablished with the brotherhood, he was unduly accommodating while staunchly defending his own convictions.

Elder Wolfe apparently never let his subordination to the church dull his fearless zest for life. Of course, in the eyes of God, faithfulness and boldness are not incongruous, but in the hearts of the Brethren they had an uneasy relationship.

Wolfe and his "Far-Western Brethren," as they were called in the east, were almost completely isolated from the brotherhood and Yearly Meeting for several decades. Some practices, particularly the mode of feetwashing, diverged over those years. In the early 1850s, dialogue began between them and the eastern Brethren who had begun to settle in Illinois. It was not until 1859 that complete reconciliation occurred. In these debates, Wolfe was definite, yet very courteous. The upshot was that where division might have occurred, mutual respect grew instead. Yearly Meeting made a remarkable decision in 1856—to respect the Far-

Western Brethren's unique practices and to continue their own. That was unusual flexibility for those days when pluralism among the Brethren on practice was unheard of. Undoubtedly, Wolfe's firmness, candor, and openness had a lot to do with the outcome. The eastern elders were surprised to find a large, well-disciplined congregation and a powerful elder where they had expected to find a few disorganized pioneer brethren. These same elders would have been even more surprised to learn that the whole brotherhood would eventually adopt the Far-Western Brethren's so-called "single mode" of feet washing, the method still used in the Church of the Brethren.

This chapter recounts many events during Elder Wolfe's fifty-three years of active leadership, but nothing of his activity in the 1840s. We know little about what he was doing in that decade except that he was the strongest and most respected elder in all of Illinois, Missouri, Kentucky, and Iowa. His whole life is told here so you will know what kind of man was keeping watch out on the frontier during the 1840s.

George Wolfe was born in Lancaster County, Pennsylvania, in 1780. He moved with his family in 1787 to Fayette County, Pennsylvania, ten miles west of Uniontown, on the Monongahela River. There his father built flat boats for settlers moving downriver to the Ohio. George and his older brother, Jacob, helped when they grew old enough. In 1800 George's father, who was also named George and was a Brethren elder, put his family on one of his boats and cast off down the Monongahela and on into the Ohio River, heading for new land in Kentucky.

The following was written by Elder J. H. Moore and published in *Some Brethren Pathfinders* in 1929.[1] Elder Moore was himself a pioneer, knew George Wolfe when he was an old man, and has a narrative style I could not possibly match. Accordingly, I am reproducing his marvelous description. I have edited the original story to make it fit this chapter and have occasionally changed a phrase or two to make the edited version flow properly. Otherwise, the words are all Elder Moore's and while I wish I could take credit for them, I am satisfied at least to pass them on to you as the penwork of a man who was himself something of a sturdy pioneer preacher.

In the rush of emigrants from the east into Kentucky, there were many more unmarried men than single women, so that getting wives for the men was a problem. It is said that when young George reached the age of twenty-three there was in his community but one single woman of matrimonial age, and that her hand was most earnestly sought by two men, one a young lawyer and the other George Wolfe. The woman was of typical Dunkard ancestry, and so was George, both raised on farms, and this gave the farmer young man the advantage in the contest for the young woman's affections. Well, George won out, so on March 3, 1823, George Wolfe and Anna Hunsaker became husband and wife. This so exasperated the young lawyer that he threatened to give Wolfe a thrashing and told him so. George tried to reason the case with him, saying that Anna had made her choice, that the knot was now tied, and there was no use in having any trouble over it. Finding that the lawyer would not listen to reason, George told him that if he thought a little spindling lawyer could whip a strong man like himself, he could have the satisfaction of trying it. This settled the matter for all time. Young Wolfe was a man of peaceful methods, almost to the extreme, but he was large enough, strong enough and brave enough to take care of himself and his rights should it become necessary to resort to the physical.

Sometime after George was married, he and his

brother Jacob, three years older, along with Abram Hunsaker, talked matters over and decided on looking beyond Kentucky for a place of residence. They had heard of the wonderful prosperity of the country around Kaskaskia and Cahokia, where more than half of the white people in Illinois Territory were then living, and decided on looking into the situation. So it was decided that George and Abram should take a hunting trip up through southern Illinois and, if practicable, pick out a good place for a settlement, nearly all of the country at the time being a perfect wilderness, abounding in wild animals, and from which all of the Indians had but recently been driven, though still somewhat exposed to Indian raids from southwestern Kentucky.

Having thus decided the two young men, strong and resolute, fitted up their boat, supplied themselves with plenty of ammunition, good guns, some provisions, a few tools, in fact a regular hunter's outfit, including trap, and started down Greene River, then down the Ohio River until they came to the mouth of the Cache River, and up they pushed the boat, through forests almost as dense as a jungle, always camping out of nights. Having gone up the river as far as seemed advisable, they hid their boat in some nook, then started out on foot, guided alone by their sense of direction. And by the way, George possessed a faculty for direc tion almost as unerring as the compass. Day or night, on the great prairies or in the dense forest, he never lost the direction. This made of him, as he was, a typical hunter and guide. But there we have these two young hunters, within less than two miles of where the town of Jonesboro, the county seat of Union County, now stands, feasting on bear meat and wild turkey, the only two white men in all the wild untamed region round about. Here in the fall of 1803, they constructed two log cabins. The logs had to be cut, brought together, notched at the ends and put together in order. Clapboards for roofing had to be split, punching split and dressed down for the floors, fireplace built and plastered with clay, and all this done without the driving of a nail.

While constructing their cabins, clearing and fencing a few acres of ground, they lived month after month on the wild game they shot or trapped and the nuts found beneath great hickory nut and walnut trees. They had no use for money, for there was no one to pay it to; had no occasion to purchase anything, and no place to buy things even if they so desired. They had no neighbors, did not see a human being inside of a year or more. They had no books to read, no papers, no magazines, no letters to write and received none. In all this time young George Wolfe had no word from the young wife he left in Kentucky, nor could she hear from him. She simply knew that he was somewhere in the dense forest of Illinois Territory, dead or alive, she did not know which, and that it might be a year or even more before she could have the pleasure of greeting him. She was a brave woman and had faith in George.

But candidly, why all these privations, experiences and hardships in a vast wilderness cut off from friends, relatives and even common civilization? It is simply a process, under the management of God and nature, for the making of a marvelous preacher, different of course from the present day college and university method.

These young men were located about forty miles north and a bit to the west of where the city of Cairo now stands. In due time things were worked into living shape, and in some way they got in touch with their families and friends. Possibly by the use of the boat they had kept at a safe place they made their way back to Kentucky and then began the preparations for moving. It is more than likely that the move was an overland trip, crossing the large streams where there were ferry conveniences, and on reaching the Illinois side of the Ohio River they might have followed the old buffalo and Indian trail, as it wound its way through dense forests and across wild prairies.

Seal of Union County, Ill.

Our story takes us now to the year of 1811 when Kaskaskia on the river of the same name, and near where it empties into the Mississippi, was the seat of government for the Territory of Illinois. At this date the population of the entire territory was just a little in excess of 12,000 and more than half of the people lived within twenty miles of the capital. But as the year was drawing to a close something startling happened. In fact two things took place, one belonging to nature and the other to art, one of the work of Providence through nature, and the other the work of man.

Far-seeing men, men of wealth and business, had reached the conclusion that the great Father of Waters (Mississippi) and all the other rivers entering it, were to become the wonderful arteries of commerce for the central part of the nation. Boats by the score were appearing upon the rivers, all however, propelled by long oars and sails.

But early in December, 1811, a steamboat, the New Orleans, was launched at Pittsburgh, Pa. It was the first steamboat to plow the western waters. Down the Ohio River it came, puffing, whistling and lashing the water. The news of the river monster traveled faster than the "fire boat," as many called it, and here and there the banks were lined by people, some of them coming quite a distance to see the floating craft go by. To all of them it was, of course, the opportunity of a lifetime to look upon the first steamboat to venture out upon the great waters of the untamed and in part the unexplored West. On December 18, just as the boat was entering the waters of the Mississippi, occurred the greatest and most remarkable earthquake ever known in the history of the country east of the Rocky Mountains. Those on the boat could see the trees waving and nodding in the absence of wind. Some trees would bend half way over, then spring back again. The earth rose and fell like laboring in great pain. Islands disappeared and others came upon the scene. In places the earth opened and streams of water and mud rose to a great height. At one great upheaval the waters of the Mississippi River were seen to run up stream only to come rushing back a bit later. Day and night the convulsions continued. At New Madrid, on the Missouri side of the river, and a short distance south of where Cairo now is, a large tract of land, timber and all, sank to a considerable depth, forming a lake sixty miles long and from three to twenty miles wide, and now in sailing over the waters of this lake one is astonished at beholding, far below, gigantic trees in great numbers, all looking like a mighty water-covered forest, miles and miles in extent, constituting one of the most remarkable under-water scenes on the American continent. For three days the earth and waters heaved and groaned and sometimes roared like the sound of heavy artillery. Some of the boats on the river were sunk, others were tossed out on the shore and many lives were lost, and a vast amount of property destroyed. The steamboat lived through it all, and continued her course down the river.

The disturbance, however, continued more or less for six months before everything in nature quieted down. The incident caused an immense sensation in all the adjoining sections and gave rise to many fears, some theories, and a bit of superstition. Some of the more superstitious said that this thing of trying to run a boat by "bilin' water" so greatly displeased God that he, in this earthquake, gave proof of his disapproval of such business. With the two things happening on the same date, the credulous had what seemed to them a self-evident point that they made use of in conversation as well as in the pulpit, for all there was in it.

Right here we come to the real turning point for good in our far-reaching story. The excitement resulted in a wonderful religious awakening all over the country. It spread to every settlement and into every town. The preachers took advantage of the conditions and people of every grade were swept into the churches by the

dozens. In the Wolfe community a Methodist minister
held a revival, probably in the spring of 1812, and many
of the settlers, most of them being of Dunkard parent-
age, applied for membership. Among the number were
George Wolfe, then thirty-two, his wife, his brother
Jacob and his wife, fourteen in all. George Wolfe was
naturally of a religious turn, but very argumentative and
a man of decided views. The preacher at once organized
his converts into a class and appointed Wolfe as class
leader. Agreeable with the rules of the Methodist
Church they were to meet regularly for worship and the
study of the Scriptures. In due time the new leader had
his class assemble at one of the homes. He had no experience in such meetings and therefore had to map out
his own course.

The first thing he did at the opening of the meeting
was to address his people about as follows: "Brethren
and sisters, we are now organized into a church. I have
pondered and prayed over this matter, and I conclude
that if John Wesley is the savior we are all right, but if
Jesus Christ is the Savior we are wrong." It is said that
this laconic speech from the young leader filled the
hearts of the other members of the class with amaze-
ment. They hardly knew what to think of such an abrupt
way of approaching a matter needing consideration. But
some of them were thoughtful enough to say: "Christ is
our Savior," and then asked, "But what shall we do?"
Then it was Bro. Wolfe said: "Let us send to Kentucky
for a Dunkard brother to come and baptize us." This
pleased all of them, and to it all agreed. In the assembly
was a young man about twenty-four years old named
Hunsaker, probably, Jacob, a brother of Wolfe's wife,
and with him it was arranged that he should go to Kentucky for a minister. The trip was a long one and meant
not less than a week, or even more on the road. The
meeting closed with a happy feeling on the part of all,
but they felt sure they were doing the right thing.

Everybody soon learned that young Hunsaker was on

his way to Kentucky. A considerable part of the route lay through sections that were still in the wilderness stage, with only here and there a small settlement and not even the semblance of a village until the Ohio River was reached, and then after crossing the river on a ferry boat a long ride to near the middle of Kentucky. His people would hardly be looking for his return short of ten or more days, but to the surprise of everybody, after an absence of only a few days, he returned, accompanied by the preacher, Eld. John Hendricks. They had met on the road, Eld. Hendricks being on a visit to his friends in the territory, for he had a number of friends in the Wolfe settlement. The meeting of the two men was a surprise to each, and after the necessary explanation there was much rejoicing.

This Eld. Hendricks was another typical pioneer preacher. He was born probably in Pennsylvania or Maryland, emigrated to North Carolina in an early day and from there he moved into Kentucky. He knew the Wolfe family when they lived in Kentucky, and had probably visited Jacob and George Wolfe, some of the Hunsakers and others in Illinois a few times, so on this special occasion he was not an entire stranger to the people of the community. But the news of his arrival was soon carried to every settlement within reach, and on the day appointed for the meeting everybody was present.

Eld. Hendricks never had a more attentive audience. We have no information regarding the text for the occasion and the subject treated, but the Brethren preachers of that day were no men to shirk duty or sugarcoat their sermons for the sake of a little popularity. They knew the gospel and then they knew how to present it so people could understand what it meant for them. So after the close of the services the entire congregation repaired to the bank of Clearwater Creek, where there was plenty of clear water and a good place to administer the rite of baptism. There were fourteen men and women to be baptized. None of them were in their teens. All were

people of mature age, and knew what they were taking
upon themselves. A season of prayer at the water's edge,
and then the elder entered the stream, leading George
Wolfe by the hand. George was tall, well proportioned,
strong, a fine specimen of real American manhood. The
elder had him kneel, then after taking his confession,
renouncing Satan and the sinful pleasures of the world,
and promising to live a life of obedience until death,
proceeded to administer the rite, immersing him in the
name of the Father, and of the Son, and of the Holy
Ghost. Then came the consecration prayer. One by one
all the others were thus baptized.

The occasion was an impressive one, exceedingly so.
It was the first baptismal service for the Brethren in
Illinois.

After holding a few more meetings, comforting and
instructing the new converts, Eld. Hendricks left for his
Kentucky home, but in the course of several months
returned and proceeded to effect an organization. When
it came to holding a choice for a minister, George Wolfe
stood out against it strong, saying, "I have looked over
the Brethren carefully and I conclude that there is no
one of us qualified for the ministry." And when chosen
it took some plain talking on the part of the elder in
charge to induce him to accept the call and take up the
work. He probably received unanimous vote of the
other members, and had their perfect confidence. This
made him the first and only resident Brethren minister,
save one, in the vast region west of the Wabash River.
At the same meeting, and the same time, his brother
Jacob and George Davis were installed as deacons, thus
placing the little congregation in good shape for work.
Eld. Hendricks was doubtless retained as the elder, and
had intended to return shortly and ordain George
Wolfe, but he died the following spring, so it was
arranged for Eld. Adam Hostetler of Shelby County,
Ky., to come and complete the work.

This ordination service took place in the spring of

Elder George Wolfe

1813, when Eld. Wolfe was thirty-three years old, and
only about one year after he was baptized. Here was a
properly organized congregation of fourteen members,
far out in the wilderness, so to speak, and every one of
them, preacher and all, young in the Christian experience. We do not recall another like instance in the
history of pioneer mission work. The little band of
believers, while in the very flush of their first love, was
put in shape to take care of themselves, and to push out
in the Lord's work. Most assuredly the hand of the Lord
was in all this as we shall see in the further development
of this story.

Eld. Wolfe seems to have demonstrated marked ability as a religious leader almost from the very start. The
little band of believers had been entrusted to his care
and he fully realized the responsibility resting upon him.
As the years of experience came to him he grew in favor
with God and man. Historically speaking he was, in
company with his friend Abraham Hunsaker, the first
man on the ground, struck the first ax in the interest of
the settlement, and was now the only resident minister in
the community, in charge of the first organized church
to come upon the scene, ready to preach the Gospel, to
baptize believers, to solemnize marriages and help bury
the dead. He appears to have been a man of ample
means, industrious, economical, a thoroughgoing
business man, farmer and stockraiser.

He had from early manhood known much about the
Bible, especially the New Testament, and was well acquainted with the history as well as the faith and the
practice of the Brethren. Following his conversion he
got down to study. He was always a close thinker and a
natural logician. Into his community moved members
from other parts, some from Kentucky and others from
the eastern states. Not a few were received by confession
and baptism, and as the year came and went the church
grew in size and influence.

Eld. Wolfe took a broad view of his mission as a

leader. He visited and did some preaching for the
Brethren in Kentucky, 150 miles distant. To the
southwest of his home, forty miles, and on the other side
of the Mississippi River, was a small band of members.
This little group had been cared for by his old Kentucky
friend, Eld. John Hendricks, who had died in the spring
of 1813, just as he was getting ready to move with his
large family to Missouri. His family, however, made the
change of location and in the number was a talented son
named James. Bro. Wolfe visited these members, and on
Saturday, Oct. 17, 1818, ordained Bro. James Hendricks
to the eldership. The two became very close friends and
visited each other quite frequently.

Elder Wolfe was now (1818) becoming a man among
men and as such was held in confidence by his
neighbors. The day had come for his ability and influence to be recognized more distinctly. The population
of Illinois had increased from 12,282 in 1810 to 40,146.
He could recall the day, fifteen years before, when he
and Hunsaker were the only two settlers in what is at
present known as Union County, but since then the
number had grown to 1,800 souls. On Dec. 3, 1818,
Illinois became a state with the capital at Kaskaskia.
Union County was duly organized and a commission
appointed to select and fix a permanent seat of justice
for the county. Eld. George Wolfe, then a Dunkard
preacher of five years' standing, was the first one named
on the commission. The commission made choice of ten
acres of the farm of John Grammer, within three
quarters of a mile of Eld. Wolfe's residence, and the
town of Jonesboro, named after a Baptist preacher by
the name of Jones. Later the figures of Wolfe and Jones
appeared on the county seal. And until further provision
could be made the court was to convene in the home of
Jacob Hunsaker, Jr. Among the names handed in by the
sheriff for the first grand jury was George Wolfe. People
had gathered from all surrounding sections. It was the
first term of court, held in a large log cabin, belonging to

a member of the Dunkard church. With the first case in hand the sheriff marched the jury out to the edge of the woods, where they found the grand jury room on a log lying beneath a great forest tree. Here in the edge of one of nature's great forests they, with becoming solemnity, thrashed out their verdict; whether guilty or not guilty, we are not advised.

Of the crowd that had assembled, the historian says, it being near the middle of May, some were barefoot, not a few wore coonskin caps, some were dressed in buckskin, and practically all of them reached the place either on foot or on horseback. It was indeed a typical pioneer gathering, in a community that had been a veritable wilderness only a few years before.

In the country was a Baptist preacher named Jones, of considerable influence. About the year 1817 the two held a joint meeting in the community, each man remaining true to the doctrine of his own church. Both of them were able men of splendid standing and their meetings produced quite an awakening for miles around. At the close of these meetings, with their hats on it would seem, they stood in the presence of the large audience and shook hands, indicating that as Christian ministers they were on the best of terms with each other, regardless of their clear cut denominational differences. So deeply and so permanently did this impress the hardy pioneers of every class that thirty-three years later, in 1850, when it was decided to adopt a seal for Union County, the scene of the two preachers, Wolfe and Jones, shaking hands, was engraved into the seal, and now every time the seal is made a part of a Union County official document, Wolfe and Jones may be seen standing side by side. Thus the impression made by Eld. Wolfe in his pioneer days was such as to perpetuate his name, and even his appearance for centuries to come.

While Eld. Wolfe took an active part in building up the community in which he lived, and in helping to put the affairs of the county in shape, he declined all political honors, even refusing later on to be considered as nominee for governor. He told his friends and admirers, and he had many of them, that he was a preacher and not a politician, that his mission in this world was to preach the gospel. Mounted on his trusty horse he went from point to point delivering his message. He had a strong, graceful and impressive way of speaking and the people of every class, common and educated, heard him gladly.

In his rounds he ran up against the Catholics in Kaskaskia, the then strongest hold of Catholicism in all the west. Here they had a well attended college, and other Catholic institutions for the training of priests and nuns. The town was founded by them, built up by them and had become the religious, political, commercial and military headquarters of the upper Mississippi Valley. Eld. Wolfe was challenged to a debate with a gifted Catholic priest. To accept the challenge would be like attempting to beard the lion in his den, with all odds in the lion's favor. But when it came to a matter of duty in defense of his religious claims Eld. Wolfe backed down for nothing. So far as we can get at the date it must have been in the year 1820, at which time Wolfe was forty years old and had been in the ministry seven years.

The elder was then in prime condition for his best mental efforts. He possessed a marvelous personality, stood erect and was thoroughly self-possessed. He had associated with men of distinction and was perfectly at home with the most gifted and influential. He feared God but neither man nor beast. The debate as it progressed created a wonderful excitement. The people turned out in great numbers. The new governor of the new state, Shadrach Bond, was there and is said to have presided. Tradition says the governor of Kentucky attended the discussion. Wolfe understood his Bible, and knew how to tell its story, and all through the debate held his gifted opponent right down to the Book, telling him what the Word of God demanded, and that the Catholics were not in their teaching, claims and manner of life doing what the Book said. And so skillfully and forcibly did our pioneer preacher meet his opponent at every point that after the discussion was over Governor Bond was heard to say that for an un-educated man Wolfe was the profoundest reasoner to whom he ever listened.

The victory was so complete and the excitement and feeling so intense, that the governor knew the life of Eld. Wolfe would be in danger as he proceeded on his way home, so entirely unknown to him and without his con-sent, he ordered a bodyguard for his protection. On the morning of his departure from the tavern where he had been stopping, and after bidding his friends good-by, he mounted his horse only to immediately find himself sur-rounded by a band of soldiers, under the command of an officer to serve as an escort on a part of his journey. This act of itself created no small sensation. But the governor had great admiration for one who had done as much for the state as the elder had accomplished, and meant to make his return to his people as safe as possi-ble.

The debate gave Eld. Wolfe quite a reputation in Kaskaskia, among the state officials, military officers and others, as well as in other parts. As a preacher no man in southern Illinois had a finer standing.

Eld. Wolfe was soon to grapple with two other big propositions. A number of his Union County members had moved to Adams County and it looked as though the rest of them might follow suit. When Illinois entered the Union in 1818 she came in as a free state. A little later Missouri was admitted as a slave state. Kentucky was also a slave state. A large per cent of the early im-migrants came from slave territory and now began agitation in favor of so changing the constitution as to permit the owning of slaves. The legislature decided to put the question of amending the constitution up to the people. For eighteen months the excitement ran high.

Newspapers took sides and the state was flooded with pamphlets, tracts and circulars. Public speakers were everywhere. Fearing the possibility of freedom losing out, Eld. Wolfe took the field in opposition to making Illinois a slave state, and such an influence did he wield that a writer in the Quincy, Ill., *Herald*, some years later, said that Wolfe did more to make Illinois free soil than any other man in the state. The slaveholders were defeated, and the Brethren as well as others congratulated the Dunkard preacher, as he was called, for the part he had so ably taken in the interest of freedom.

After having resided in Illinois for twenty-eight years, reaching out in his labors to Kentucky, Missouri and several counties in southern Illinois, there came to Eld. Wolfe a turn in the road. For him the hand of destiny pointed to Adams County, to which part of the state the majority of his flock had already emigrated. He sold his possessions in Union County and the year 1831 finds him domiciled on a large tract of fine farming land eighteen miles east of Quincy. He was then fifty-one years old, right in the prime of his physical and mental manhood, and one of the most brainy preachers in all the region round about. In a little while a love feast was held on the premises of one of the well-to-do farming members. A meetinghouse was erected near the village of Liberty and the work of the church started in good earnest.

Eld. Wolfe was not long in building up a reputation. The people in Quincy heard about him and on Sundays some of them would drive out to the church, eighteen miles, to hear him expound the Word. Hearing so much about what was going on out at the Dunkard church, one of the Quincy clergymen decided that he would go out and see for himself. That day Wolfe preached on the love of God, touching on nonswearing, nonconformity to the world, and the atonement. His discourse was a long and able one. He often preached two hours, and always kept his congregations interested to the end. He

never used notes. The clergyman returned to the city and
told his congregation that Eld. Wolfe knew more about
the true principles of Christianity than any man he ever
met, and further said, that if we had more like him we
would have better churches and a better world. He concluded his report in this way: "I heard more gospel from
that peculiar man than I ever heard before."

The church being well established in Adams County,
known as the Mill Creek church, Eld. Wolfe proceeded
to broaden out in his work. He made some trips to Cape
Girardeau County, Mo., where Eld. James Hendricks
was in charge, visited the members in Pike County, to
the south, and then extended his labors into Hancock,
the county north of his own. Here he was laboring
among the churches, his field of operation and personal
acquaintance extending from middle Kentucky to near
the northern limits of Illinois, and his great intellect easily overshadowing that of any Brethren preacher in all
the west. His deep personal piety, childlike simplicity
and marvelous ability as a preacher of the gospel had
won the love and even admiration of every member with
whom he had come in contact. He had accumulated
considerable property, and was in a position to devote
practically all his time to the interest of the church. His
son David was a member of the state legislature, and
this, along with his fine standing otherwise, gave the
family a considerable degree of prestige not only in the
rural sections but in the city of Quincy itself. So
favorably did he impress the leading men of the county
that Senator Wm. A. Richardson was heard to say that
he regarded Eld. Wolfe as one of the profoundest
thinkers the state of Illinois ever produced.

This is the man who was going here and there confir-
ming the churches, and teaching principles, though a bit
unorthodox at the time, that were, under the direction of
the One who sees the end from the beginning, destined
to become the general practice of the Brotherhood. For
some decades, the Brotherhood in the east seems to

have, in a great measure, lost sight of him and his work, and still he was pushing ahead and taking care of the Lord's flocks as he came in touch with them, a task which only a strong man could accomplish during the period in which he labored. Then later on when he came in touch with members that had moved into the country from the eastern churches, news of the man and his work began to be sent back to the home congregations, some of it correct, but a good deal of it not. This gave rise to rumors and much widespread prejudice. Even Eld. Henry Kurtz, editor of the *Gospel Visitor*, our only church paper at the time, took sides against him. This intensified the opposition. The feeling was not solely against Eld. Wolfe and his large congregation in Adams County, but against all the churches in Southern Illinois with which he was closely affiliated. He had himself in a limited way lost sight of the Annual Meeting and her proceedings. Living as he did on the extreme west side of Illinois made it very inconvenient for him to attend nearly all of the Annual Conferences. The first one he ever attended was the one held in Montgomery County, Ohio, in 1850.

Beginning about this time, Eld. Wolfe's friends in Illinois, and among them some very influential elders, got busy with a view of bringing about a complete union of the general Brotherhood and the Far Western Brethren, as the churches in Adams County, Macoupin County, Bond County and some others in Illinois, Iowa and Missouri were called. In this movement Wolfe's own church took part, and in a special way Dr. Sturgis of Bond County and Christian Long of Carroll County. As a result of these repeated efforts the Annual Meeting of 1855 appointed a committee of eleven strong elders to visit these western Brethren, look into the situation and report to the next meeting to be held in Northern Illinois. Eld. Christian Long, a special friend of Wolfe, was a member of the committee and was authorized to make all necessary arrangements for the meeting of the committee and those representing the Western Brethren. The visit was arranged to be held during the first week of May, 1856, in the meetinghouse in Adams County, Ill., Wolfe's congregation. For some reason four members of the committee did not attend. The seven present, with Eld. David Hardman, chairman, went into the investigation and with the exception of one minor incident, the investigation was a most satisfactory one, and ended with four statements as a basis of union to be presented to the Conference the week following. A member of this committee writing us about the proceedings, says that the whole committee was taken by surprise. Here they found a large congregation, possibly 200, of intelligent and prosperous members, and as for Eld. Wolfe himself, he was in intelligence, personal piety and devotion far in advance of anything they were anticipating. Intellectually speaking, he was easily the peer of any one on the committee, and yet in dealing with him they found him as gentle as a child. During the investigation the matter of the single mode of feet-washing came up. Eld. Wolfe told the committee that the claims of the western Brethren in this respect, were fully as good as theirs, for they could trace their descent back to the first Brethren in America. Just then Eld. John Umstead [sic] a member of the committee from near Germantown, Pa., spoke up saying that his church always practiced the single mode. Bro. Christian Long says that the statement from Eld. Ulmstead was like a bombshell in the meeting. Here was a member of the committee testifying in Eld. Wolfe's favor. That settled the feet-washing question.

No committee was ever more thoroughly welcomed and more kindly treated than was this one. There being a few days to spare before starting to the Annual Meeting, the time was taken up in preaching, and during these meetings the two sons of Eld. Wolfe, David and John and their wives made application for membership and were at once baptized. As before stated, David was a very prominent man in the county, having been a member of the state legislature. The ending of the committee's work with such a fine feeling and the coming of these four prominent members to the church caused much rejoicing, not only in the church but in the community as well.

From here the seven members of the committee, with their report in hand, accompanied by Eld. Wolfe went direct to the Waddams Grove Conference. The report being thus signed by the seven acting members of the committee made the paper regular. It was not, however, until three years later that the perfect union was completed.

Elder Wolfe was seventy-nine years old when the union was fully consummated.

Many did not fully accept his views regarding the better methods of conducting the love feast services, still he made friends wherever he went. However, those who stood opposed to him little thought at the time that the day was not so far off when his views would be fully accepted and made the general practice of the Brotherhood from coast to coast.

While differing with the main body of the church regarding some methods, he never for a moment questioned the correctness of her outstanding principles. On these points he stood foursquare, and stood firm. He was very spiritual, almost intensely so, highly devotional, and an uncompromising advocate of all the New Testament institutions. During his life he had formed but one habit which we in all these days of advanced Christian ethics would call bad, but not thought much of in his day and generation. He smoked a pipe.

Eld. D. B. Gibson, who was personally acquainted with Eld. Wolfe, had heard him preach possibly more than a score of times, gives this description of him: "Bro. Wolfe was almost gigantic in proportions; six feet or more in height, very broad shoulders, slightly round, deep chested, heavy limbed and weighed, I should judge, about two hundred and seventy-five pounds. His head was large, very broad and protruding brows, indicating strong intellectuality; forehead receding, high and full. Hair rather auburn until whitened by age. Nose aquiline but not large. Mouth broad and jaws wide. Lips flexible. Eyes blue and deeply set under overarched brows.

"His manner of preaching was like his personality, commanding, and yet as gentle as a child. His language was simple, easily understood even by a child, while a philosopher would sit spellbound under his preaching. I have often heard him preach two hours, but never saw a man or woman leave the congregation because not interested. In some respects he was the grandest preacher I ever heard. His great theme was the love of God. He would plead the great cause of Christ, his doctrines, his precepts while great honest tears would course their way down his cheeks. I never saw the man who sat under the spell of his artless eloquence but what rose up with the feeling, 'I will be a better man.'

"He visited the churches in Morgan, Sangamon and Macoupin Counties every year for twenty-five years in succession. The ferryman at Naples on the Illinois River in 1858 said he had ferried him over the river nearly every year for twenty-five years. He seemed so uniform in person and deportment that anyone who ever saw him never forgot him. His coming was looked for by old and young, and from all he received the most cordial and affectionate greeting. He was one of the most highly reverent men I ever met. No man ever swore in his presence. He impressed almost with awe every beholder.

"He always wore the peculiar garb of the Brethren. In 1864, near the close of his life, at a District Meeting in Southern Illinois, he was heard to say, 'Why do I wear the Brethren garb? I answer. When in 1812 I came to the church the church did not come to me. I weighed well her doctrines, her rules and her order. I joined her communion because I loved her. I became one of her number. I turned away from the world. In fact, I withdrew from it. I reasoned that I did not love the world, but I loved the church. I will not be like the world I hate, but will be like the church I love.'

"When preaching the funeral of my oldest sister he made the world look smaller to me than I ever saw it before. Heaven, home, eternal life and eternity were made more glorious than they ever before appeared. I left that meeting resolved to live for God.

"The last time I heard him talk, and while the stillness of the grave swept over the assembly he said: 'I have preached the gospel for over fifty years. I labored much when Illinois was a wilderness. My work is now nearly done. I have, like Paul, finished my course, and if when eternity shall dawn, and as I gaze with enraptured vision on the mighty hosts of the redeemed, if in that mighty throng one soul should be numbered with the blest because I worked, prayed and preached, I shall be fully requited for all my labors.' Having thus spoken he sat down while his congregation wept."

This was probably his last public utterance and shows the feelings of the man, as he by the eye of faith took a longing look into eternity. He died Nov. 16, 1865, and thus passed into eternity one of God's great and noble men.

CHAPTER 8

Chapter Eight
A Virginia Slave

I f Elder George Wolfe was most of his life masterful in the best sense, Elder Samuel Weir began his life as a slave in the worst sense. Both were courageous, but circumstances called for a different kind of courage from Elder Weir. Where Elder Wolfe always had the freedom to move and the respect of men, Elder Weir could never move freely and knew the prejudice of men. George's methods were imperious; Sammy's were meek. Both did good things for the Brethren. This is the story of Sammy Weir, born a slave, the first black man to be elected to the ministry and ordained to the eldership. It was written by Landon West, father of Dan West who created the Heifer Project after World War Two. Elder West published this in tract form in 1897 under the title "Life of Elder Samuel Weir."[1] I have edited it somewhat to adapt it to this book, but it is reproduced here largely as it originally appeared in print.

Samuel Weir was born a slave, in Bath County, Virginia, April 15, 1812. In his second year his family, with their master, William Byrd, moved to Botetourt County, of that State, where he remained a servant of Mr. Byrd until twelve (12) years of age. At this age and in the year 1824, he was sold at a private sale to a Mr. Andrew McClure for the sum of two hundred and eighty dollars. He then lived with and served Mr. McClure till the winter of 1843. When nearly thirty years of age the following event occurred, which, although a sad one, yet resulted in good—the conversion of a father and mother, the freeing of a slave and then in his conversion also.

A little son of the master, and the favorite of the family, was, about this time, thrown from a horse and killed. The event at once marked a change in the lives of both the father and mother, and soon afterward they made application to the Dunkard Brethren for membership. They were told that the Brethren did not receive anyone who held slaves, and that they could not be received until they would first give freedom to Sammy, their only slave. Such terms of Christianity were at that time and in old Virginia, thought to be severe, for it was then that members of the church thought to justify Slavery by the Gospel, and to oppose Slavery then was thought to be a sin. But the terms named by the Brethren to this penitent father and mother, were accepted by them, and Sammy was set free.

Mr. McClure had been, in the fullest sense, a worldly man, as I learn from Brother B. F. Moomaw, of Virginia, but kind to his family and also to his servant, laboring with him in the field, and as a servant of all. And the fact being known to the Slave Traders and drivers, that he would be required to give up his slave upon coming to the Brethren, these did much to obtain Sammy by purchase, offering for him the sum of fifteen hundred dollars. But it was refused with a declaration that he was now opposed to the sale of humanity, and that the slave should go forth a free man. So freedom was given him, but he remained with the family, laboring as before, until an opportunity offered to send him safely to a free State.

About this date, brother Peter Nead, of Virginia, began preaching in Botetourt County, and during his ministry there, Brother and Sister McClure were baptized in February, 1843.

Soon after their baptism, in 1813, Sammy met a Methodist minister and his wife, and of this interview, Sammy gives us the following: "Sam, is it true that McClure and his wife have joined the Dunkards?" I told him it was true. He said, "Why Sam, we have been fishing for them this long time, but we did not get them." I told him they did not fish in deep enough water. "And that sets you free, does it?" I told him I was free. The wife then spoke up and said: "Well, Sam, I wish to God that all men were Dunkards, for that would do away with this awful curse of Slavery."

The great and serious changes in the family and that in his own life, had a marked effect upon the mind of Sammy also, and soon after the baptism of the brother and sister, he too made application to the Brethren for membership. He now felt that he owed his love and service to God during his life; for the sudden death of the little son, the conversion of the father and mother to the Gospel of Christ and, above all, the freedom now given to himself, were enough to lead him to the one Savior of all; and Sammy felt that to give himself and his life to the service of God was no more than was due, and he loved the church that had given him his liberty. He applied to the Brethren for membership, and was baptized by Brother Nead on Sunday, May 14, 1843. And, he being the first colored member received by the church in that part of Virginia, it was soon a question as to how he should be received by the Brethren after baptism—whether with the right hand and kiss of charity, or with only the right hand of fellowship. But after some consideration by the church, it was decided to receive him with the right hand of fellowship, but without the salutation; and in this manner he was received as a member.

We have in this case, both with Sammy and his former master, a spirit of submission worthy of our imitation. Sammy, although a free man, remained with and worked as a servant for his former master—and that, too, without a murmur—for eight months after being set free, and when baptized and in full relation with a royal priesthood; he was willing to be received on any terms his white brethren were ready to take him.

And his master, but now a brother, although in but moderate circumstances in wealth, refused a large sum of money for the servant, now one of the most valuable; and not only gave him his freedom, but a good suit of clothes, a valuable horse, saddle and bridle, with money and all things necessary for Sammy in his journey to Ohio; and they parted as Brethren, with their best wishes and prayers for each other's welfare. They met no more in this life.

And Brother B. F. Moomaw, of Virginia, coming to Ohio in October of that year (1843), it was decided by the Brethren in Virginia, that Sammy should come under his guidance and protection to Ohio. It was urgent, too, that he should come that year; for the laws of Virginia at that time held all liberated slaves liable to be sold again into slavery, if found within the State one year after being set free. And it was all important, too, that he should have a guide and protector during his journey; for some who had been set free before, and who had started without protection to the free States, did not reach them, and were never again heard from by their friends, who supposed that the lost ones had been captured and sold again into slavery.

Brother Moomaw and his valuable charge came away from that part of Virginia in the latter part of October, and coming at the rate of thirty-five miles per day, reached the Ohio River, then the Jordan to slaves, and the line of the Slave and Free States. They crossed at the mouth of the Big Sandy on Sunday, October 29, 1843, when Sammy and his faithful guide passed over from slave territory into the land of freedom.

Upon reaching the Ohio shore, Brother Moomaw said to him: "Sam, you are now a free man and on free soil, where you can enjoy your freedom as all other free men." We can only think that we imagine what the feelings of this humble believer were, but none of us can know them, and much less can we describe them.

Brother Moomaw speaks thus of the event: "He did not, while on the way, seem to be affected in the least, but now, it appeared to me, that his whole being was affected, and that he now felt as he had never felt before."

It was another era in Sammy's life. He was now a free man and on free soil, and his heart swelled in gratitude to God for his deliverance. And none but pardoned sinners can ever know or share in the feelings of a liberated slave.

From the place of crossing they came down the Ohio River, reaching the home of Brother Thomas Major, living then in Sicioto County, Ohio, on Monday. But Brother Major being away from home, they were received and cared for very kindly by Sister Sarah. This was Sammy's first meeting with Sister Major.

On Wednesday, November 1st, they reached the home of old Brother John Moomaw, in Twin Valley, a few miles north of Bainbridge, Ross County, Ohio, where they remained until the next Sunday morning, November 5th, when they left that part and came north twelve miles, to the Brethren's meeting at the Busch Meeting House on Paint Creek, three miles west of Frankfort, in the same county. Upon their arrival at the church, they were met by the Brethren, among whom were Elders Robert Calvert, John Cadwallader and John Mohler. A statement of the facts connected with

Sammy's coming, was given by Brother Moomaw to these Brethren, and after the regular services, a council with the members was held, to determine what should be done for the brother now offered to their care by the Brethren of Virginia.

It was soon decided to receive Brother Sammy into the Paint Creek Church, and over which body Brother Calvert was at that time the Elder in charge. It was also decided that Brother Calvert should act as a Guardian for Sammy for at least one year, and see that he obtained a home and all his wants be provided for. And Sammy being the first and only colored member of that church, and in that part of the State at that time, the one great question was, "Where can we find a home for him?" When this was offered, an older brother, William Bryant, a minister, and one of the most zealous, came up and said: "I will find a home for him if he will come and live with me." Upon hearing this offer, the council decided that Sammy should go and make his home at Brother Bryant's.

Brother Moomaw and Sammy dined that day, November 5th, with an old Brother, John Bush, who lived near the church, and that afternoon this pilot and his charge parted company, to meet again on earth no more.

The attachment formed betwixt Brethren Moomaw and Weir during this their journey to Ohio, was both warm and strong, and must have been, in the fullest sense, such as only Christians feel; for, in speaking of the journey and of the pleasant associations had by them while thus on their way, they both seemed to regard each other with the best of feeling and respect. The lesson shows, too, what the pilgrims' feelings for each other can be, and also what they should be.

Sammy lodged that night with Brother Jacob Eyeman, near the Fairview Church, in Fayette County, Ohio, and on the next day went to his new home at the residence of Brother Bryant, on Paint Creek, some six miles above Frankfort. And here, at this home, he lived and worked as a farm hand for almost two years. Of the home and treatment received at Brother Bryant's, we feel that it must have been fully satisfactory to Sammy, for in speaking of the family and also of Brother Bryant, he seemed to regard each one as a member of his own household. And of Sammy's character, some conception may be had from the respect ever shown him by the family of Brother Bryant, and also from a statement made by Brother Bryant himself, who said, "I regard Sammy as an example to me in many things, but especially so in that of religion."

It was here that Sammy's education began, and none but the hand of God could have so well directed events to the gaining of that end, as is shown in this case. When consulting with him as to his education, we learned that he, with the thousands held in slavery, had by law been denied the benefit of learning to read or to know even a part of the alphabet; and now, upon being set free, and especially after coming into the church and a new State, for a home among strangers, Sammy felt the need of an education more than ever before. It was all-important to him, and to acquire this, was to mark one of the most important changes of his life, and it was to destroy the last effect of slavery with him. But this great change in his life did not begin until after his arrival in Ohio, in the winter of 1843-44, and when he was upwards of thirty-one years of age.

Of the many changes in his life, he spoke with pleasure, but especially so, of that of his education. I give the event in his own words: "We were all sitting around the fire one night, when I said, 'I wish I had had a chance to go to school when I was young.' At this, old Mother Bryant spoke up and said, 'Sammy, you are not too old to learn, and you can learn yet; and if you will say you will try it, I will have Katy to learn you.' This Katy was their little grandchild, Catherine Long, then ten years of age, who at that time was living with the family. I said I would try it, and Katy went and got the book, and we commenced. We got along very well at times, but not very fast, for she would often get out of heart, and sometimes very angry at me, because I did not learn faster; and then she would tell me that I was nothing but a black Negro, and that she could do nothing more for me. The work would then stop, but on the next night, after she had been to school and I to my work, with the old alphabet leaf in my pocket, and we had all come together again, and supper was over, and Katy in a good humor again, then I would say, 'Now, Miss Katy, please try me again; I will do better this time.' So she would get the book and begin again, but sometimes I did no better than before. But we worked at it that way all winter, and I learned my letters. After this I went to school two winters, and to a colored teacher over in Highland County, were I studied spelling, reading and arithmetic, but I could never make any headway in writing. I stopped going to school too soon, for when I found that I could read the Bible I felt satisfied, and I gave up all other books but that. The Bible has been my delight, and I have read it through several times."

From Mr. Henry Bryant, of Ross County, a son of old Brother William, I learned the residence and address of Sammy's first teacher, now Mrs. Catherine Bryant, of Montgomery County, Indiana, and in reply to me, she wrote July 30th, 1885: "I learned him his A B C's when he was at our house, and when I was but ten years of age, and Sammy got for me a red cotton handkerchief."

From Brother John Mohler, of Clermont County, Ohio we learn that Sammy, while attending school in Highland County about 1843, boarded at the home of Elder John Mohler, the father of our informant, and who, at that time, lived on Clear Creek, some eight miles north of Hillsboro. We learned from Sammy, and also from Brother Mohler, that the teacher was a colored man named Jacob Emmings, and a minister in the Baptist church; and it is to him that Sammy owed the completion of the education obtained by him, and also the beginning of his work as a minister. His life was one of great variety, and thus was another change and a great one, but it was not all.

Of the beginning of his public ministry—a work he seemed slow to engage in at first—he spoke: "My teacher in Highland County was a Baptist preacher, and at their meetings, where I often went, he would urge me to get up and talk. At last I told him I would try; but when the day came I felt so very weak that I thought I could not, and did not get up. But I did not feel well over it, and I then thought I would never do so any more."

This was in 1845, or 1846, and, being the only colored member then in that part of the State, and the sentiment among the whites not favorable for admitting the colored people into the meetings with the whites, Sammy was compelled to meet mostly with his own race, and they always of other denominations. It was under these circumstances—and they were the most discouraging—that his work in the ministry began; but with a firmness and zeal that many of us do not yet possess, he won his way over every obstacle. He was spoken well of by people of other denominations; he had there none of his own to go to hear him. And well should his zeal be commended, for he, with none to stay by to cheer and support him, still labored on for the one Master, whilst scores of white ministers, with friends and help on every side, have given up both faith and work, and have gone down in despair.

Of his election to the ministry, he said: "I had been preaching around at the meetings of the colored people, and of other churches for four or five years; so when the Brethren heard that I was trying to preach, they told me to come out from town, and preach a sermon for the whites at the Bush Meeting House. And they said if they then thought that I could preach, they would put me at it in earnest. The minister, Joseph Kelso, also asked me to come and I told him I would. So one day when I was present, he gave it out for me, and some five weeks before-hand. When he gave it out, I thought everybody tried to look me in the face, but I thought it was nothing that I should be ashamed of.

"The meeting was held in August, 1849, and there was a great crowd present, and all of them white but myself. I spoke thirty-nine minutes by Kelso's watch, and from the words in Hebrew ii, 1-2; and I have never seen prettier behavior in all the preaching I have done than I had that day."

After the trial sermon was delivered, the members present were asked if they were willing that the colored brother should take part in the ministry, and their voices were unanimous in his favor. He was then given his charge as a minister, and instructed to go to his own race and hold meetings wherever opportunity was offered.

Of his work and life as a minister, he said little, but that little expressed much in the life of a minister, and especially so with one placed as he was; for his public life was at that time, and in his situation, well calculated to bring out all the variety found in the brief period of one man's life. He said: "I then preached just wherever I could find a place, and they would argue with me, and they do yet. I would tell them what the Word said about these things, and then they would say, when they saw that I wanted what the Word said: 'Why, Sammy, it is only some of your notions of it.' "

His work as a minister went on thus with all its discouragements for a period of sixteen years and without a brother or sister for an assistant, but apparently with as great zeal for the work as at the beginning.

The mission and cross of Jesus Christ have been borne by many, but very seldom have they been borne by one alone, but in this case we have an Ethiopian to begin the work alone, and then for the greater part of his public life to manifest his love to his Savior with as little aid and encouragement from this world as it is possible for one in our day to conceive. And while others, with their troubles, have turned back or given up in despair, when surrounded with friends, this humble servant of God went steadily and cheerfully onward and upward, without a murmur or word of complaint.

And of his knowledge of the Bible, the whites say there was no one in the village or neighborhood who was better acquainted with the reading and sense of the Scriptures than was Sammy; and if any question or dispute arose among his neighbors as to a Bible subject, he was their reference, and his decision satisfactory.

Thus it continued until in August, 1865, when Brother Harvey Carter and Martha, his wife, became satisfied that Sammy's teaching was nearest in accordance with the Words of Jesus, and they made application to Sammy for baptism. Arrangements were at once made for a meeting at Frankfort, Ross County, Ohio, where Sammy and the applicants all lived, and Brother Thomas Major and Sister Sarah, then of Highland County, were sent for. This brother and sister attended at the meeting in August, 1865, and Brother and Sister Carter were baptized in Paint Creek, near Frankfort.

The event occurring just at the close of the Rebellion, and while the feeling was yet excited on the subject of Slavery, the great question of trouble, it made the reception of these colored people into full relation, and into the same church with the whites, a cause for some stir, but that soon passed away. It was a matter for a sinful world to talk of, and to find fault with, but it was a cause of thanksgiving to God by Sammy; for he then felt as he had never felt before—he was no longer alone in his work for his Master.

In October, 1865, a Love Feast was held by these few members in Frankfort, and embracing but five members; two whites and three colored—Brother and Sister Major, Sammy, and Brother and Sister Carter. It marked a new era in Sammy's life and also with his race, for it was the first feast held by the colored Brethren in the State of Ohio, and for all that we can say, it was their first one of the Earth. But it was a feasting on the Body which was broken for the Races, and this feast marked a new point in the extent and goodness of the great salvation.

Sammy was given authority to baptize and to solemnize marriages by Brother Thomas Major, when at a meeting of the Brethren at Fairview, some miles west of Frankfort, in the year 1872. He then continued meetings in and around Frankfort, and also at or near Circleville, on the Scioto River, with an increasing interest, and the reception of some by baptism, and one or two colored members from Virginia by letter.

We have already noted many changes and events for one short life, but we have yet a few more, and they are of greater importance than those already given.

The first we name is that of the choice of Brother Carter to the ministry, on Wednesday, February 9th, 1881. The meeting was held at the residence of Brother Carter, in Frankfort, and was conducted by Elders Thomas Major and the writer; and while all seemed to enjoy it much, no one present enjoyed it so much as did Brother Sammy Weir. And it was not at all to be wondered at for after a period of thirty-two years in the ministry, separate and alone, he now felt that he had an assistant in the work. None of us know what the poor brother's feelings were, and none but God can tell how grateful he felt in the thanks he gave.

And it was at the same meeting, and on the day above given, that Sammy was ordained an Elder and was given the fully ministry. This position—the highest and best the Church can bestow—was here given to one as well worthy to receive it as we need now to look for. This gave to Sammy the oversight of the colored members in the Scioto Valley, and while he lived but a short time to enjoy his position, yet we feel that none who may ever enjoy a membership in that district, need ever to feel ashamed of their first elder.

And here, dear reader, is to be seen another one of the Lord's ways. And we may well ask: Who would or could have thought, when Brother Nead led a slave into the stream in Old Virginia, nearly forty years before, that he was then baptizing the first minister and Elder of the church among the colored people! And who could have seen that all the steps I have described were all leading on to the full ordination of a man of God. But so it was, and so it is; the Lord's way is the true one, and always the best one.

And here let us all gather strength and take courage by considering well the noble example of this humble servant of God, and let all of us who possess so many more of the blessings of God than did this poor slave, try to use our gifts and blessings to glorify God as well as Sammy did his.

After his ordination, in 1881, he did but little more in public life, for his days were ending. He, with Brother Carter, kept up their meetings regularly at Frankfort, and occasionally at Circleville, where the work had begun; but Sammy's desire now was to leave his house and lot as a donation to the colored people for a church. But there being a debt unpaid and a mortgage on the lot, and his health failing, he felt that he must give up in despair unless God would aid him in this also. And so here, as all along the way, the Strong Arm was seen just at the right time, and Brother William D. Mallow, of Ross County, assumed the debt, and Sammy's life was left to close in peace, and at his old home.

Of his Bible, he at one time spoke to me as follows: "After I had learned to read, I got a large Bible, and read it through several times. And the Methodist preacher here having no Bible, I loaned him mine, and he POUNDED IT TO PIECES." The Bible was in scraps, and the matter being stated to the sisters of the Lower Twin Church, of Preble County, Ohio, they made him the gift of another Bible. And at the close of the Love Feast held at Frankfort, November 9th, 1883, and

the last one Sammy attended before his death, the gift
was presented to him, with a statement as to the ones
sending it. He accepted it gladly, and with tenderness
said: "I am very thankful to them for it, and all I can do
to pay them is, I can pray for them."

I now pass on to speak of his death, the greatest event
of his life. His time was full of important changes, and
all for the better, but this, the greatest of all, I have no
power to describe, for I know not yet the glory to which
he has gone. But I feel that that change was also for the
better for Sammy had nothing to lose by dying; it was all
gain to him.

His last illness was Gangrene, and began in
December, 1883. And learning of his sickness, Brother
Henry Frantz and the writer, with Brother Mallow,
visited him several times in February, 1881, giving him
farewell March 1st, and did all that was possible to cheer
him in his last days on earth.

Brother Mallow met him last on the morning of his
death, and gave him farewell for the last time. Brethren
Carter, Jones, Sowers, and Sister Carter, were his atten-
dants night and day until his death, besides many others
in and around Frankfort, who visited and cared for him
as the day of his life was drawing to its close.

He seemed at all times fully resigned to the will of
God, and left the world, being at peace with all its people. He went down slowly, but patiently, and fell asleep
at 9:00 A.M., on Saturday, March 15th, 1884. His age
was 71 years and 11 months.

His funeral on Sunday, March 16th, was attended by
many friends of both Races, and the sermon was
delivered by Brother Mallow, from the words: "Thou
shalt come to thy grave in a full age, like a shock of corn
cometh in his season." Job vs. 26. The Brethren at
Frankfort, not yet having a church house, the colored
Methodists gave theirs for the occasion.

The body was laid in the cemetery, just east of the
town, for its last sleep, and to await the morning of Eter-

nity. It will then be aroused from its slumber by the call of the one great Master from Heaven, and another great change for the slave will occur. His tomb was erected by gifts from the Sisters of the Western Churches of Ohio.

Of Sammy Weir's character as a Christian, I will let others speak. Dr. Galbraith, Sr., a Gentleman of Frankfort, and a physician of experience, who had been Sammy's physician for years, and who visited him and dressed his limbs daily in the last illness, said to Brother Frantz and myself during our visit to the sick room: "I can say of Sammy what I can say of no other man; I have known him for thirty years, and I have never yet known any harm of him."

During the visit made to the feast at Frankfort, November 9th, 1883, and the last one Sammy attended, a number of Brethren and Sisters lodged at the hotel, which was then under the care of our friend, John Adkins; and he, learning the aim of our visit, said to the Brethren while there: "Sammy Weir is the best man in our town."

The testimony of our friend Gilmore, a neighbor of Brother Mallow's is as follows: "I was once with Sammy at Judge Rittenhouse's adjoining Brother Mallow's, and working at the threshing machine. Sammy and I were together on the straw-stack. Whenever the machine stopped and work for a time ceased, while others were idle or engaged in conversation, Sammy sat by himself on the straw, learning to spell from the scrap of an old spelling book, which he carried with him. He was never idle."

And when he had become so low in health and the care of him so great a burden, it was suggested by some that he be taken to the County Infirmary and cared for there; but our Brother Mallow coming in at the time this was proposed, said: "Never, I will care for Sammy myself, before he shall go and die in a poorhouse." This righteous man was never forsaken of God, nor did he ever come to want.

From Brother John Jones, near Frankfort, who attended Sammy till his death I learn by letter, that his last word was the name of Brother Mallow. And just before he passed away, Brother Mallow came in as he was passing to take the train. Sammy was speechless, but gave his hand and smiled. It was their last farewell. Brother Mallow left for the train and in ten minutes more, Sammy Weir had taken his departure, and that, too, for another world.

Of Sammy's ancestry and family, we know but little, for but little can be known. Slavery has kept a sealed history of its work, and allows us to know but little of its victims.

His father's name was James Weir, and his mother's name was Lucy Bird; the grandmother's name was Rosa Bird. Sammy took the name of his father, contrary to the slave rule, because he was unwilling to take the name of a master, and thus recognize the rule of Darkness.

From Sister Grabill, of Clarke County, Ohio, I learn that Sammy's mother remained in Virginia, and died a slave. Sammy never saw or heard of her after coming to Ohio in 1843; nor do I know that his mother ever again heard of her son. He was the eldest of seven children whom he knew, and he gave me their names as follows: Samuel, Rosa, Harriet, Anna, Warick, Allen, Charlie Walker and Robert. Of his brothers and sisters, he heard no more after leaving Virginia. He was never married.

As a preacher, Sammy was not an eloquent man, but was honest, humble, patient, courteous and well versed in the Scriptures.

I pass now in a hasty review of Sammy's life, that you may again see some of the Light which has come down from Heaven.

Sammy was born a slave, but when he turned to God for liberty, it was given him; when he asked to become a Christian, there were those who received him; when a pilot to the free States was needed, there was one at hand who brought him safely through; when a home for this lonely pilgrim and stranger were asked for, one of the best was given him; when a Guardian for the oppressed was sought for, there was one at hand who, in the fullest sense, was a friend to the needy; when a teacher was desired, there was one present, able and willing, who, although but a little child, yet she did her work as faithfully as a mother; when there was an opening for a church amongst the colored people, there were both a brother and a sister ready to go and give this Pioneer brother their aid; and finally, when strength and life were both failing, and it was said to take him to the Infirmary, there to die, there was one at hand to say, "Never shall he die in the poorhouse." Surely, none but God could have directed so well, and at every point met the wants of the needy, as we see here in the life of this Virginia slave, Samuel Weir.

Commentary

There are two ways to view the reception the Brethren gave Samuel Weir. Against the background of American slavery, they were courageous to make Mr. McClure free Samuel, to accept him as a member, to transport him to free soil, and then to elect him to the ministry—all this before the Civil War. The church had been officially on record against slavery for years. They were ahead of their time and on the way to accepting black people as brethren. Christian love was overruling natural prejudice.

However, prejudice was there in the hearts of the Brethren. The church in Virginia did not receive Samuel with the kiss, only with the hand of fellowship. In Ohio, he could not worship freely in the churches and had to worship with black Christians of other denominations. After elected to the ministry he was told to preach to his own, not invited to sit on the ministers bench in a white church. His meekness and long suffering were extolled,

as if more along that line was to be expected of him than
others. Viewed against what we know today about the
subtleties of prejudice and against the knowledge that
legal freedom and token positions are not the same as
full respect and equal opportunity, the Brethren in the
1840s still had a long way to go.

Yet there were a few Brethren who had considerably
overcome this subtler bias. And in their official
judgments the Brethren did the right things even if some
members were not fully in accord. Article two of the
1845 Yearly Meeting minutes is a good example. They
judiciously balanced a clear statement of Christian conviction with forebearance for the "weaker" brethren.

In regard to receiving colored members into the
church:

> Considered, to leave it to the counsel of every in-
> dividual church, as it is done in all cases; but if colored
> persons are once received as members into the church,
> the members should be at liberty to salute them in like
> manner as white members, at the same time having
> patience with those who may be weak in the faith and
> can not do so. The assembled elders, however, consider
> it as the more perfect way, to which we all should strive
> to come, viz., that love, which makes no distinction in
> the brotherhood in this respect. (See James 2:1-10)[2]

The 1840s were probably the most formative decade
in Samuel Weir's life. We learn much about the Brethren
of that time by seeing how they responded to this man.
They showed more largeness of spirit than most in their
day and less than they might have. They were good people, and they were, like us, sometimes too small of heart.
We also learn much about an extraordinary man, who
quietly accepted the harsh terms life set for him and who
became in spite of them a man of love and an elder.

Samuel Weir was an unobtrusive man whose accomplishments were probably more obvious to God than to men.

CHAPTER
9

Chapter Nine
Two Doctors and a Fisherman

Elder John Kline

Anyone who knows the least bit about Brethren history has heard of Elder John Kline. He is one of three or four most oft-referred-to persons. He is remembered because he was murdered in 1864 at the hand of Confederate supporters who took it upon themselves to rid the countryside of all supposed Unionists. It happened at the peak of his career just after he had been moderator of the Yearly Meeting for four consecutive years. He was a great man, respected even by those who did not share his nonresistant ways. Frequently, he corresponded or met with political leaders on behalf of the Brethren, especially during the Civil War in order to negotiate exemption for young Brethren from the Confederate conscription. He was not as bold as George Wolfe had been in the Black Hawk War, but he knew his way around.

He was born in Dauphin County, Pennsylvania, on June 17, 1797, and moved with his family at the age of fourteen to Rockingham County, Virginia, on Linville

238   THE OLD BRETHREN

Creek, where he lived for the rest of his life. In 1818 he married Anna Wampler; they had one child who died in infancy. Anna became deeply disturbed emotionally sometime in the 1840s, but Brother Kline kept her with him at home and cared for her with touching solicitude.

Benjamin Funk, the editor of Elder Kline's diary, gave a vivid physical description of him.

> His height was very nearly five feet six and one half inches. His normal average weight was, to the best of my recollection, about one hundred and seventy pounds. He was what may be called a well-proportioned, symmetrical man as to personal form.
>
> John Kline had a full, square face, dark eyes, and dark hair in his earlier years. His hair was usually long enough to cover the back of his neck, was slightly curled by nature, and wavy, and beautifully parted over the middle of the head from the forehead. He carried a pleasant countenance, and his social habits were very agreeable.
>
> He had a light beard, which from some cause was never more than a few inches, say three or four, in length, and this was mostly limited to his chin and lower jaw, back to the throat. He shaved his upper and lower lip.[1]

He was called to the ministry in 1830, probably advanced to the second degree before 1836, and ordained an elder in 1848. He served on Standing Committee three times in the 1840s. From 1851 until his death he served every year. The many preaching trips he made covered an estimated one hundred thousand miles, all on horseback. Many of those miles were on Nell, whom he rode from 1849 until his death. In addition to all this he was known as a country doctor and often ministered to the body as well as the spirit. Much more could be said of him and in fact has been. But I am going to ig-

Harvest time

nore his achievements and give you an intimate picture
of his everyday life. You can find several excellent books
and articles elsewhere[2] that will tell you what he did and
since much of it was achieved after our decade, I will
leave that for another story.

The following was written in the 1930s by Annie
Zigler Bowman, Elder John Kline's grandniece, then in
her eighties. It appeared in *The Gospel Messenger* in
April, 1836. Annie was born in 1849 so her childhood
reminiscences are from the 1850s, not the 1840s, but we
may presume that Elder Kline, a man of steady habits,
had not changed much. It gives a pleasing glimpse not
only of Annie's beloved "Daut," but of life in that age as
well.

He traveled much in adjoining counties on preaching
tours. I remember of his often going to Page County
which is east of Rockingham. He began the work there
with just one member, a sister. He soon had a congregation built up. The people were principally Old School
Baptist. Then he went west, often to Hardy and
Hampshire Counties, where much of the country was
thinly settled and heavily timbered. He would tell us of
hearing the wolves howl at night and of desperate roads.
He also often spoke of the kindhearted hospitality of the
people through the mountainous part of Virginia. The
primitive simplicity of their mode of living appealed to
him and he loved to go among them to visit and preach.
In fact he was not satisfied long at home: he soon felt
called to go again.

My earliest remembrance of him is of his continual
going away and coming home. My father's home was
quite near his.... We often ran to meet him as he rode
in and up to the hitching rack, always sure of a kindly
greeting from him as he drew the saddle pockets from
the large roomy ones in which he often carried food as
well as medicine to hungry and sick patients. He would

go into the house with them and almost immediately reappear with a bottle of liniment of his own make, remove the saddle from Nell's back and treat the saddle galls, for invariably when he came home from those long trips Nell's back would need attention. But he was careful to keep her well fed and she always came home spry and full of life. He often spoke in German to her and I verily believe she understood German as well as the English Language.

He was a man of wonderful ability, but of the most primitive and simple habits. He never had one bit of use for tobacco and was strictly temperate in all things. He never used intoxicating liquors in any form and I don't suppose he knew the feel of broadcloth. He always wore homespun and homemade clothes for that was all we could get those days, and thought ourselves fortunate if we had a good supply of them. We spun and wove wool for winter clothes and spun and wove flax for summer wear and for bedclothes. There were no felt or hair mattresses to be had and we filled our linen bed ticks with wheat or oat straw. An entry in his diary says he very much preferred oat straw. . . . He was such a busy man, always doing something for somebody. He invented and made a spinning jenny to lighten the labor of making our clothes. . . . He was my great-uncle, but we never called him uncle, but always called him Daut. . . .

I remember as though it were yesterday how we children liked to visit in his room. His medicine cabinet, with its many bottles both large and small, was always a source of interest to me. Then, too, he would sometimes gives us a small vial of cinnamon drops, or sometimes peppermint, which greatly pleased us because a vial was a rare toy for our playhouse. While the drops lasted we never got tired of playing doctor. One of us would play being very sick, one would be nurse and another would be the doctor, and when he called his cinnamon drops would answer for all kind of medicine, and we always got well immediately. Then Daut used to make a kind of pepper cake which he called the "Bread of Life." He often gave us bits of this and said it was healthy for us, but it did not take much of this to do us, for it consisted chiefly of pepper and we soon had enough of that.

Then the open fire in the Franklin stove with the shovel and tongs in the corner was always so cozy in winter. There was a clock on the mantle; and the sundial just outside of the south window (which was one of his own make) was where he could compare with the clock to see if it was with the sun. His chair was immediately inside the window where he had a good light to read or write, for he did much of both when he was home. He had the right arm of his chair made very wide so he could lay a large book on it to read. It was large enough to write on comfortably. It was not a lazy man's chair by any means; it had neither rockers, springs or cushions . . . and the low back would never suit a lazy man. Daut was always such a busy man. Within easy reach of his chair was his bookcase and the little stand at the head of his bed. There was his old-time desk with his medicine cabinet on the top of it, and a well-worn rug carpet with "Moms" chair in the corner by the shovel and tongs. There you have Daut's room as it is indelibly impressed in my mind. There was nothing expensive—except possibly the books—or gay; but it was all comfy and homelike and he was always so glad to get home again after some of his protracted preaching tours. . . .

Daut was deprived of much joy of the average man's homecoming because of Aunt Anna's mental condition. Sometimes she would not know him; other times she would not see him. She would convey herself away where none knew, and if we wanted to hunt her up he would say: "Let mom alone, she will come when she gets ready." He always seemed to know what was the best thing to do, for after everything got quiet she would come in and go to her room as usual.

Daut loved to sing and on summer evenings about dusk he would often sit on the long porch and sing the hymns he loved. . . . There at the south end, against the banisters on the bench (for porch swings and rockers was an unknown commodity then), he would sing: "What Wondrous Love Is That," "Happy Day," and many other hymns he loved. Sometimes he would sing his own verses. "He Died at His Post," which he had set to music. I think he had Joseph Funk of Singers Glen compose the music.

Daut did much for the poor among his patients and membership. He gave about all his share of wheat to his people. Let an idle, shiftless man come begging a grist, if his family was suffering, and he usually got what he asked for, but when Daut got through he felt more like going to work than to stand for another such lecture like Daut gave him.

He had a pleasant smile and friendly greeting for every one, but I never remember him to stop long enough to jest or gossip with anyone; he always seemed to be busy but never hurried or rushed unless he was called to see a very sick person. He was our doctor, our minister and uncle, and such a fatherly friend to every one! It is no wonder we looked up to him and took our troubles and problems to him, for which he always found a ready solution. . . .[3]

Elder Jacob Fahrney

It might appear that all elders were physicians. (You met D. B. Sturgis in Chapter One and now you have met John Kline.) That is not true, but in order to confuse you further, I will introduce still another elder-physician, Jacob Fahrney. As far as I know, there were very few men in the fraternity who were doctors as well as ministers or for that matter doctors at all. I do not want you to get the impression that there were many professional people among the Brethren; there were not, and the professions were not encouraged.

In those days a doctor was not always what he is to-day. None of these men was trained in a medical school; nor had any gone to a college or university; nor hardly had public schooling. But each was intelligent and inquisitive and took up the study of medicine on his own. What each became was a kind of herb doctor, proficient in administering natural remedies compounded from plants and roots and accompanied by whatever book-learning he could acquire or experience he could get from apprenticeship to another self-made physician. This training was decidely unsystematic, and standards for practicing medicine hardly existed. His practice was determined by how well he was trusted and respected and whether his crude remedies worked.

Yet these men were not quacks either. Fahrney and Kline were well thought of and widely sought after. Elder Kline combined his herb lore with something called the "Thompsonian method," which stressed natural remedies and avoided "active depletion of the body by copious blood-letting, blistering, drastic cathartics and starving,"[4] which were still practiced in the profession. Elder Fahrney augmented his herb lore with preparations and knowledge gleaned from some ancient medical books that had come over from Switzerland with his great uncle, and did his apprenticeship under his father. These men were not doctors as we know them, but they were humane men who did people good with what they had.

Young Jacob wanted to go to medical school but the church kept him from it. If records are correct, there were at least six doctors in the Fahrney family. Jacob was the second; his father Peter Fahrney was the first, and a well-loved doctor he was. Peter was the son of John who with his brother Abraham, came to this country in 1727 from Switzerland. Abraham had begun studies to be a doctor, but death took him shortly after arrival here, and John carefully saved his books. John's son Peter took an interest in them although he became a tanner. One day he fell from his horse, crippled his back, and was forced to abandon his trade. He returned to the old books and began to train himself to be a physician. He was known as the "walking doctor," and there are some good stories about his life which I will not tell here.

Jacob was born in 1798 at Chambersburg, Pennsylvania. In his youth, he could not fail to be interested in his father's work. But he was also "deeply impressed with the religious spirit of the community and being of a somewhat grave and contemplative mood, his development took a spiritual rather than a scientific turn."[5] Peter had been reared an Amish Mennonite, but when they took a dim view of his interest in medicine, he decided against joining them. He lived for a time in a Dunkard family, Durnbaugh by name, married the daughter Eve and that way came to embrace the Brethren. He found them not quite so hardened against his books and profession as the Amish. His son grew up in strong Dunkard country, the Antietam congregation in southern Pennsylvania and northern Maryland, and was deeply impressed. That impression was reinforced by his early discovery of the *Martyr's Mirror*.

Nothing could exceed the rapt enthusiasm with which Jacob dwelt on this ponderous volume, his heart being stirred especially by the heroism and sufferings it recorded of his Swiss forefathers, so many of whom, for their faith, had perished by the axe and stake or pined away to death in the dungeons of Zurich and Schaffhausen. Again would he peruse the records with flushed and tearful face, of the droves of hapless exiles who had to

forsake their Alpine homes, wandering among strange
people in search of religious peace, but only to find it in
graves on the plains of the Palatinate or "by the blue
Alsatian Mountains." It was a moving and pathetic
chronicle for a piously-disposed youth, and it so cap-
tivated the intellect and sympathies of Jacob Fahrney
that even to his dying day, as his son affectionately
remembers, he would point his most casual discourse
with touching allusions to the sorrows and stern fidelity
of the early brethren in Switzerland.[6]

This vivid story of the sufferings of the European
Mennonites did not draw him back to the denomination
of his grandfather. Instead it endeared him more deeply
to the Brethren.

Meanwhile Jacob decided to follow his father and
become a doctor, and, further, to seek his training not
only as his father's apprentice but at the University of
Pennsylvania medical school. This was announced with
rather extraordinary effect:

This fell like a thunderbolt among the quiet Dunkards
at Beaver Creek, who were a branch of what was known
as the Antietam Congregation. However sacred were
family rights, the voice of "the church" was omnipotent
on education, and some pious but unprogressive elder
stated that somebody said, that he heard from
somebody else, how a student could not graduate at any
of the state colleges without joining the Freemasons,
and therefore taking an oath! This was quite too much
for the oath-abhorring Dunkards, and in deference to
the fears and scruples of the brethren, Jacob had to
forego the course that would have given him a state
diploma.[7]

While the Brethren were more open than the Amish,
they were not that open.

However, Jacob managed to reconcile his two interests, medicine and the church, and to continue his own rustic medical course. The death of his father saw the surrounding community beginning to address him as Doctor Fahrney. And the church was noticing his religious zeal. They elected him to the ministry in 1824. In 1841 upon the death of the presiding elder, he was ordained and made elder-in-charge of the Antietam brethren, at the age of forty-three, younger than ordination usually occurred and very young to be the "housekeeper." He died in 1848 also at a young age. He served twice on Standing Committee at Yearly Meeting during the 1840s.

Doctoring remained his principal livelihood throughout life, but he also served the community as a notary or scrivener (a professional copyist). He was one of the few Brethren who knew English, and his son claimed this assisted his advancement to bishop. This son, who was named Peter after his grandfather and who was only eight when his father died, became a well-known producer of patent medicine and by the end of the century a Chicago millionaire. He used the old family medical recipes for his products, the most famous of which was "Dr. Fahrney's Blood Vitalizer." Ads for this wonderful elixir along with glowing testimonials from Brethren elders were not uncommon in the pages of *The Gospel Messenger* in the last quarter of the nineteenth century.

His son wrote that Elder Fahrney was "distinguished even outside his own people for a spirit of philanthropy and social reform."[8] Whether this is true we do not know; his son's biography is somewhat inflated and, I think, less than objective. We do know that in at least two ways he was a bit progressive. He was, along with Brother Isaac Price of the Greentree congregation in

Resting at harvest time

Eastern Pennsylvania, one of the first Brethren to open-
ly advocate temperance.[9] This was unusual, for the
Brethren, while very sober folk, were not teetotalers.
And they were especially shy of the excessive enthusiasm
of the American temperance movement.

> He was also a zealous and outspoken friend of
> temperance, and was the leader in that section of the
> crusade against "harvest tippling" which has since so
> widely prevailed. Early in this century even the frugal
> Dunkards used to serve out rations of "schnapps," in
> the long, sultry harvest days, to the field hands who did
> their work, and the results were often so mischievous
> that the abolition of the custom was a genuine blessing.[10]

His second bit of progressivism was probably a
regretted accident. He was by "friendly force" made to
sit for a Daguerreotype, one of the earliest forms of
photography. "Such a vanity was ill-fitting a preacher of
the word of life."[11] He commented, but he acquiesced
anyway. Apparently others in the church agreed with his
assessment, for H. R. Holsinger reports there was a
great stir, which so upset him that it hastened his death.
His son's account makes no mention of the disturbance,
but we know that he died in 1848 and that in 1849 the
first query appeared at Yearly Meeting in regard to
photos: "Whether brethren can be allowed to have their
likeness or profile taken" (Article 17)[12] The Brethren
gave this laconic reply, "Considered as not advisable."
Whether the photo, his death, and the query are connected we do not know, but the thought makes for interesting speculation. Holsinger reports that the
Daguerreotype was taken early in 1848. It could not
have been later than that, for he died on April 12 of that
year. It could not have been too many years earlier, for

Elder Jacob Fahrney

Elder John H. Umstad

the Daguerreotype process had been published only in 1839. There is no reason to dispute Holsinger's date.

What was Elder Fahrney's misfortune is our good fortune because he furnished us with what is to my knowledge the earliest extant photo of a member of the fraternity and the only one I know of from that decade. It is an extraordinary photograph showing the flowing hair and thick chest-length beard that the old Brethren wore, the shaved upper lip, and the somber dignity of an elder. It is reproduced here along with his son's epitaph: "A gentle, sincere, and high-minded Christian, plain of speech, but prompt in sympathy and ever willing to help others by deed or counsel."[13]

Elder John H. Umstad

Elder John H. Umstad was a fisherman, and a man I should like to have known. There are two Old Brethren for whom I feel that; one is George Wolfe; the other is Elder Umstad. He was an eccentric and entirely lovable man. There are here and there men by whom God himself cannot help being charmed. Elder Umstad was one of these.

He was born on New Year's day, 1802, in Philadelphia. His parents moved to Montgomery County, Pennsylvania, when he was nine, and he lived there for the rest of his life. They were not members of a church, so he never received much religious instruction. It was said in later years that he was naturally religious, but if so, that quality did not show itself for some years. He was a very lively young man. The following story is told:

John Umstad in his early days possessed a vivacity

bordering on wildness. . . . His father owned another
farm beyond the Perkiomen Creek. The barn was old
and did not appeal at all favorably to John. One day it
took fire and was well up in flames when John arrived
on horseback. Putting the spurs to his horse he galloped
at high speed round and round the barn swinging his cap
in the air and shouting: "Now, we'll have a new barn;
now, we'll have a new barn!"[4]

In the 1830s there was a religious awakening in the
community, and in 1831 John's sister, Isabella
Fitzwater, joined the Brethren. John made fun of her
until later that year the revival touched him and the
scoffer, probably with some chagrin, joined the scoffed.
His sister's husband and Isaac Price were also converted. He apparently entered into his religion as heart-
ily as his fun, gave up his fashionable clothes, and helped
convert others. By 1834 they were ready to found a
church in that neighborhood, and Brother Umstad and
Isaac Price were elected to the ministry. The church was
called Green Tree, and they each served it until death.

He retained his lively disposition throughout his life
and was known everywhere to be very cheerful, a good
talker, and an enjoyable companion. He was thoroughly
uninhibited and said whatever came into his head. When
he met young people, he would say unceremoniously,
"Well, does thee love Jesus?"[15] There was a certain un-
converted man who once said, "I hate to meet that man
for he always says: 'Well, Bub, do you love Jesus?' "[16]
One time H. R. Holsinger was traveling by train with
him. As Holsinger got up to disembark, he offered
Brother Umstad his hand. The old man rose and said,
"Brother Henry, I want to kiss thee," and did, to
Brother Holsinger's embarrassment and his fellow
passengers' interest.[17] George D. Zollers, a minister in
Illinois, told the following story. The good elder was in

Carroll County to preach at Brother Zoller's church, Hickory Grove. Zollers knew he had arrived, but had not yet seen him. They had met only twice before. Zollers writes:

> I saw Bro. Umsted [sic] hasting toward me, and he surprised me by his sudden unexpected approach. He greeted me with his countenance gleaming with the sunshine of heavenly love, and poured out the effusions of his heart in these memorable words: "Hold fast that which thou hast, let no man take thy crown." Then in a whisper he added: "It's a noble calling," meaning the ministry.[18]

This most unorthodox greeting only endeared him more to Brother Zollers.

Elder Umstad was a good preacher. The Brethren always enjoyed his lively oratory. One writer notes with a touch of dry humor:

> Bro. Umstad developed into a speaker of excellent ability, noted more however, for his earnestness, cheerfulness, and winning ways than for his depth of thought and logic.

This same remarks:

> His preaching did not cover a broad field. He preferred to limit his lines of thought and do good work. This led to his having a number of favorite texts and themes that he used quite frequently.[19]

His brethren must have fondly indulged his peculiar ways and enjoyed his sermons the way one looks forward to a good story that an old uncle tells repeatedly yet always to the satisfaction of his nephews and nieces. Holsinger notes:

> He had a few favorite texts. . . . One of them was "Mene, mene, tekel, upharsim." Dan. 5:25. From this we heard him speak several times and he handled it well.[20]

Elder Umstad was a good businessman and farmer and active in his community. He was well enough off to be free to do considerable church work and often traveled among the churches. His preaching had marked effect.

> He believed God to be a loving Father, and he presented him as such to his hearers. His appeals to the sinner were almost irresistible. He told them what the Gospel demanded of them, pointed out the danger of rejecting the easy terms of pardon, then presented his earnest appeals in such a pleasing manner as to almost captivate those who listened to his discourses.[21]

He was an untiring fisher of men.

But he also liked to take fish from the water. There is a story about that: He was appointed to preach at the Green Tree church on a week day. Early that morning he went to the river to fish. He so loved fishing that he took no notice of the passing time and fished well into the evening. Then he remembered his appointment to preach. He hurried to the meetinghouse, where the congregation was waiting for their preacher, walked quickly down the aisle rubbing his hand, and entirely nonplussed announced his text, "I go a-fishing" (John 21:3). He preached, it is said, one of his finest sermons.[22]

When Elder Umstad did something, he never did it half way. He was thoroughgoing to a fault, and was particularly known for unlimited liberality. He took the New Testament instructions and did exactly as they directed.

On one occasion a poor woman came to his home begging. He gave her five dollars whereupon she went to the house. His wife then came to him and asked what she should give. Not saying anything about what he had done, he replied: "Mother, just give her what you think is right." He carried out to the letter the Savior's command that when one makes a feast he should not invite his rich friends but the poor who could not recompense him again. On a certain Thanksgiving Day, he invited all the poor of the neighborhood to his festive board. He became so liberal that interference was deemed necessary. Unprincipled people would take advantage of his goodness of heart by borrowing money and never repaying. One such one told him that he would never pay till he was sued. "Very well," replied Brother Umstad, "then you will never pay." The man was afterward converted and paid the money.[23]

He served on Standing Committee three times during the 1840s and was loved and respected everywhere. H. R. Holsinger said of him: "He was blunt and outspoken even to eccentricity, but these qualities were but a spice to his exuberant honesty and kindness of heart."[24]

He was a memorable character. The Brethren Almanac said of him in 1909:

Many of his apt remarks have come down to the present generation, and in the community where he lived he will be quoted for generations to come. He so impressed others with his originality, peculiarity, aptness, agreeableness and love for his Master that he will not soon be forgotten.[25]

He died April 27, 1873. He is, I should like to think, now seated in heaven regaling God and his angels with his pithy sayings and glad heart.

CHAPTER

10

Chapter Ten
Two Gifts of the Spirit

Elder Peter Nead

Peter Nead was a theologian and a man of contrasts. In a day when few Brethren wrote books, Brother Nead wrote books. In a time when there were no Brethren theologians, he did theology. To be sure, his theological writings were amateurish when compared to university theologians, but decidedly polished for the rural Brethren. You have sampled in chapters two and three his vivid imagery and sometimes lofty phrases. Peter Nead was a blessing to the Brethren of the mid-nineteenth century. It was said that his book, *Theological Writings on Various Subjects, or A Vindication of Primitive Christianity*, published in 1850,[1] brought more people into the brotherhood than any other book. He is also credited with the first Brethren book on their faith and practice, called *Primitive Christianity, or A Vindication of the Word of God*, which he published in 1834.[2] All this writing when the Brethren

German dunkers on their way to Shenandoah

were little given to bookmaking would seem to make
him a bit "fast" for his brethren, yet he was the leading
spokesman for the "Old Order" element of the church in
the 1860s and 1870s until his death on March 16, 1877.

He was born January 7, 1796, the son of Daniel Nead
of Hagerstown, Maryland. The family was Lutheran
and probably descended from German immigrants.
Peter's grandfather offered to pay for Peter to educate
himself for the Lutheran ministry. Why he turned this
opportunity down we do not know, for records indicate
that he was a deeply religious young man. Instead he
clerked in a store, and later, after his family moved to
Frederick County, Virginia, he was apprenticed to a
tanner.

Those early years of Peter's religious pilgrimage are
murky. Sometime in his twenties, he joined the
Methodist Episcopal Church and because of his zeal and
ability was elected a class leader as George Wolfe had
been. Like Wolfe, Nead was not satisfied, although not
having George Wolfe's Brethren background or
forthright methods, he followed a more circuitous route
into the Brethren.

He was a restless and uncertain youth who
nevertheless had a strong feeling that God had
something in mind for him. He felt a call to be an
itinerant preacher and for well over a year in 1823 and
1824 traveled up and down the Shenandoah Valley in
Virginia, preaching to anyone who would listen and living off the hospitality and handouts of his hosts. He
would send word ahead that he was coming and make
an appointment to preach. Or he would sometimes just
show up. He was oft-times well received and sometimes
greeted with arguments or suspicion. In homes,
schoolhouses, meetinghouses, and even a wagonmaker's
shop, he preached dozens of sermons and attended

Elder Peter Nead

countless meetings and he was still not satisfied.

He wrote a diary of those months, and we have the good fortune to have most of it. Often he was in despair. Like many sensitive young persons who have a keen sense of calling without yet a clear substance to the calling, he was pummeled with doubts and overwhelmed with a sense of his own inadequacies. Sometimes he could hardly preach, and he wrote that his memory abandoned him. Into the vacuum left by the uncertainty and depression, unpleasant and uncomfortable thoughts often crowded. We do not know what they were, but it is not uncommon, when a young person's commitments are not yet firm, for fears and uncomfortable desires (Nead called them his "carnal" nature) to rush in past the not yet strong bulwarks of his personality. Today we know enough about the psychology of the unconscious not to be so disturbed by unpleasant or even perverse thoughts. We know that they are a part of human personality and that while they should not be indulged, neither should they be violently suppressed. Rather they must be endured with the knowledge that they will pass as the person takes up lasting commitments and a growing faith. Peter did not have such an assurance, so his wandering desires, sharpened by the loneliness and unconnectedness of his itinerant life, caused him some discomfiture. There were also a few moments of joy when he felt he was on the right track.

His diary entry for November 10, 1823, shows him in great distress: (Excerpts from his diary are presented with the original spelling and syntax.)[3]

November 10th left Burtons for Madison court house and arrived in that village about 3 o'clock, and a early candle light Preached in the house of Jacob Miller; for two or three days Back i Have been Sorely Tryed, i have

been so bound up that I could barely preach, Pray, or
converse upon any subject. O Lord have Mercy upon
me, come to my help, scatter my enemys, and let my
Soul into the lights of the Gospel revive my droping
speerits—

He was still in this state two days later.

November 12th Madison City, i still remain bound in
mind, not at liberty, as though the Lord withdrew his
Sperret from me . . .

Yet he doggedly continued his traveling and preaching.
On the fifteenth he writes:

November 15th Shennendoah county Massan(e)tta
Valley, Preach at Hays School house, and was
measurelybly at liberty—

His binds are loosening and he writes the next day:

. . . before meeting as usial retired to the woods, and
supplicated a Throne of mercy, entreating God to
prepare me for the Solemn dutys of the day—the Lord
answered my Prayer and gave light and liberty to his servant . . .

Then on the nineteenth, this exuberant entry:

November 19th This has been a day of light and liberty
to my Soul. i had sweet communion with my God while
Traveling through a Desolate mountaineous country . . .

But by December 1, his somber stiffness has returned:

December 1st I have been for one or two days back
Tongue Tyed, the Lord knows what is best for such a

short sighted mortal as i am, Lord ever guide me by the
unceasing wisdom, victory victory, o Lord i must obtain, or never be what i ought to be, o that my eye may
be single, that my whole body may be full of light . . .

God answered his prayer for he eventually achieved
victory over his passions and his doubt, and in later
years was known for his singleness of vision. There were
two things yet to happen to put him on that course—
joining the Brethren and getting married.

His dissatisfaction brought him eventually to the
Brethren. It is said that his first introduction to them
was a booklet entitled *A Brief and Simple Exhibition of
the Word of God* (1823) written by Elder Benjamin Bowman (1754-1829) of Virginia.[5] His diary shows that he
visited Daniel and Samuel Arnold in Hampshire County
(then Virginia, now West Virginia) in July, 1823, and
requested baptism. Peter had been searching for people
who practiced their Christianity the right way, and the
Brethren met the test. He wrote: "i told him (Daniel) i
wanted to conform to the ordinances of Christ Church i
therefore wanted to be baptised."[6] Samuel Arnold's reply is instructive.

After some conversation he told me that there would
be no meeting in the neighborhood for some time.
Therefore I would have to wate, that it was contrary to
there order to baptise any person, until they had a council of the church.[7]

The Brethren were not quick to add members even when
a forthright request was made. They followed a
deliberate and cautious procedure. Nead himself was to
write later: "The true church will never make it her
business to 'creep into houses and lead captive silly persons,' (2 Timothy 3:6)."[8]

But here the person was not silly and had come voluntarily, and still Elder Arnold would not baptize without first consulting his brethren. It would have been a rare evangelist who would have displayed Elder Arnold's caution.

Peter, however, did not have matching patience, and despite the good elder's invitation to stay in the neighborhood until the next meeting, he wanted to move on and not be "burdensome to the Brethren." He also told Brother Arnold about his call. ". . . i told him that it was impressed upon my mind that i ought to labour in the vinyard of the Lord, and that when i left home i promised to obey the call."[9]

The elder gave a suggestion to cover both of Peter's wishes. He knew the young man was traveling to Rockingham County, so he offered to give him a letter to an elder there, David Garver (or Garber) since there was a large church in that county. He cautioned Peter that in order to preach he would need to be called by the church council. He suggested Peter find a school teaching job there.

> . . . where i would have an opportunity of being better acquainted with the Brethren and they of me, and if the Lord had designed me to preach that i would have after. Sometime the church to approbate me and that I could certainly then labor with more success.[10]

The Brethren were very cautious to put men in the ministry especially at their own request. The call had to come not only individually but through the church as well. Peter did not take Elder Arnold's advice. Instead he rambled and preached until winter and then commenced again in April, 1824. In June he returned to the Arnolds, and was baptized (June 14th) in the Potomac

River by Elder Daniel Arnold.

Still he did not stop preaching or traveling. What the Brethren thought of that we do not know, but finally in 1825 he settled down to a more steady and acceptable life and married Barbara Young of Broadway, Virginia, at Linville Creek. Though she was nine years older than he, their marriage was a good one. In later years he remarked, "I have a little wife, but she has a big heart."[11] Joining the Brethren and marrying Barbara must have brought his life into focus, for while we have no diary entries to rely upon, we know he settled down in Broadway to farming, tanning, and teaching school. Finally, in 1827, the Brethren got around to electing this hasty preacher to the ministry at the same council meeting when John Kline was made a deacon.

A good story is told of Brother Nead's early years as a preacher when he was still a bit "fast" for the Brethren.

Bro. Nead's manner of dress was more stylish than was the custom of the Brethren. One feature of his attire, offensive to the Brethren, was a tall, white hat, often the style of the clergy of those days. Bro. Nead was so earnest in his work, and enjoyed his church relationship so much that they were slow to ask him to put the hat away. Finally old Bro. Benjamin Bowman decided that he could remove that hat without offending Bro. Nead. So, one Sunday, after the close of the preaching services at his own house, he asked Bro. Nead to take a walk with him. Entering the barn, he closed the door, and took him to the farther end of the floor, where he approached a fanning mill. Reaching into the mill, he drew out a new, low-crown hat, and said, "Bro. Peter, the Brethren feel that the hat you wear is not in harmony with the humble profession you have made. We love you, and desire that you may do a great deal of good in the church. Now, Bro. Peter, here is a new Brethren's hat that I bought for you." Holding the hat close to his

face, he said, "Will you wear it?" Bro. Nead said, "Yes,
I will." He took the hat and never wore any other kind
of hat as long as he lived. The kind manner in which
Bro. Bowman approached him, had such an effect upon
him that he changed all his clothing and came in the full
order of the church.[12]

Peter moved a good bit in his lifetime: From
Broadway, Virginia to Augusta County in 1840; then to
Botetourt County in 1843; next to Ross County, Ohio,
in 1848; in the same year to Montgomery County, Ohio,
near Bear Creek; and finally in 1850 to another location
in the same county, nine miles from Dayton, near the
Lower Stillwater church where he became the bishop. It
was this church that Julius Hermann Mority Busch
visited (See Chapter Four). He met Bishop Nead,
accepted an invitation to spend several days at his farm,
gratefully accepted a copy of his *Theological Writings*,
and had this to say to him: "Here I learned to know in
him not only a childlike and loving spirit, but also a man
much more informed in theological matters than I had
anticipated."[13]

In addition to the book in 1834, another written in the
same year, a third published in 1845, and the *Theological
Writings* of 1850, he published still another book in 1866
and many articles for *The Gospel-Visiter* and the *Vindicator*.

No other person, with the exception of Henry Kurtz,
used the printed word more than Elder Peter Nead. And
hardly anyone could equal his wide reading. Yet it was
this same man who opposed higher education in his old
age. His book writing could certainly be called
progressive, yet he was one of the leaders of the "Old
Order," helped found the *Vindicator* whose purpose it
was to uphold the old ways. His son-in-law, Samuel

Kinsey, was the editor, and after the division of the denomination in 1881 the paper became the official organ of the Old Order Brethren and remains so today. When he joined the Brethren he was much more hasty than they, yet by the end of his life, he was the bulwark of the old ways. He wore a fashionable hat as a young preacher, but became a strong advocate of the order of dress.

This is really not so difficult to understand. It is not unusual once a young man masters the vagaries of his personality to become a bit over-zealous in suppressing them. Sometimes the heartiest sinners become the greatest saints. St. Augustine not only abandoned the sexual promiscuity of his early life, he became celibate. Paul, former persecutor of Christians, became their zealous apostle. Brother Peter, even when he was a rambling preacher, exhibited a decided doggedness of purpose. He loved the early life he had with the Brethren in Virginia in the 1830s and 1840s, fastened upon it, and would not let it go. It was so much better than the confusion he had known as an itinerant Methodist. He was sure it was best for all the other Brethren as well. It may have been, but not all agreed. The 1870s saw increasing change, the 1880s the schism; and where they had been one, there were now three churches that continued to grow apart, at least in life-style and practice if not in spirit.

Elder Nead served on Standing Committee six times in the 1840s and twelve times in his lifetime. He died in 1877 at the age of eighty-one. We may safely presume that had he lived until 1881, he would have gone with the Old Order. He would no doubt not approve of today's Church of the Brethren, but it may be grateful for his early articulate leadership.

Sister Sarah Righter Major

Sister Sarah Righter Major

Sarah Major was entirely out of place among the Brethren and yet remained entirely in her place. And that is how she became the first and, for decades, the only woman preacher in the fraternity. We do not know much about her, but there are some things we can learn about the Brethren by seeing how they responded to her. She was born August 28, 1808, near Philadelphia, Pennsylvania. Her maiden name was Righter, daughter of John Righter, who was a member of the Philadelphia church. Being near the city, she received a fair common school education. In her teen years she was gay, fashionable, and carefree. When she was eighteen, she heard Harriet Livermore preach, and the event changed her life. Miss Livermore was a well-known preacher whom the Brethren sometimes allowed to preach. This would never have been permitted out in the rural areas, but the Philadelphia and Germantown Brethren were always a bit more progressive.

Apparently Harriet Livermore did more than convert young Sarah. She also set a provocative example, for shortly after she joined the church she herself felt called to preach. She knew how the Brethren felt about women preachers. They took Paul's admonition in 1 Corinthians 14:34-35 very seriously:

> Let your women keep silence in the churches: for it is not permitted unto them to speak; but they are commanded to be under obedience, as also saith the law. And if they will learn anything, let them ask their husbands at home: for it is a shame for women to speak in the church. (KJV)

So she suppressed her calling for a time, but without much success, for she soon fell into melancholy and her father noticed that something was wrong. He questioned her and she confided her strange calling. You can imagine her relief when she found him sympathetic, and her surprise when even her elder was supportive. Her father went to see Elder John Keyser, bishop of the Philadelphia church, after which the bishop talked with Sarah and encouraged her to follow the calling. She began to preach publicly at the Philadelphia church. Elder Israel Paulson at the Amwell church in New Jersey also took an interest in her and asked her to preach at his church.

We know very little about those early years of her preaching, but she must have confined it mostly to the churches near her home. How much resistance she faced we do not know, but we do know that by 1834, eight years later, she was well enough known across the brotherhood to draw the attention of Yearly Meeting. She found them not as open as her home church. In that year a query was submitted:

> Concerning a sister's preaching. Not approved of; considering such sister being in danger, not only exposing her own state of grace to temptation, but also causing temptations, discord, and disputes among other members. (Art. 13, 1834)[14]

Sarah, however, continued to preach. The elders at Yearly Meeting decided to send a committee to silence her; one was duly appointed and dispatched. After considerable discussion, the elders came away without enforcing the meeting's decision. Elder James H. Tracy of Indiana, one of the committee members, asked about the matter, replied bluntly, "I could not give my voice to silence someone who can outpreach me."[15] And so the brotherhood and Sarah came to a tacit understanding.

The nature of that understanding was mentioned in passing by Sister Sophia Lightner of the Pipe Creek Church, Maryland, in the letter she wrote on July 12, 1840, to her uncle John Bonsack in Virginia. (See Chaper One, p. 37). Sister Lightner knew Sarah Righter, corresponded with her at least once, and referred to her in three different letters between 1837 and 1869. Sophia's letter is delightfully colloquial.

> St. [Sister] Sarahs case was brought forward at the yearly meeting. If I understand correctly it was settled in this way: That in her own parts she can speak when ever they think proper, but other churches, that is the br. [Brethren] in other parts or districts durst not send for her unless that family of the church in which they live are in union. If there should be one or two private members not reconciled, they could not prevent, unless it should be an Elder opposed, why then she durst not come. I feel sorry that it is pind down so close, and yet I rejoice that God did not permit her to be entirely put to silence . . .[16]

And that remained the practice throughout her life.

On November 18, 1841, two men were elected to the ministry in her home congregation. One was her father, with twenty-nine votes; the other was Thomas Major, with twenty-seven votes. Less than a year later she married Thomas and once again had the good fortune to have found one of the few men in the brotherhood who could support her preaching. Throughout their long life together, he consistently encouraged her ministry and stood aside to make way for her. We have heard countless incidents of the faithful "little woman" behind the "great man." Hers is a case in reverse. Sarah's preaching career was considerably assisted by her husband's patient deference. However, Sarah was a

Elder Thomas Major

quietly determined woman and we may presume that
she would have persisted without her husband's support. She made a wise choice when she married Thomas
Major.

They moved in 1843 to Scioto County, Ohio, and
several years later to Highland County, same state. Here
they formed, served the church, and ended their lives.
They had five children; only three lived to adulthood,
and curiously none joined the Brethren.

There are several accounts of Sarah's preaching. They
usually agree upon her ability and the unique method
she and Elder Major used to deal with the cautious
Brethren. The earliest is from the pen of Sohia Lightner
in a letter to her Uncle John Bonsack on November 3,
1837.

> [we had] ... the pleasure to hear from Brother
> William Price and Dear Sister Sarah Righter ... Sister
> Sarah spoke about 1 ½ hours ... she spoke a powerful
> summons ... and that evening they had a meeting at
> Brother Joseph Foutzs and the next day the meeting was
> at Old Uncle John Roop. They said that Sister Sarah
> spoke two hours and a quarter. There some confessed
> they had never heard such a summons before ... They
> expected to have near forty meetings before they would
> arrive home . . .[17]

Brother J. H. Warstler of Indiana gave this description
of her appearance in his church:

> When she entered the church house of Solomon's Creek
> congregation, she took her seat down in front of the
> stand while Elder Shively and Major [her husband] went
> up on the stand and, after some little talk and arrange-
> ment among themselves, Brother Major invited her up,
> and she took her seat at his right side. In dress she was

neat and plain—a very plain bonnet, which she soon laid
aside and a little shawl around her neck and over her
shoulders extending down the back and over the breast.
Her face showed marks of age and care and labor. She
was the picture of meekness and humility, completely
subject to the will of her husband.

After the opening exercises she was invited by Brother
Major to preach. She arose, and slowly announced her
text, an old, plain, simple one. I was disappointed. I expected something new, at least something out of the ordinary course of texts, and here was one of the common
ones. I was disappointed in the text, but was interested in
the preacher, and I gave attention. It did not take long to
discover that out of the common came forth the sublime.
I could see a wonderful unfolding of the text. I think I am
safe in saying that I never heard a text so expounded, il-
lustrated, and so transformed into newness of life as was
done in that discourse. The sermon was a masterpiece of
workmanship.[18]

Note the way she carefully deferred to Elder Major's
lead. This careful respect for the leadership of the men
helped to endear her even to the crustiest Old Brethren.

However, she did run into resistance. Edward Frantz,
former editor of *The Gospel Messenger*, told this story
from the 1880s when Sarah was over seventy and had
been preaching for well over fifty years.

On a summer Sunday of my boyhood, about 1880
perhaps, came Sarah Majors and her husband Thomas
from their home in the hill country farther south, to the
Donnels Creek Church of Southern Ohio. It was common knowledge that Sister was the better preacher of
the two. Besides that, she was a woman. The younger set
was unanimous in hoping she would preach, but some
uneasiness was apparent in the gathering congregation.
A council of the members present was called at the west

end of the church under the maple trees, a spot well accustomed to consultations on problems of procedure. I
recall that in the brief interchange of opinion one
brother referred with emphasis to Paul's words: "It is a
shame for a woman to speak in the church." The result
was a decision to ask Brother Major to preach and Sister
Major, taking her place behind the table with the
ministers, to lead in the opening prayer. So it was done.
I remember being impressed with the eloquence and fer-
vor of her prayer. I recall nothing of the sermon. I think
I was too busy nursing my disappointment to give it
proper attention.[19]

Sarah always deferred to the order of the church and
the authority of the elders. Though her desire to preach
was decidedly out of place, she was very careful to keep
her place and consequently no fault could be found with
her. It is said that once she preached the Brethren always
wanted her back. She had this to say in a letter written in
1835 about her deference to men:

You once thought this liberty I use an assumption not
belonging to the female character, because the Head of
the Church in sending out into the world, chose his first
herolds from your sex. My dear brother, I shall ever
acknowledge the head of the woman to be the man, and
the head of every man is Christ.[20]

But she also said this:

I believe man to have been first in creation, but I also
believe woman was made to be an help meet for or equal
to him, having a soul and body, capable of helping him,
in his natural and spiritual world, the companion of his
joys and sorrows, in heaven and on earth, who looks up
to him as for her power and protection, and on whom he
is bound to look with feelings of care and love, so as

to secure that confidence to himself which belongs to his high station.[21]

She was saying tactfully yet with telling directness that, while men have the priority in creation and the biblically ordained authority, women are equal in *capability*. And she gently reminds her correspondent that a man is dependent on a woman for the confidence and security that allows him to be high and mighty. Not exactly a radical women's lib position by today's standards, but out of the ordinary, perky, and staunch for her time. While Sarah did not usurp power or position, she certainly did not give ground either. She was a solid and courageous woman and widely respected. In her long letter of 1835 (written when she was only twenty-seven), she argues her position with considerable eloquence. She even goes so far as to suggest that if Paul's instructions to the Corinthians are taken as his final word on the matter, he contradicts himself.

> Therefore, I conceive it would be very inconsistent in an apostle, who had laid his hands on men and women, and pray'd over them, that they might receive the Holy Ghost, because it was given to a woman in answer to prayer—when at that time it may not be given in such measure to more experienced Christians.[22]

She preached wherever she was received. People loved to hear the "woman preacher," going out of curiosity and returning with appreciation. It was Sarah who converted Isabella Fitzwater, sister of John Umstad, and started the awakening that resulted in his conversion. She converted Abraham Cassel, and was a good friend of James Quinter who in the 1870s and 1880s was a prominent editor, college president, and member of

Dunker girl in the fields

Standing Committee. She gave Quinter, eight years her junior, a copy of the New Testament when he was sixteen years old. It was a year later that he joined the church. She was known for her concern for black people, and she and Elder Major were two of Samuel Weir's most consistent supporters. They were the only (See Chapter Eight, page 225) two white people at the first love feast of the black Brethren. She would sometimes preach in infirmaries and the penitentiary as well.

H. R. Holsinger had his own encounter with Sarah, and with his usual inimitable style recounts it as follows:

> I had the satisfaction of sharing the Philadelphia pulpit of the Tunker Church some time during the sixties of the nineteenth century with Sister Major. It was my turn to preach in the afternoon, and I confess guilty of a feeling closely akin to humiliation, at the thought of being in the same stand with a woman preacher. In the evening Sister Major preached, and I now humbly acknowledge that I was very much ashamed of myself and of my effort, but most of all was I dissatisfied with myself because of the prejudice confessed to above, but which I am thankful to have the assurance I had carefully concealed. She preached an excellent sermon. Her style was simple, her manner perfect, and every gesture in place.[23]

About Sarah Major's activities during the 1840s we know very little except that she had already been preaching for some years and was known across the brotherhood. That was the decade when she married and moved to Ohio. We may assume she was preaching with her usual quiet force. She wrote in her 1835 letter:

> God always gave his gifts freely where they were willing to use them, and I believe in Christ Jesus male and

female are one, just as Jew and Gentile are made one. Every one should do as much as they can to glorify God with the different gifts of the Spirit of God.[24]

And that is what she did.

CHAPTER 11

Chapter Eleven
Vintage Brethren in the East

I t is obviously not possible to chronicle the untold numbers of unique personalities in the whole fraternity in a whole decade. There were stuck away in the backwoods many old elders, farmers, deacons, and hard-working, colorful sisters who went unnoticed by all but those who lived and worshiped with them. The past five chapters have presented the Brethren who stood out. The story of the others cannot be told, but you may be sure that there were many interesting persons.

It is just as obvious that the story of every congregation cannot be told because there were too many and because so little is known about them. Just as the majority of the Brethren must of necessity go unchronicled, so must the congregations.

The foregoing five chapters were about people, not all people but prominent or interesting persons whose biographies also tell something about the church. This

and the next chapter are about four churches none of which was prominent (individual congregations were not prominent across the brotherhood as they are sometimes today) and all of which are interesting for different reasons. I have chosen them for their human interest, for what they show about congregations in general in the decade, and because there was enough information available on them to make telling their story worthwhile. The two churches in this chapter were in Lancaster County, eastern Pennsylvania. They will give you an idea what an older, well-established congregation was like. The next chapter is about two churches nearer the frontier, in areas little or undeveloped.

White Oak

The White Oak church had an early history of conflict. By the 1840s things had settled down somewhat, but not entirely. The first German Baptist minister within the bounds of what was to be White Oak was Peter Hummer, who in 1753 bought almost two hundred acres about three miles west of Manheim. It is thought that his election came shortly thereafter, for a minister was needed there being none nearer than ten miles.[1] Peter Hummer had an unusual daughter named Catharine who had visions and claimed to communicate with the dead. Today we would call her a medium. Peter had great confidence in his daughter's powers, took her with him on his preaching tours, and was known to remark upon the wonderful way God was manifesting himself in his family. Dr. M. G. Brumbaugh reports that this "made a wonderful stir in the colonial church."[2] The matter was brought before the elders at the Yearly Meeting on May 28, 1763. They admonished Peter Hummer, who they said had "brought too much of his human nature into those doings,"[3] they reproved

Catharine's critics for harsh words; and amazingly they left the validity of Catharine's visions up to each member's judgment, counseling each side not to judge the other and passing no judgment of their own upon these spiritualistic experiences which were unquestionably well out of the ordinary.

Catharine, however, got some of her own "human nature" into the matter. It seems that only one person, a young man, could enter her room when she was entranced without breaking the trance. It came to the attention of the Brethren that this young man, Sebastian Keller by name, was aroused by more than Sister Catharine's visions, and that not all of Catharine's interests were on the spiritual plain. One historian puts the matter delicately yet without wasted words: "In the summer of 1763 it developed that she was not true, and the church took up her case, and dealt with her."[4]

Catharine was disgraced, her father crestfallen. The blow was so great that he refused further to preach and thus ended the ministry of the first preacher of White Oak County. Catharine afterwards married Sebastian who became a well-known herb doctor and member of the state legislature. Catharine is in marked contrast to the cautious decorum of Sister Sarah Righter Major.

All this happened before White Oak became a separate congregation. In 1772 the old Conestoga congregation, which included almost all of Lancaster County and dated back to 1724, was divided into three—Conestoga, White Oak, and Swatara. At this time there were two ministers in White Oak—Christian Longenecker, who was an elder (ordained in 1769) and Johannes (or John) Zug, who was eventually ordained in 1780. These two men together had the oversight of the church from 1780 until 1808, and for at least a third of that time they found it nearly impossible to get along. It

appears that of the two, Elder Longenecker was more at
fault, but Elder Zug contributed his part. Three Yearly
Meetings, 1799, 1803, 1804, took up the matter at length
and on each occasion handed down a remarkably
balanced judgment[5]—none of them, however, to much
avail. Elder Longenecker either assumed too much
authority or absented himself in sulky indignation. Yet
the long-suffering Brethren in Yearly Meeting continued
to try to reconcile them and followed a policy calculated
to make them work together. It never succeeded; they
never did; and it is surprising that the congregation was
not torn up more than it was. We have no records but
the Yearly Meeting minutes, so perhaps it was badly dis-
rupted, but it survived and grew anyway. The situation
was relieved finally by the death in 1808 of Brother
Longenecker, who was still not fully reconciled to the
church.[6] Elder Zug lived on into his ninetieth year
(1821). The two elders were born the same year and served for twenty-eight years in mutual disapprobation.

The 1840s also had two co-laboring elders. They were
however, different. "Each of them labored in the
ministry for about 50 years, nearly the whole time
together. They lived only about three miles apart, and
were never known to disagree."[7] Their names were
Daniel Fretz (1775-1864) and Jacob Haller (1777-1865),
and their peaceful "housekeeping" must have been appreciated. Yet White Oak's preacher problems were not
yet over. Daniel Fretz took charge in 1822, after
Johannes Zug died, and Jacob Haller joined him soon
thereafter, although the date is not known. They continued to share that responsibility until their respective
deaths in 1864 and 1865, although for many years
someone else had practical charge of the church, for
they were old. Elder Fretz was not a farmer, but a shop
carpenter, turner (lathe operator), and undertaker, the

latter not being a common occupation for a Brethren elder. He was fluent and quick to speak, always in German; yet he was mild in church council. His voice was not strong, and he was sometimes so overcome with emotion while preaching as to weep. Then his voice was hardly more than a whisper. In 1840 or thereabouts, he was kicked by a horse and walked ever afterward with an uncomfortable limp. He would often say in his preaching: "We have three principal enemies to contend with, viz.: The Devil, the world, and self, and when we have once conquered self, then the other two cannot affect us much."[8]

Elder Jacob Haller was by contrast blunt and short-spoken. He was not entertaining or fluent. The following story is told of him.

> On one occasion when a Brother who was a little forward had consumed much time, and said but little, Elder Haller arose and said: "I will say something too, if something comes to me worth saying." Then he stood a little, looking on the table, and again looking up, said: "I believe nothing comes, so I will give the time to others who may have something to say." This, no doubt was meant as a reproof.[9]

When he was eighty-four years old, in 1861, he stood up at a love feast in the presence of several strange ministers and perhaps anticipating their thoughts about such an old preacher said in German: "I believe I could guess what you all think. You think I might keep my seat, and let others talk, but if I can I will try to say much in a few words."[10]

In addition to being not fluent, he was sometimes obtuse; he liked to speak in parables and allegories, the meanings of which were not always clear to this otherwise appreciative audience. When he was young he

was keenly aware of his preaching deficiencies and when
he was first elected they gave him considerable discom-
fort. He was pleased that the church had such confidence in him to elect him, but each time he preached he
would go home and review the imperfections of his ef-
fort with painful torment. By his own report he stayed
away from meeting more a hundred times. In later years
he was a hardy and singular old gent. His daughter and
her husband lived in Juniata County, Pennsylvania,
eighty miles away. He often visited them and always on
foot, even after he was eighty. On one of the visits a
brother from the Lost Creek congregation asked him,
"You are reputed to be rich, and we cannot understand
why you always walk so far." He answered, "Yes, I am
rich, but I own no horse. I am content, and godliness
with contentment is great gain—the greatest wealth a
man can have in this life."[11]

In 1841, White Oak had grown large enough that it
was decided to divide it. A line was drawn across the
congregation's territory dividing it into Upper White
Oak and Lower White Oak. Elder Fretz had oversight of
the Lower church and Elder Haller of the Upper. There
were two other ministers in each congregation at the
time of the division. In the same year a portion of White
Oak along with sections of Conestoga and Swatara were
organized into the Tulpehocken Church. The separation
into Upper and Lower was not entirely satisfactory to
all members, and, in order to make it so, privilege was
granted to any member to hold his membership in the
other district if he wished. Despite that unusual measure
(or perhaps because of it) the division was short-lived.
There was some preacher trouble that weakened the
Upper district. Then in 1847 two elders from adjoining
congregations helped reorganize the Upper district
without the knowledge or counsel of Elder Christian

Longenecker (the second) who had practical charge of both districts because Elders Haller and Fretz were getting old. This caused bad feeling. A committee from Yearly Meeting was sent. They recommended reuniting the two churches which recommendation was accepted and instituted in 1851. It was not uncommon during this period for churches to be growing so fast that dividing was necessary, but it was unusual for the division to fail. The need for two congregations must have been real, however, for in 1868 another division was made which was successful.

Elder Longenecker was the grandson of the contentious Elder Longenecker who had caused Johannes Zug so much trouble. He must have been nearly the opposite of his grandfather.

> In conversation once, in a company of Brethren, he said he never was angry. When the others expressed surprise, he said there was one occasion when he had a horse that balked, and refused to work, he felt a little different. If that was not anger, then he was never angry.[12]

He was also peculiar in that for a time he wore a full beard. The Brethren custom was to shave the upper lip and sometimes even the lower lip, leaving the beard full and long on the chin and sides. One explanation was that the mustache was a military symbol and therefore to be shaved off. Brother Longenecker, however, said his conscience required him to wear his beard full—that is, until one day a choking spell seized him. He thought he would die and became so frightened that he vowed that if God spared him he would shave his mustache—and that is how he came back into the order of the church. He was born 1791, elected 1828, ordained in 1841 at Elder Fretz's request, and died in 1855.

While the eldership of Fretz and Haller was har-
monious, they were not without their own preacher
problems. One problem went as far back as 1822 and
was partly David Fretz's fault. In or about that year an
election was held and Elder Fretz, newly in charge of the
congregation, was conducting it. When the members
came in to vote, one after another said, "Jacob Myers,
Jacob Myers."

> Now Jacob Meyers and his brother [not a member]
> had a store in Petersburg, and kept liquor, as all rural
> stores did at that time. Then Elder Fretz became excited,
> and said: "Something must be done. We dare not elect a
> man to the ministry who sells liquor," and went out
> among the members and asked them: "Have you been in
> to vote?" If they said: "No," then he said: "Well, go in,
> but don't vote for 'Yoke Moyer,' " and when the votes
> were all in, Brother Gibbel had a majority, and was
> declared the choice.[13]

This was highly unorthodox and contrary to the order of
the church. No one, elder or otherwise, was to discuss or
influence the election. Apparently Elder Fretz got away
with it. What the members thought of his action we do
not know, but you may guess that "Yoke Moyer" was
not happy. He went to Brother Gibbel and asked him
to decline to serve, but Gibbel replied that he had not
asked for it and would not renounce it. The historian
gives this trenchant report of Jacob Myers' reaction:
"The result was that Myers left the church, joined the
Universalists, preached for them, and made political
speeches, was a ready talker, and lived to an old age."[14]
The White Oak Brethren lost if not a potential leader at
least a colorful character.

However, whom they got by averting "Yoke

Moyers' " election was not without his own imperfections. Elder Fretz avoided a trafficker in liquor and got something at least as bad. The historian says cryptically, "Brother Gibbel prospered in the ministry for about ten ·years when for some mistakes he lost his membership."[15]—not the ministry only but his membership as well. (He was "placed in avoidance.") What his mistakes were we do not know, but they must have been serious. Soon he was restored to membership and not long after reinstated in his office. But in 1846 he made another mistake and was "churched" again. Another minister, Peter Werner, was disowned at the same time. Again we do not know why. In 1847, they were reinstated, but as private members. Nine or ten years later they began to press to be restored to the ministry. Elders Fretz and Haller and a third elder, David Gerlach (ordained 1856), by this time had little faith in them and moved slowly. Gibbel and Werner became impatient and contrary to the order of the church, began to make their own appointments to preach; they were disfellowshiped again. This time they tried to start their own church. They failed, and the long-suffering White Oak Brethren reinstated them once again in 1862. Perhaps Elder Fretz, had he known in 1822 what the next forty years were to bring with Abraham Gibbel, might have settled for "Yoke Moyer" despite the liquor on his shelves.

Abraham Gibbel died in 1864, aged seventy-four; Peter Werner in 1867, aged seventy-four. The good old elders whom they gave so much trouble died in 1864 (Fretz, age eighty-nine) and 1865 (Haller, aged eighty-eight). The historian writes: "Thus four conspicuous characters were removed from the White Oak Church, by death, in a ripe old age, in less than three years' time."[16] While its preachers were not always White

Oak's richest blessing, they certainly were interesting.

It would be fascinating to know more about White Oak in the 1840s—council meeting issues, unusual community events, special times like love feasts or baptisms, Brother Gibbel's mistakes, the personalities of Elder Fretz and Haller—the things that make history come alive. Some of those things could be known through additional research, but that will have to wait for another book. Three things more should be said of White Oak in the 1840s. First it had no meetinghouses, the first being built in 1859 when two were erected. Second, hardly any English was spoken. When much of the brotherhood used half English and half German, many eastern Pennsylvania churches remained steadfastly German, partly because of tradition and partly because that area was so heavily German-American that English was not pressed upon them as fast as it was further west. This was true as late as 1871. H. R. Holsinger reported on the Annual Meeting of that year which was held in Berks County, Pennsylvania.

> Among the peculiarities of the meeting, may be mentioned that there was more German speaking, both public and private, than at any previous meeting we attended. There were many persons present that understood scarcely any English.[17]

In the third place, White Oak of the 1840s was the mother church of nine[18] present-day congregations of which today's White Oak is only one. Despite all its preacher problems, this congregation was a fertile and vital arm of the church.

Conestoga

There were only two churches in Lancaster County in

the 1840s. The other church was Conestoga—the first in
the county, the only one in the county until 1772, third
oldest after Germantown and Coventry, and the mother
of more churches than any other save Germantown. We
already know that White Oak was the 1772 scion of
Conestoga. There is even less information readily
available about Conestoga in the forties than about
White Oak. Elder Jacob Pfautz (born 1776, elected 1815,
ordained 1823) either shared or held the oversight of the
church for nearly forty years, dying in 1864 at the age of
eighty-seven. The forties seem to have been his most active years, during which time he served on Standing
Committee four times. (Available records show him on
the committee also in 1838.) Beyond that very little is
known about Conestoga for that decade. But two events
of interest occurred in that congregation in that period
for which we have records and which provide insight
into not only that congregation but the ways of the
Brethren as well—the Yearly Meeting of 1846 and the
construction in 1847 of the first meetinghouse in the
county.

The 1840s were a great decade for building—approximately fifty-eight meetinghouses were built across
the brotherhood. The Lancaster County churches were a
bit slower than other areas where congregations much
younger already had houses. The procedure they followed however, was much like that of many other congregations. Isaac Steinmetz, a lay brother, provided
eighty perches (one-half acre) for which he received thirty dollars. (Often the land was donated.) Then a
building thirty-six feet by fifty feet was erected and completed in 1847. Usually the members gathered and built
the meetinghouse themselves, or they hired a carpenter
in the congregation to do it. The records do not tell who
built this house, but we may guess that Isaac owned the

Steinmetz's Meeting House

nearby Steinmetz brickyard and contributed the brick.
Building with brick was a bit unusual, for most
meetinghouses in eastern Pennsylvania up to that time
were log or stone. The Conestoga Brethren were very
careful to organize the use of their meetinghouse well.
Theirs is one of the few meetinghouses of the period for
which a constitution is recorded.

Memorandum Book of the German Baptist brick
meetinghouse, near Isaac Steinmetz's generally called
Steinmetz's meetinghouse.

Ephrata Township, January the 12th, 1847.

Constitution

We, the undersigned, having agreed to form a constitution of a meetinghouse to be erected on the land of
Isaac Steinmetz, in the township of Ephrata, Lancaster,
county, at the crossroads near Steinmetz's brickyard, as
follows, to wit:

The said house to be called "German Baptist
Meetinghouse." It shall be for the use of the religious
denomination, called German Baptists, for them to hold
religious meetings in the same at any time. Any preacher
or preachers of any other denomination, or some person
for him or them, must obtain permission from all the
Trustees of said house before he or they can go into the
said meetinghouse, with the intention of preaching.

A part of said house may be occupied for teaching a
day school any time it is considered necessary by the surrounding neighbors.

No kind of exhibitions or lectures shall be allowed in
said house.

One half acre of ground shall be given to build the
said house thereon, and for the use of a graveyard.

Three Trustees shall be annually elected by the con-
tributing subscribers to said house, every year on the
second Saturday of every March, in the afternoon,
between the hours of one and four.

The election shall be held by the Trustees then in office.

No votes shall be accepted at any of the said elections held as aforesaid, which are handed in by proxy. The election shall be held in said meetinghouse.

Any man elected Trustee must live within one mile of said house.

Witness our hands, the day and year above written.

> Isaac Steinmetz
> David Martin
> Charles Bauman
> George Frantz
> Samuel Wolf
> John E. Pfautz[19]

On April 18, 1848, Isaac Steinmetz, in exchange for $30 deeded over the property and meetinghouse to the trustees, David Martin, George Frantz, and himself, who, according to the constitution, had been duly elected on March 11, 1848. The cost of the house was $686.87 which was met by subscriptions from 206 neighbors.[20] While most of the neighbors were Brethren it is likely that some were not. This was unusual, for unless they were building a "union" building cooperatively with another denomination (which they sometimes did), they built their meetinghouses with their own money. In this case, while it was clearly a German Baptist meetinghouse, it was just as clearly intended by the constitution for the use of the community as well.

Today, if a congregation builds a church, it is automatically the only place it worships. This was not so in the 1840s. The new house became the place of meeting for those members who lived near it, which meant that it may have been used every two to four Sundays, depending on how many preaching points there were and how many preachers. The other parts of the Conestoga con-

gregation still met in houses. It may not have been used
for love feasts at all, barns still being in use. The
Brethren in that neighborhood must have been proud of
their neat new house. It was variously called Steinmetz's
Meetinghouse, the Brick Meetinghouse, and the German Baptist Meetinghouse. It stood until 1939, when it
was razed.

The second event of interest in the Conestoga congregation was the Yearly Meeting of 1846. To Abraham
Cassel who was then twenty-six, we owe this informative
account.

Friday morning May 22, 1846, to yearly meeting with
the Rev. Samuel Harley and wife and Samuel M.
Harley, passed through to Boyerstown and Reading to
Bro. Isaac Smuckers. Next morning through
Adamstown and Reamstown to Samuel Landes for
dinner. From there through Ephrata and Lititz to Bro.
Christian Longenecker's all night. Met many Brethren
there from Franklin County and elsewhere. Had
meeting there next morning. Samuel Harley spoke about
the woman of Samaria; after him old Jacob Haller,
Daniel Fretz, and David Gerlock. Through Manheim to
Philip Ziegler's. But I went from Longenecker's with
Bro. John Young near Mt. Joy, eighteen miles. Con-
versed till nearly 3 o'clock in the morning, principally
concerning the Essenes whether they were Christians or
not, and the Millenium. Next morning, he took me to
Elizabethtown where we had meeting in a
Winebrenarian Church. Our horses were all ungeared
and stabled at the tavern and hay and water ordered and
paid for by Bro. Jacob Rider. Went with him from
meeting for dinner to Bro. Isaac Eshleman's. For tea
and all night at John Keyser's. Meeting there next morning where Harley spoke from Hebrews 2:3. Ziegler and
Hoffer also spoke a word of testimony. From there we
all went to John Young's overnight. Had meeting next

morning in a school house close by. Text Phil. 2. In the
afternoon we had a large Council Meeting at his house
concerning the affairs of Abraham Gibble. Next morning to Sister Shoemaker's where many Brethren,
ministering and others met us from Maryland, Virginia
and other places. Had a very interesting meeting there in
the barn. Jacob and Daniel Saylor were also there and
spoke with such power and energy that I never heard its
equal in my opinion. From there to old Bishop Pfoutz's
and the next morning to Konigmacker's in the vicinity
of the Yearly Meeting. Left our horses and baggage
there during the meeting which commenced on Friday
morning 8 o'clock. Present about twenty-five bishops,
one hundred and twenty-six preachers and perhaps
10,000-15,000 hearers. Regular worship lasted till noon.
Then the Council commenced which lasted till Saturday
dinner when regular worship began again and the
balance of the queries were decided by the Standing
Committee in a private room after which two candidates
were baptized in Royer's Meadow. Then began the
preparation for the lovefeast. They erected a large can-
vas tent for an eating saloon with five tables for two
hundred and forty to sit up at a time. The cooking was
performed in a large wash kitchen where they had two
fifty-gallon kettles over the fire to heat water for coffee
and to boil meat and broth for the communion supper
which was partaken of by at least two or three thousand
communicants. Next morning (Sunday) public worship
began at 7 o'clock and closed at half past twelve during
which time twenty sermons were preached from
different texts. The principal speakers were George
Hoke from Ohio, John Kline from Virginia, James
Tracey from Ohio, Israel Poulson from New Jersey,
Peter Nead from Staunton, Virginia, Henry Kurtz,
Ohio, Adam Brown from Missouri, James Quinter,
Philip Eshelman from Chickahog Valley, Cristel Funk
from Greencastle, Pa., the two Saylors from Maryland,
Henry Koons from Washington, Andy Miller, old

Place of Annual Meeting, 1846. John Royer Farm.

Spanogle, old David Shollenberger, Peter Long, Lorenz
Etter and Jacob Brown and Samuel Harley. From there
we went that afternoon yet down to Isaac Smucker's.
From there home the next day. Arrived at about 8
o'clock in evening; absent thirteen days and traveled
about two hundred miles—was much refreshed and well
pleased with the journey—been well all the time and had
very favorable weather.[21]

This is the best account of a Yearly Meeting for that
decade, not only the Meeting itself but the traveling,
visiting, and meetings that usually preceded it. We are
fortunate that young Abraham overcame his father's
resistance to education and became not only well read
but a careful recorder of detail. There are many familiar
names in his account: White Oak Elders Haller, Fretz,
and Longenecker, "old Bishop Pfoutz" (Pfautz) of
Conestoga, George Hoke, John Kline, Henry Kurtz,
and Peter Nead. Reference was even made to the errant
White Oak minister Abraham Gibbel (Cassel spelled it
Gibble). He was disfellowshiped in 1846 for the second
time and the council meeting Abraham Cassel reports
must have been where it was done. The order of events
followed in this meeting was different from that explained in Chapter Five. In 1847, the meeting adopted a
new procedure, instituted it for the first time in 1848,
and that year amended it further. The description in
Chapter Five was of a Yearly Meeting in 1850. It was
also highly irregular for the Standing Committee to settle the "balance of the queries" in a "private room."
Perhaps this was done to conclude business not completed in the available time.

The Big Meeting was a great event, and the restrained
excitement of the Brethren lies just below the surface of
Brother Abraham's meticulous detail.

Commentary

The Brethren of the 1840s kept few records. But what we have shows them to be very human—disagreeing, giving in to desires, delighting in a new church building, visiting at Yearly Meeting. They were sober and straitlaced, but their humanness sometimes burst the laces as it did among the White Oak ministers or lightened their sobriety as it did in the excitement at Yearly Meeting.

The eastern churches were a bit more ingrown than the western churches. Minister problems in the west were sometime solved by one of the parties moving on further west. The peculiarities of the people in the east tended to take a slightly more pedestrian form unlike the flamboyance of George Wolfe, or the Old World liberalism of Kurtz, or the forward-looking missionary activity of Kline, or the widely read theological conservatism of Nead. The Lancaster County Brethren were ingrown not so much in thought, tradition, and practice as in culture. Their life was much more heavily German flavored. The strong "Pennsylvania Dutch" culture, mixed with the distinctive Brethren order, seasoned by fertile land and freedom of faith, and circumscribed by the settled richness of Lancaster County life aged these Brethren to a peculiar vintage found nowhere else.

CHAPTER
12

Chapter Twelve
Venturesome Brethren in the "West"

The west" in the 1840s was Ohio, Indiana, and Illinois. During that decade alone, at least eighteen churches were created in those states. This chapter is about two of those churches, one in Ohio, the other in Indiana. We have the good fortune to have some detailed descriptions of early life in each. You will see that life was different from the settled prosperity of Lancaster County—more treacherous, more exciting, less domestic. The churches were not less faithful, but they were sometimes less stable. No sooner was a congregation gathered, an elder secured or advanced, a minister or deacon elected, than the elder or minister or several members might pull up and more further west. If the eastern Brethren were settled and sometimes ingrown, the western Brethren were sometimes restless. Fortunately the two churches herein described did not suffer from itinerant members. This decade was a vigorous one for each of them.

Pioneers' first winter

Painter Creek

In the 1820s and thirties, Brethren from North Carolina, Tennessee, and Kentucky settled along the Stillwater River and the Brush Creek that flows into it, in Miami County, Ohio, near West Milton. They were organized as the Brush Creek Church in or about 1817, with Elder Philip Younce in charge. The congregation soon began to expand into the area north called Ludlow and in 1835 that was added to its name.[1]

In 1833 Brethren began moving into an area still farther north and west in Darke County on Painter Creek about eight miles from West Milton. They were from Pennsylvania, Virginia, and Maryland and became the nucleus for a third extension of the Brush Creek church. They took the name of the stream so that by 1840 the congregation went by the cumbersome name of Brush Creek, Ludlow, and Painter Creek, but was known more simply as "Younce's Church" after their elder whose strong influence was felt for many years.[2] This congregation has gone through organizational and geographical changes since then, but the Painter Creek section retained that name, became a separate congregation in 1914, and continues under that name today.

The following description was written in 1941 by Levi Minnich, to whom we may be grateful for a graphic portrait of frontier life and worship.

The first members of what we know as the Painter Creek Church came mostly from Pennsylvania, Virginia, and Maryland, about the year 1883. The land was heavily timbered, low and wet, some of it covered with water much of the year, making it conducive to ague, chills and fever. That is why it was later in being settled than surrounding communities. Among the families who first settled in this community were the

Stauffers, Swingers, Layers, Joneses, Youngs, Makers, Newcomers, Shuffs, Hellers, Pennys, Hesses, Shafers, Minnichs, Fourmans, Spidels, Heckmans, Brookinses, Kinseys, Olwines, Crowels, Kreiders, Finfrocks, Brandts, Holsopples, Mishlers and Hollingers. As a rule the families were large, some having as many as ten or more children. They had migrated by covered wagon over the Appalachian Mountains to what was then the far west. Many families brought all their belongings on a two-horse wagon or two-oxen. To lighten the load some of the adults and the older children walked much of the distance. Upon their arrival their first task was to secure their claim or ownership to a parcel of ground, then erect a log cabin. In many instances a new family would move in with another family until the new cabin was erected. Those who came first gladly assisted newcomers and in a very short time a log cabin was sufficiently completed to move in. At first there was no ground cleared, no bridges, schools or churches.

Our early brethren were in limited circumstances. They sought to get as much of their living as well as food for their livestock from the surrounding forest. There was an abundance of maple trees. These were tapped in the early spring when maple sap began to flow. A sufficient amount of maple sugar and syrup were made by each family to last throughout the year. Luxuries were scarce. But the oldtime taffy pulling was enjoyed by all and provided a social function for the young folks that young folks of today might well envy. Money was scarce. Hoop poles the right size to make barrel hoops were plentiful. Dayton had a good market for these poles. This was the first money crop for some of our early brethren. So common did this traffic become that these hoop poles gained the name of "Darke County Currency." Game was plentiful. The unbroken forest was the home of the deer, wolf, bear, fox, panther, wild turkey and other animals. A few hours strolling through the woods with his breech loading gun brought the early

settler good returns and added greatly in maintaining a
supply of provisions for the family. Their cattle were
turned into the open woods to graze. A bell was
strapped onto the boss cow to indicate their
whereabouts at eventide, when one or more of the
children were sent to bring them home. As the children
went on their mission the echo "coo boss, coo boss, coo,
coo, coo," could be heard rebounding through the
woods. Soon the cows were found in their usual place in
the open barnyard standing in the smoke fire to take
refuge from the pesky mosquitoes during the milking
hour. Their hogs too, were usually marked for iden-
tification, then turned into the open woods to get their
living largely from the abundance of mast consisting
mostly of beech nuts, hickory nuts and acorns. The
children enjoyed the smaller chestnuts known as chin-
quapins. It was quite an achievement when some grain
was grown for family use and for their livestock.
Stillwater Mills was the nearest place they could get
wheat or corn ground. Much of the year roads were
almost impassable. Some would go to the mill on horse
back, or with a sack of grain on the fore part of a wagon.

As more people moved in there was an increasing de-
mand to have public religious services. About 1839 or
1840 they asked Philip Younce, a circuit rider who lived
near the village of Nashville a few miles east of West
Milton, to come and preach for them in one of their log
houses. The request was granted. He made the trip on
Saturday on his horse named Barney. The meeting had
been well advertised among the settlers. On Sunday
morning, hungering for the preached word, they came
by wagon, on foot and on horseback following the trails
through the woods to the home of Bro. Fred Stauffer
where the first sermon was preached in this community.
Many of these early settlers became discouraged because
of sickness and the repeated drowning out of their crops.
Some of them were homesick to return to their native
land. Bro. Younce not only gave them an encouraging

gospel message but he pointed out the possibility of this densely timbered forest land being transformed into many, happy, prosperous homes for their children and grandchildren. This was a great day and a happy occasion. They made unanimous request to have Bro. Younce preach for them throughout the year. He promised to do this every eight weeks. Just before one of these appointments heavy rains had caused Painter Creek to rise over its banks so as to endanger one's life in attempting to cross. On Saturday afternoon before the Sunday appointment Bro. Jacob Stauffer, accompanied by his son David 10 years old, went to the point of crossing to warn Bro. Younce of the danger. Scarcely had they arrived at the water side when they saw Bro. Younce coming on his faithful horse that had carried him through hundreds of miles of mud and swamps and water. As Bro. Philip approached the water Bro. Stauffer with his strong voice gave the following message—"The creek is past the point of fording." Bro. Younce replied "Barney is a good swimmer" and across the water they started and soon Barney verified the statement that he was a good swimmer and delivered his passenger to the place to where Bro. Stauffer and his son were standing. Bro. Younce's clothes were soon dried by the log fire in Bro. Stauffer's home. He preached the next morning according to previous announcement, returning in the afternoon.

Philip Younce had three sons who were also preachers, John, Abraham, and David. They too did a great deal of pioneer preaching over a wide range of territory of Ohio and Indiana. Meetings were held not only in the homes of people but in their barns and in the shade of the forest trees. As the years passed the young people became more numerous. There was little opportunity for social gatherings. The young people suggested the idea of erecting a log meetinghouse in which to hold singing schools and debates. The old people were not so friendly to this movement except Fred Stauffer who

became one of the most liberal contributors. A well
preserved 44-page leather-bound subscription book
dated 1849 given to Levi Minnich by David Stauffer
shows that some gave labor, some money and some
material ... John Fourman ... who operated a water
power saw mill on what is now known as the Dan Fourman farm, furnished the flooring and the slabs for the
seats. John Schwinger was the treasurer. Fifty cents a
day was paid for carpenters. When the old folks saw that
the building of a log meetinghouse was going to be a
success many of them joined the enterprise and a
building about 24 by 30 feet was erected. This was one
mile west of the village of Painter Creek on what is now
known as the Orville Beane farm. There were two windows on each side and one at the east end and a door at
the west end.

There was a box stove in the middle of the building.
The seats were made of slabs with two pins at each end
and one in the middle for legs. Two planks were used to
make the long table. The ministers sat on one side of the
table and the deacons on the other. Each minister present was expected to be prepared to preach and to respond if called upon. One of the deacons was usually
called upon to read the scripture selected by the speaker.
After the sermon, or sermons which were much longer
than in our present day, the other ministers and deacons
bore testimony to the spoken word. The hymn books
used were pocket size. The minister would line the hymn
in couples of two. If any of the deacons were gifted in
singing they would "set a tune" and all the congregation
would join in singing. Benjamin Longenecker and John
Swinger did much of the leading. Many times and especially during the summer the church house was too
small to hold the people. It was a common thing to see
crowds of people standing outside at the open windows
to hear the word of God proclaimed. Sometimes when
the attendance was unusually large the men and boys
would pick up slab seats and carry them across the road

A Pioneer meetinghouse

north and east where there was a favorite shady place in
the woods where services were held under the trees in the
churchyard. The smaller trees were used for hitching
posts. These outdoor services were very enjoyable and
there was plenty of "standing room for all." For a score
of years this log meetinghouse was quite a community
center for young and old. The membership increased by
immigration as well as by baptism.

Though there were some crop failures and much
sickness the most of the brethren met with some
prosperity. Year by year and with much hard labor they
added a few acres to their farming land by clearing away
the timber.[3]

Elder Philip Younce had, for a Brother, an unusual
young manhood. He was born in Ashe County, North
Carolina, in 1775 of German parents by the name of
Yontz. (Philip always used the Anglicized "Younce.")
At eighteen or nineteen he joined the U. S. Army and
was a member of the force that General "Mad
Anthony" Wayne led against the Indians in 1794. He is
reported to have marched from Wilmington, North
Carolina to Fort Wayne, Indiana. He apparently liked
what he saw on his march, for after returning to North
Carolina and marrying Margaret Byrket in 1808, he
started west again in 1813 with his wife and two small
boys,[4] settling at Nashville, three miles east of West
Milton, Ohio. He must have changed his mind about
military service—for we find him in 1816 a Brethren
elder—and about Indians as well. A story is told that in
1814 shortly after he arrived in Ohio, three or four thousand Indians were camped around Greenville, which
was about twenty miles northwest of Nashville, while
the second treaty of Greenville was being negotiated.
Sister Younce is said to have baked a large basket of
sweet cakes and taken them to the Indians. Elder

Younce was known to be well respected by the Indians.[5]
It seems that this erstwhile Indian fighter had become a
friend to his beleaguered former enemies.

Elder Younce labored for over fifty years in southern
Ohio, and the churches in Miami and Darke counties
owe much of their early growth to him. He died at the
home of his son Elder Abraham Younce near Pleasant
Hill, Ohio, on April 16, 1864, aged eighty-nine years. He
had ten children, two daughters and eight sons, three of
whom became ministers. His eldest son John figures in
the second half of this chapter.

Mississinewa

Indiana became a territory in 1800 and a state in 1816,
but Northern Delaware County was not settled until
about 1820. Before that it was wilderness.

> Everywhere present were the towering monarchs of
> the forest, along the wooded streams roamed the
> predatory wolf, and the restless red man parted the
> water of old Mississinewa with the prow of his birchen
> canoe.[6]

A bit romantically stated, but true in substance. The
name of the country came from the Delaware Indians
who once lived along the Delaware River in the east and
who stopped long enough in the area to give their name
to it before being pushed still farther west. The land was
rough, and the best places to settle were along the
Mississinewa River, which provided mill sites, livestock
watering places, communication, and transportation. A
Delaware County historian gives a good description of
the latter use:

> . . . boats for carrying freight were built and sent down

the river loaded with the products of the country along the stream as early as 1838, and for a number of years afterward. The first of these voyages we have any account of was made in 1838 by Jacob Gump and Joseph Snider. Their vessel was not fashioned after the model of our transatlantic steamships, nor was it so commodious or comfortable as our modern floating palaces on the Hudson, the Mississippi or the Ohio Rivers.

The boat of these early settlers was a flatboat, fifty or perhaps sixty feet in length, four feet wide and three feet deep. On this were placed one hundred barrels of flour, two barrels of lard, three barrels of linseed oil, together with a quantity of bacon, coon skins, ginseng, and in fact anything that would bring cash on the market to which the craft was bound, which in this case was Peru, Ind., some sixty miles down the river, and a short distance below where the Mississinewa empties into the Wabash River. The pilot of this board was one Abraham Gray, who was supposed to know the river . . .

The crew consisted of four men, each of whom manned an oar. The trip down was supposed to consume two days and as it was not considered safe to navigate at night, the boat was tied fast to a tree, the crew went ashore and cooked and ate their supper, rolled up in their blankets and slept until morning, when after a hearty breakfast, they would resume their voyage. Reaching their journey's end, they sold their cargo for cash, sold their boat to some one who wished to proceed still farther down the river, made what purchases they could carry, and then started for home on foot, where they would arrive in two or three days, to the delight of waiting wives and children, and the envied of all the neighboring boys.[7]

Jacob Gump and Joseph Snider were not only hardy riverboat men; they were also good Dunkers and charter members of the Mississinewa congregation. They were the earliest of a number of Brethren families who came from Miami and Darke counties, Ohio, west into Delaware County, Indiana. Brother Snider came first, settling his family along the river in 1835. Brother Gump followed one month later. By the fall of 1838 there were enough Brethren in the area that Elder Isaac Karn, John Darst, and John Crumrine visited them from the Miami Valley and advised them to hold meetings even though they had no preachers or deacons. In 1841 in the spring John Younce, son of Philip, moved into the area from Miami County, Ohio, and the church, now having a minister was organized and given the name of the river. In 1846 Brother Younce was ordained and the church, now complete with its own elder, was fully on its way. In 1841, George W. Studebaker and John U. Studebaker were elected deacons and launched into the many years of service they were together to render to this church. Ralph G. Rarick has given us a well-written, if a bit florid, account of the life and worship of the good Brethren on the Mississinewa.

Amidst the throbbing scenes of our twentieth century we find it restful to reflect on that more quiet epoch when people were so very differently environed. Sundry trees of the forest, animals of the wild, log dwellings, the fireplace, the tallow candle, grandmother's spinning wheel and grandfather's clock that measured time with the tick of its long pendulum—these and many of a kindred nature were components in the scenes that every day greeted the sturdy pioneers.

In the period of which we write, wild game was very plentiful. The wood homed the deer, wolf, fox and wild turkey, and the river abounded with fish. A few hours devoted by the early settler to a stroll through the woods with his muzzle-loading rifle usually brought him good returns. Not infrequently would some article of "store" food become exhausted from the provisions; but meat, secured in the above way, maintained a prominent place on the backwood bill of fare.

Sister Nancy J. Snider once told us two incidents which are indicative of the presence of bears and deer. When a girl she went out one evening through the path of the wood to bring the cows, which were left to graze at random. One cow had a bell strapped to her so as to indicate their whereabouts. She stopped to catch the tinkle of the cow-bell. What she really heard was something stirring in a fallen tree-top, and a bit later a member of the bruin family emerged and stood up to better view the passer-by.

In the second instance, it was a beautiful Sunday morning. All was quiet about the settlement with the exception of a wild turkey which would express its good feeling with a continuous gobble. The man of the house endured the same for a season, but finally ceased to restrain himself longer. Grasping his gun, which he always kept in readiness with a load, he stepped without his cabin door and was on the point of ending the joys of the gobbler when something came to pass that changed his plot. A buck was spied within good range, and when the rifle cracked it was the buck that fell.

A word with regard to the marketing. It stands much in contrast to our time to note that the people of those days were paid in the market an average of about fifteen cents per bushel for corn, ten for oats and forty for wheat. The grocer paid five cents per pound for butter and four cents per dozen for eggs. It was common to exchange a pound of the best quality butter for a spool of thread. In addition to this, the trading center was no nearer than Muncie, ten to twelve miles distant through the wooded way, and their big-wagon travel required that an entire day be set apart for the trip. Some travel was of course done on horseback, and bob-sledding was usually good through the winter months. Bro. John R. Rench tells us that he went many times with his father, David Rench, on the two weeks' trip of hauling grain to Ohio.

In the epoch which this chapter covers, the Mississinewa congregation were without a meetinghouse. But this fact occasioned no curbing of their worship, for they had a right conception of the building as being secondary to the . . . glory that should pervade it, and that the presence of the Lord could as well be brought into the quarters which they could only yet afford. So in the winter their convening was in cabins and in the summer time it was in barns.

In accordance with the plan adopted, all the members' names were written on a sheet of paper, and each family had the meeting as it came their turn. The housewife of the home where the meeting was scheduled would, on Saturday, prepare the dinner for all the members and friends that would remain after the service on Sunday. Only the coffee and tea were prepared on the Lord's Day. . . .

There were three barns in which the greater number of Love Feasts were held. The one most centrally located for all the members was that of Bro. Joseph Snider, who lived near the plot where the first churchhouse was later located. The largest barn of the vicinity was that of Bro. Jacob Cunkle, and some of the Love Feasts were held in the barn belonging to Bro. David Rench, Sr. These were blessed times for the church. Many people were usually in attendance at these special services, traveling via horseback or the vehicle of a big wagon. It was an age when the neighborly spirit was strongly prevalent, and many hearts were made happy thereby. As Sister Nancy J. Snider has put it, "Those were good old days and we enjoyed them so much!"

Before Sister Nancy became a member of the Church of the Brethren, she was one time present at a Communion service, held at the home of Bro. Jacob Cunkle. In speaking of that service she said, "If there ever was a heaven on earth it was there!"[8]

The church was very special to those pioneer

Brethren. Hardy, isolated, with a great thirst for fellowship and a vigorous faith, they relished their meetings which were rich with love and meaning.

There were three men who gave Mississinewa its leadership in the 1840s and for many years thereafter. Elder John Younce, about whom little is known, was the overseer from 1846 until his death in 1865. At that time Elder John U. Studebaker was placed in charge and Elder George W. Studebaker was designated a sort of co-overseer. These two had been elected together back in 1841 as deacons and served together until 1882 when George moved to Kansas. Elder John continued to serve until 1895 when, because of old age, he resigned, living on until 1901 when he died at age eighty-five. He was of Pennsylvania Dutch stock, born in 1816 in Miami County, Ohio, elected to the ministry 1847, and ordained in 1859. He confined most of his activity to his home congregation.

It was good that he did, for Elder George's confines were farflung. While John ran things at home, George preached from Alabama to Wisconsin. He was born March 2, 1818, in Bedford County, Pennsylvania. When he was eighteen months old, his parents moved to Miami County, Ohio, and in 1835, when he was seventeen, they moved again, to Delaware County, Indiana, where he remained until 1882, whereupon he moved to Kansas. He had little schooling and after being elected to the ministry he felt its lack, so he offered to provide board for a school teacher in order to study grammar with him. He was in later years noted for his prodigious memory, being able to quote nearly all of the New Testament. Brother Studebaker loved the scripture so much that he once considered a bad cut on his foot a blessing because he read the Bible through several times in both English and German while convalescing.[9] He

Elder George W. Studebaker

was elected to the ministry in 1842, ordained in 1850, loved mission work, and traveled extensively up until a few years before his death.

Among his many labors was a missionary trip through the South after the Civil War; and in 1854 he organized the first church in Ash Ridge, Wisconsin. The 1840s were the formative years for Brother Studebaker's long and fruitful ministry. Ralph G. Rarick has another.

> We opine that our readers will want to pause and study the engraving (photo) of Elder George W. Studebaker. Those features are radiant with suggestions of intelligence, altruism and piety, a firmness coupled with kindness, and a happiness as if his walk with God had been through a summer's day of bliss. He had a pleasing personality, and was usually to be seen wearing a smile. The incident is given us that a certain man one time left his place of residence for Muncie, somewhat out of humor, for things had not gone to suit him in his home. On his way to the city he was to pass the home of Elder Studebaker. Be it accidental or providential, we are at least told that Brother George W. met him there and presented the customary smile. The man testified that all his ill feelings left him and he felt so much better upon meeting the genial old man.[10]

He was a robust man who outlived four wives, thirteen brothers and sisters, and five of his own nine children; he died July 27, 1905, aged eighty-seven.

Commentary

The brotherhood must have been exciting during the 1840s. Every year new churches came into being where Brethren had never been before. The country was growing and expanding at a tremendous rate. Opportunity, good land, new vistas, seemed endless. If you did not like where you were or whom you were with, you moved on west. George Wolfe, Henry Kurtz, George Hoke, Sarah Major, John Metzger, and George W. Studebaker all started in Pennsylvania and moved west. Peter Nead began in Maryland and went west via Virginia. Even John Kline was born in Pennsylvania and moved into the then undeveloped Shenandoah Valley. It must have been a good world in which to be a farmer and to be in the church. The Brethren were drawn west by both. They liked the opportunity and the land; they were people of the earth and they liked new earth. But they were people of the spirit too and they liked the wide open west where they could receive God's spirit in their own way, unencumbered by culture or tradition other than their own.

They were a disciplined people, and the discipline was harsh enough that it could pinch and bind. It did that sometimes in the east; perhaps White Oak's preacher trouble had something to do with this. It probably did in the west too sometimes but there it went well with the harsh life. It gave symmetry and shape to the vastness, while fellowship gave warmth and intimacy to the emptiness. Clearing wilderness was a straightforward matter of hard toil, and the man who did it preferred his religion unvarnished and severe like the benches he sat on. And when he was fresh from the emptiness of unpeopled land he relished the tangible fellowship of the love feast. But in spite of his severity he could still have charity for the outsider or backslider, for he was not crowded by them. Space makes tolerance easier.

Those early years on the frontier must have been rich indeed. But they were short-lived, because hard work brought prosperity, development, culture, and a more settled domestic life. The severity so well-adapted to the frontier hardened in some places when growth hemmed

Apple-butter bilin'

it in. Forty years later it was not the eastern Pennsylvania churches that championed the old order with unrelenting tenacity. It was the former pioneer churches in Miami and Darke counties, Ohio. On August 24, 1881, the first organizational meeting of the old order group (The Old German Baptist Brethren) was held in the Ludlow and Painter Creek church.

The tide swept on west and the "west" became the "mid west." If this book were about the 1860s or 1870s, this chapter would be about Kansas and California. Today the Brethren are in no sense a pioneer church and our problems are a lot different—less backbreaking, but in many ways more heartbreaking. However, we may look back on the pioneer Brethren with frank appreciation for their toughness and faith and perhaps with thanksgiving that we do not, like Elder Philip Younce, have to ford a stream on the way to church.

CHAPTER
13

Chapter Thirteen
Geography, Dress, Schism, and Die Grosse Versammlung

This chapter is a potpourri in which I will take up in turn all those things I wanted to discuss but left out of previous chapters. Sometimes an author writes a chapter, not for the reader, but for himself—when he cannot stop himself from dishing up all the oddments that he has gathered during his journey through the book. Whether the reader likes them or not, they are irresistible to him, so he stirs them together and comes up with a stew that is as satisfying to him in the cooking as it may be unpalatable to the reader in the consuming. This chapter is that kind of stew and while taken together the ingredients are hardly the recipe for a gourmet chapter, taken separately each has, I hope, enough succulence, and or perhaps I should say nourishment, to sustain your interest.

Geographical Spread
As you have gathered from this book, the Brethren

Annual Meeting, 1876

spread out tremendously during the nineteenth century.
In 1800 there were an estimated thirty-six congregations
with between two thousand and twenty-five hundred
members.[1] In 1900 there were an estimated eight hundred congregations with approximately seventy-five
thousand members.[2] The actual size of the Brethren
communities was greater than these estimates, because
most joined the church in their mid-twenties, and
because there were persons who attended worship
sometimes, but who for reasons of stubbornness or in-
dependence refused to join. If these two groups, plus
children and interested nonmembers, are included, I
would estimate there were in 1800 between three thousand and four thousand persons in all the Brethren communities. The church was very small when it entered the
nineteenth century.

The Brethren were in only six states: Pennsylvania,
with twenty-three congregations, Maryland with four,
Virginia with five, West Virginia with one, North
Carolina with two, and Ohio with one. Missouri had a
small colony at Cape Girardeau as early as 1795, but it
was not at that time a properly organized congregation.[3]
By 1900 they were all the way to the West Coast and
well-established there. Nineteen states had at least one
congregation and there was a District organization.[4]

That growth was geometric, not arithmetic. By that I
mean that not only were new congregations formed each
decade; but the number of new congregations formed
each decade increased. The rate of increase increased as
well as the number. For instance, between 1800 and
1840, a period of four decades, approximately eighty-five
congregations were formed. Between 1840 and 1850,
only one decade, forty-one congregations were formed,
double the previous decade average.[5] This accelerating
rate continued through the end of the century when the

last eighteen years, between 1882 and 1900, saw an estimated three hundred three congregations begun.[6] This rapid formation of congregations tapered off after the turn of the century, but the growth in membership continued.

Growth was vigorous in the decade of the forties, which started with one hundred twenty-one congregations in 1840 and ended with one hundred sixty-two in 1850.[7] These forty-one churches were formed in one of three ways: (1) Brethren moved to new territory and started their own church there; (2) a congregation grew so large that splitting into two or more small units was necessary; (3) a congregation sometimes had a few members out on the edge of its territory who started a sort of mission point which was served by the ministers of the main congregation until the new group could stand on its own. I would estimate the number of members in 1840 at eight thousand five hundred and in 1850 at twelve thousand (based on an average of seventy members per congregation in 1840 and seventy-four members per congregation in 1850, recognizing that some congregations might have several hundred and others less than fifty members).

This was an important decade for meetinghouses too. The Brethren had been reluctant to build church houses but overcame this reluctance in the 1840s at a rate that must have been alarming to the older Brethren. There were an estimated forty-one meetinghouses in 1840 and an estimated ninety-nine in 1850. Those figures do not, however, tell the whole story, because some congregations had more than one. Actually only thirty-five congregations contained those forty-one houses, meaning that eighty-six congregations (more than two-thirds) met in homes or school houses. In 1850, the ninety-nine meetinghouses were scattered in seventy-four con-

Indian Creek Meetinghouse

gregations, meaning that now nearly half the one hundred sixty-two congregations had church houses.[8] Building houses for worship was an important change for the Brethren, who had valued for nearly a century and a half intimate worship in their homes. This decade was important because it saw that change accelerate sharply.

Statistics do not measure what is important in a Christian community. The only progress really worth having is not in numbers but in faithfulness, unselfishness, clarity of vision, and integrity. Numbers do sometime indicate the respective vigor of these, for a church without them dies; but numbers can also mean superficial growth, evangelism without substance—what Peter Nead called "creeping into houses and leading captive silly persons."[9] This the Brethren wanted to avoid. So we will take the numerical growth of the 1840s not as a matter of pride but as a matter of fact. There were so many good things about the Brethren that we do not need to point to their numbers to justify them; and they themselves would have resisted such pride. We can be sure that in this decade they did not allow their growth to become more important than their convictions and practices. People, when they joined, came in under strict discipline.

Growth as fact, though, cannot be ignored, for the church in that decade cannot be fully understood without knowing that it grew rapidly and that many congregations were in newly developing areas. The Brethren thrived in the vigor of the young nation where they could worship and farm as they pleased, for they loved the earth and its goodness almost as much as the Lord and His ordinances. Their ways must have been amenable to some of their fellow Americans as well, for while their families were large it was not offspring only that joined their fraternity.

Other denominations, however, were growing too and we must not take the Brethren to be one of the most sought after pioneer churches. On the contrary, they were not widely popular, for they were a bit more thoroughgoing about their religion than most people cared to be. We must take them to be vigorous among other vigorous peoples and growing among other rapidly growing denominations. And we must remember that the whole population was growing quickly with the consequence that there were increasing numbers of people who hadn't the slightest interest in the Brethren or any other Christian group.

The Order of Dress

The Brethren have often been known as *plain* people who wear plain clothes of distinctive style. I discussed in Chapter Two the principle of nonconformity which is the basis for plainness, but I said nothing about how they dressed. There are two reasons. In the first place, this was not spelled out precisely in the 1840s. The Brethren were to be plain to be sure, but the exact clothing styles were not specified. Later, toward the end of the century, these details were spelled out sometimes with dreary precision. When we remember their plain dress, we tend to think of those latter years rather than the 1840s when plainness was a flexible practice, not a specified regulation. In the second place, we know very little about what the Brethren of that decade wore.

That their dress was plain there can be no doubt. Article 6 of the Yearly Meeting minutes of 1845 mentions clothing first:

In regard to members conforming too much with the world in fashionable dressing, building and ornamenting houses in the style of those high in the world.

Considered that it is a dangerous and alarming evil, and ought not to be among the humble followers of the lowly Jesus.[10]

Also it is clear that the men were to wear beards, particularly ministers. Article 11 of the 1846 minutes discusses this at length and reaffirms two earlier precedent-setting Yearly Meeting decisions from 1804 and 1822.[11] Women were expected to cover their heads when praying (Article 6, 1848).[12] Men were counseled not to wear fur or cloth caps and women not to wear "trimmed-straw or leghorn bonnets" (Article 3, 1849).[13] Beyond these there were few specifics on dress. Article 25, 1849, is revealing:

Whether it would not be agreeable to the gospel, to advise those members, who have been in the church two or three years, and are still conformed to this world, not to come to communion until they deny themselves, and become transformed from the world, after being admonished thereto?

Considered, that conforming to the world presents itself in such various ways, that we cannot erect a standard in regard to it, so as to authorize the church to prohibit such members from partaking of the communion; but such members should be admonished and reproved by the church, again and again.[14]

With great wisdom, the Brethren recognized that conforming to the world is more complex than clothes only and that to exclude a member solely on this basis would be unwise. The Brethren in the 1840s were more flexible on dress than their children in the 1870s when the right to speak at the 1877 Annual Meeting was denied a brother because his mode of dress was wrong.[15]

Young man's style of dress

The Brethren in the 1840s urged each other *not to conform* to the world, while the Brethren of later decades expected each other *to conform* to the order of the church. The difference is subtle but important. Nonconformity in the forties was an overall intention to keep life simple. It was an attitude, not a set of regulations, and could therefore differ in practice. Exactly how a brother or sister was plain varied somewhat across the fraternity according to economic situations, regional peculiarities, and accessibility of merchandise. The Brethren in the latter quarter of the century were more prosperous, were selectively sampling parts of the broader culture, and were living in a nation of increasing luxury. The temptations were greater, so apparently the restraints needed to be more specific. Uniformity within the church became at least as important as nonconformity between the church and the world, because the Brethren now had to protect their identity as well as avoid worldly evils. Perhaps that shift is why the Brethren eventually lost their plainness. Dress became a badge of membership, no longer an act of gospel simplicity and the Brethren rightly discarded it. Had the emphasis stayed on simplicity rather than uniformity perhaps today's members of the Church of the Brethren would still wear a plain attire.

A brother wore ordinary trousers, shirt, suspenders, usually a vest, and leather boots or shoes, like those of any other man. His coat, beard, hair, and hat are what set him apart. Two kinds of coats were worn by brethren in the 1840s; both were frock coats, cut away in the front with long skirts in the back. One kind had a standing collar; the other had a turned over or rolled collar with lapels like today's suit or sports coat.[16] In 1877 there was a lengthy debate at Annual Meeting as to which of these was the "ancient order"; the moderator, D. P. Saylor,

James Quinter in
3 different types of coats.

who was noted sometimes more for his eloquence than for his objectivity, made a lengthy statement tracing the standing collar back to his great-grandfather in the mid 1700s, ostensibly to prove that it had always been the order.[17] Nearly everyone agreed with him (at least those recorded), and it was of course the standing collar that became the distinctive mark of the plain coat and remains so today among the Old Order Brethren and those few members of the Church of the Brethren who retain the plain garb.

However, photo after photo available from the 1850s and 1860s when Brethren began to have their pictures taken show a rolled collar and lapels (or at least lapels where the back of the collar is not visible). These were taken of men who were born in the last decade of the 1700s or first two decades of the 1800s and who were leaders of the church by the 1850s and 1860s. It is non-sense to assume that they all abandoned the order during those years only to come back to it and defend it in the 1870s and 1880s. They were not young when the pictures were taken and we will presume they were wearing attire that was customary, not innovative. James Quinter, pillar of the brotherhood in the 1870s, was photographed in 1856 at the age of forty, when he had been a minister for eighteen years, with rolled collar, lapels, and a *necktie*, of all things. That was the same year he was ordained to the eldership, and he was so well regarded that Yearly Meeting, at the request of the George Creek church in Pennsylvania, where he had served for fourteen years, directed a special committee to ordain him—an unprecedented act. Yet his attire, while black and unostentatious, was not at all what D. P. Saylor claimed had always prevailed. Even Peter Nead, the champion of the old ways, is shown with lapels (his beard obscures the collar; see p. 265). Yet the most authoritative representation we have of dress in 1850, a series of woodcuts, ironically from Peter Nead's *Theological Writings*, published that year, show the frock coat with the standing collar. (See reproductions of these in Chapter Three.)

The answer to this curious confusion seems to be that both were worn, that regions differed, that communications were poor enough that the differences were noticeable only at Yearly Meeting, and, that nonconformity being more important than uniformity, not much was said.

One further curiosity exists that may give an alternative answer. Sometime late in his life, James Quinter had more photos made. They must have been made at the same sitting because the lines of his hair and beard are almost identical. Yet one shows him with a standing collar with no lapels and the other with the same coat folded back to form lapels, with, however, the back of the collar still standing. Why he did this we do not know, although we do know that Quinter was a diplomat. Perhaps he wanted a picture that would satisfy each view of tradition. It is possible that many of the coats shown on photos with lapels had standing collars which are obscured. Perhaps the coat was designed so that out of doors the lapels were folded over and buttoned up while indoors they were laid open. However, there are enough photos that clearly show a rolled collar to indicate that the "ancient order" was not quite as clear as Brother Saylor thought.

The beard, the hair, and the hat are easier to be sure about. A brother was expected to grow a beard when he joined, although he was not disfellowshiped if he did not. A minister was especially expected to have one and the congregations were counseled not to elect or advance him if he was without a beard. Moustaches were unacceptable, particularly if worn without a beard, because that was a military style. Occasionally they were worn with a beard;[18] but more generally the upper lip was shaved and sometimes the lower as well for a half inch or so, leaving a full growth from hairline down the sideburn and across the chin. Apart from the military character of the moustache, a clean shaven upper lip was perferred because it made the exchange of the holy kiss more agreeable to the recipient.[19] Bristles were not exactly unholy, but some brethren found them a minor intrusion in an otherwise dignified proceeding.

The hair was long, embarrassingly so. If a minister or male member of any of today's denominations tracing their history to these early Brethren (including the Old Order Brethren) wore his hair on his shoulders as did Peter Nead (p. 265) or Jacob Fahrney (p. 251), his brethren and sisters would greet him with distaste, mistrust, or at best long-suffering tolerance. Finally, the hat was broad-brimmed without a cock, low-crowned without a crease, and black—flat, low, and plain like their meetinghouses. It was this hat that old Elder Bowman pulled out of the fanning mill and so gently urged on the then fashionable Brother Nead.

We can only make careful guesses at a sister's attire prior to 1850. That she wore a long, plain, dark colored dress, with a fitted bodice, long fitted sleeves, and full skirt we can be relatively sure because that is pictured in a woodcut in Nead's 1850 *Theological Writings*. (See Chapter Three, page 79.) She sometimes augmented this basic dress with a neckerchief about the neck or a dress cape that came down over the bosom and with appropriate modesty obscured her feminine form. An apron was often worn. Although Article 6, 1848, called for her head to be covered only during "praying or prophesying,"[20] she did in fact wear a cap nearly all the

Woman's style of dress

time. It covered almost all of her hair, tied under her chin with strings, and was put on at marriage. Since a woman usually joined the church only after marriage, members automatically wore caps. Her hair was long and fastened under her cap. Ornate combs or pins were not used, being fashionable and expensive. For outdoors, a bonnet was worn over the cap and a shawl or large cape over her dress.[21] Her attire was not specified and so might vary slightly from that of a sister from another part of the brotherhood except that both would be clearly plain.

The New Dunkards

No account of the Brethren in the 1840s would be complete without mentioning the events in the Bachelor Run congregation in Carroll County, Indiana. While those events were local, they were serious enough to come to the attention of Yearly Meeting, to necessitate special action by the meeting, and to result in a permanent schism.

The controversy revolved around Peter Eyman (also spelled Oiman, Oyman, or Iman) and George Patton, two ministers with ideas not entirely consistent with the order of the Brethren. The church in Carroll County was organized around 1830 and was called Deer Creek.[22] Its early leaders were Eyman and Peter Replogle, between whom trouble soon arose. Whether the differences were doctrinal or personal or both we do not know, but a division of the territory was made in 1838 to ease the tension. Eyman became the elder of the western part of the county where the Bachelor Run congregation was formed and Replogle became elder of the eastern part, named Lower Deer Creek.

This did not settle the issue. Not every member was satisfied with the minister he got, and there was some movement of members between the congregations. Whether it was from Lower Deer Creek to Bachelor Run or vice versa we do not know. It may have been in that direction because the latter was a vigorously growing congregation while the former was not.[23] However, Eyman's unorthodox ideas may have driven some in the opposite direction. These restless members revived the quarrel between the two elders.

The disturbance, however, existed inside the Bachelor Run congregation as well. George Patton was elected to the ministry in 1840. Isaac Eikenberry and Philip Moss were elected in 1842. Elder John Hart moved into the territory in 1844 and Hiel Hamilton came from the Four Mile congregation in 1846. He had just been elected to the ministry the year before and would later become prominent in brotherhood affairs. In or about 1846 David Fisher was elected, so that by 1848 there were seven elders or ministers in that congregation.[24] With that many ministers trouble is hard to avoid; and if you add Eyman's distinctive style and ideas, Patton's support of Eyman, and the older conflict with Replogle, schism is not surprising.

The issues appear to have been whether to question the applicant for baptism before he entered the water (the practice was to ask three questions in the water), whether to place the Lord's Supper on the table before the feet-washing, the single mode of feet-washing, whether to discard nonconformity in dress, and membership in secret societies.[25] Eyman and Patton either advocated or at least permitted each of these, all of which were contrary to the order. By 1848 the disturbance at Bachelor Run had become so serious that Yearly Meeting decided to call a general council. There were at least three such councils called during the 1840s. The general council was a miniature or regional Yearly

Meeting called to settle serious questions in a given
locality. It had the same authority as Yearly Meeting
and was usually presided over by the same elders (from
that area) who would normally be on Standing Committee. In this instance there was a distinguished group
including Henry Kurtz, Peter Nead, and John Metzger
and presided over by George Hoke. General council
very soon disappeared because Yearly Meeting adopted
the practice of sending committees of elders to settle dis-
putes and because district organizations began to be
formed in the 1850s.

The general council deliberated for three days and
must have expended considerable energy and suffered
some agony. They took the individual issues first and
tried to answer them as best they could appealing to the
order of the church and previous Yearly Meeting
decisions. Then finally they took up the problem that
the Eyman-Patton faction presented. The following was
their verdict:

> In regard to ... the difficulties of Bachelor's Run
> Church with Bros. Oyman and Patton, and others, the
> brethren in general council considered that there have
> been committed errors on both sides, in consequence of
> which many members on both sides made satisfactory
> acknowledgments before the meeting, and it was con-
> cluded that, with such, all that is past should be forgiven
> and forgotten, and with as many as may yet come and
> make satisfaction, and that they all should be received
> into full fellowship, and Bro. David Fisher in his office
> as speaker. Furthermore, this meeting considers and
> counsels, that Bros. Oyman and Patton, and such others
> that hold yet with them, should have yet time to reflect,
> and should they come, also, in a reasonable space of
> time, and make satisfactory acknowledgment, then the
> church should also be willing to forgive them; but if they

should persist in their contrary course, going on holding meetings in opposition to the church and even become railers of the church, there would be no other way than to put them into full avoidance, according to I Corinthian 5.[26]

As you can see, many acknowledged their complicity in the problem, including David Fisher, who had gone off with the faction for a while. A reasonable willingness to bear with Brothers Eyman and Patton was displayed, with, however, the unyielding requirement that they come back into the order of the church and make "satisfactory acknowledgment" of their errors. Peter Eyman and George Patton were already well on the way of following their own convictions and to return would have denied what they had come to regard as right. They never came back, but instead formed a group that has variously been called New Dunkards (or New Dunkers), Oimanites, Patton Brethren, and the New Dunkard Church of God.

Yearly Meeting Issues

It was called *Die Grosse Versammlung*, the Big Meeting, and in addition to its obvious importance, this meeting each year has left us with one of our richest sources of information about the Brethren in the 1840s—the minutes of the proceedings. These minutes are direct and terse, for the Brethren rarely wasted words or hedged issues. These records leave little doubt where the Brethren stood and give us valuable glimpses of what was important to them and how they handled it.

Nearly half of the articles debated from 1840 through 1850 (eleven years) were concerned with ensuring and enforcing correct order and discipline: church Council Meeting trials, avoidance, the extent and prerogatives of

church officers, elections, whether or not to lay hands
on deacons, and the correct procedure and order for
Yearly Meeting. This is not surprising at all, given the
Brethren's love of "order" and the purpose of the Yearly Meeting. The proper observance of the ordinances
was the second most oft-debated theme, again not surprising since it was here that the faith was alive and unique. The ordinances had to be guarded vigilantly and
kept pure. The third most oft-recurring block of issues
were defenselessness, non-litigation, and nonconformity—the stance the Brethren took toward the world.

There was a fourth kind of issue, not so frequent yet
demanding a noticeable amount of discussion—practical questions of everyday life, especially divorce and
alcohol. The Brethren were opposed to divorce. They
did allow a divorced person to remain in the church, but
if he remarried, the church council quickly disfellowshiped him. Remarriage was considered adultery.

The alcohol question was less clear-cut. Many of the
articles in the minutes dealt with stills because there
were some Brethren who distilled their own whiskey and
sold it. Yearly Meeting was clearly against this and
against intoxication, especially at worship. But the
Brethren had not as yet taken an exclusive stand against
all alcoholic beverages in any form. And in fact most of
the Yearly Meeting discussions were about "ardent
spirits," which are I presume hard liquor. There is no
mention of wine or beer, and we know that wine was
used in the love feast. Even these "ardent spirits" were
never clearly forbidden during this decade. (Only the
stills were expressly prohibited.) We know that "harvest
tippling" was indulged in (see Chapter Nine, page 250);
and a little whiskey for "medicinal purposes" was not
uncommon. This analysis may cause some dismay
among those Brethren today who thought erroneously

that the strong abstinence position of this century went all the way back to Schwarzenau, but they may take comfort from the fact that while not teetotalers in the classic (I'll-never-let-a-drop-pass-my-lips) sense, they were consistently sober, not given either to drunkenness or to social drinking.

There is surprisingly little mention of worship in the minutes. I am not sure why, but I am guessing that on the one hand, the exact order and form of worship was not ordained by Scripture and therefore variation was less disturbing; and that on the other hand, the traditional, simple worship service was so comfortably ingrained and so well-loved that nobody thought to question it. Doctrinal issues were least discussed of all. An article in the 1844 minutes is the only record for the decade that deals with theological doctrine apart from church order and practice. The issue was the relationship between faith and repentance and was interestingly enough one of the few doctrinal problems Peter Nead addressed in his 1850 work. This also is not surprising, for the Brethren were people of the book and the deed, not the idea or the dogma.

Concluding Commentary

This book is now finished and it is time to add a concluding word. If you were to ask me what fundamental qualities characterize the Brethren for the decade of the 1840s, I would answer as follows.

They took the New Testament as the discipline and final arbiter for their life and church, for it was the conclusive statement of God's wishes. They believed the material world was not evil, but tempting enough that a policy of caution and moderation was in order. They regarded the human world as consistently more prone to evil, demanding at critical points not moderation only but strict nonparticipation—a policy of nonconformity, defenselessness, and refusal to use the law or swear the oath. The inner life of their church community was defined and celebrated by several cherished ordinances, which were clearly called for by the New Testament and warmly appreciated.

Their worship was simple, straightforward, and apparently enjoyed despite rough-sawn, backless benches and interminable preaching. All of this was circumscribed, carefully guarded, and vigilantly upheld by the "order," which included regular council meetings, the Yearly Meeting, elections, cautious delegation of authority to church officials with well-defined responsibilities, and a healthy respect by all members for discipline. At times this blunted individuality and harshly curtailed irregularity; sometimes it resulted only in a certain sober severity; usually it produced gentle, orderly people of unimpeachable integrity and clear personal identity. The Brethren as a church and as a people were simple. They shunned adornment and excess and were moderate toward and respectful of other human beings, their animals, and the land. At their worst they were narrow and severe; at their best they loved God, each other, and the earth with simplicity and careful attention.

As individual persons they were as rich and varied as you might expect any body of people to be. This personal color was not in varieties of dress or cultural interests, or political activities, or education, or occupations. In these they possessed a dreary similarity. Their color is found rather in personal peculiarities and the unique way each made his or her peace with the church. Strict discipline sometimes produces delightful eccentricities which are subdued and hardly noticeable to the casual observer yet surprisingly varied on closer look. They are all the more fine or precious because they have been hammered out at some cost on an anvil of church order and polished by constant rubbing against the other members of the community. That is the kind of personal color the Brethren had. Surely a decade that can contain Henry Kurtz, George Wolfe, Samuel Weir, Sarah Major, Peter Nead, and John H. Umstad is not without color. When you add their fondness for getting together, their large appetite for visiting, their distinctive practices, their zest for new land, and their gentle good humor, you have a portrait not in bright colors but in rich and intricately executed browns.

That is how I have come to regard the Brethren of the 1840s. It is perhaps a bit overstated, but then that may be permitted an author in his conclusion. I have, however, tried to present these Brethren to you in such a way that, while my impressions are obvious, you can form your own opinions about them. Those in the end are at least as important as mine.

Notes:
Chapter One

1. J. H. Moore, *Some Brethren Pathfinders* (Elgin, Ill.: Brethren Publishing House, 1929), pp. 314-320

2. This is an edited and at some places reworded version of a description by Martin L. Heckman in "Abraham Harley Cassel, Nineteenth Century Pennsylvania German Book Collector," *Publications of the Pennsylvania German Society* (Breinigsville, Pa., 1973), VII, pp. 120-122.

3. Benjamin Funk, *Life and Labors of Elder John Kline The Martyr Missionary* (Elgin, Ill.: Brethren Publishing House, 1900) p. 79.

4. Funk, *Life and Labors of Elder John Kline*, pp. 159-176.

5. Moore, *Some Brethren Pathfinders*, pp. 131-134.

6. This letter is reproduced from a typed copy in the possession of Edith Bonsack Barnes, who has kindly given permission to print it. The original is reported to be in the library of Duke University, Durham, N.C.

Chapter Two

1. H. R. Holsinger, *History of the Tunkers and The Brethren Church* (Lathrop, California: Privately printed, 1901), p. 232.

2. Peter Nead, *Primitive Christianity, or a Vindication of the Word of God* (Staunton, Virginia: Kenton Harper, printer, 1834) p. 53.

3. *The Gospel-Visiter*, I (August, 1851), p. 71.

4. Peter Nead, *Theological Writings on Various Subjects, or A Vindication of Primitive Christianity* (Dayton, Ohio: B. F. Ells, printer, 1850), p. 123.

5. *Ibid.*

6. *Ibid.*, p. 122.

7. *Ibid.*, p. 123.

8. *Minutes of the Annual Meetings of the Church of the Brethren* (Elgin, Ill.: Brethren Publishing House, 1909), p. 85.

9. J. H. Moore, *Some Brethren Pathfinders* (Elgin, Ill.: Brethren Publishing House, 1929), pp. 103-104.

10. *The Gospel-Visiter*, I (May, 1851). p. 23.

11. *Ibid.*

12. *Ibid.*, p. 24.

13. Nead, *Primitive Christianity*, pp. 104-105.

14. *Ibid.*, p. 110.

Chapter Three

1. Peter Nead, *Theological Writings on Various Subjects, or A Vindication of Primitive Christianity* (Dayton, Ohio: B. F. Ells, printer, 1850) p. 54.

2. Peter Nead, *Primitive Christianity, or A Vindication of the Word of God* (Staunton, Virginia: Kenton Harper, printer, 1834) pp. 57-58.

3. H. R. Holsinger, *History of the Tunkers and the Brethren Church* (Lathrop, California: privately printed, 1901), pp. 383-384.

4. Nead, *Primitive Christianity*, pp. 75-76.

5. *Minutes of the Annual Meetings of the Church of the Brethren* (Elgin, Ill.: Brethren Publishing House, 1909), p. 97.

6. Holsinger, *History of the Tunkers*, pp. 249-254.

7. Nead, *Primitive Christianity*, p. 118.

8. *Ibid.*, p. 126.

9. *Ibid.*, p. 120.

10. *Ibid.*, p. 121.

11. *Ibid.*, p. 142.

Chapter Four

1. H. R. Holsinger, *History of the Tunkers and the Brethren Church* (Lathrop, California: privately printed, 1901).

2. Julius Hermann Moritz Busch, *Wanderungen Zwischen Hudson und Mississippi, 1851 and 1852* (Stuttgart and Tubiengen: J. G. Cotta, 1854), 2 volumes.

3. Donald F. Durnbaugh, "The German Journalist and the Dunker Lovefeast," *Pennsylvania Folklife* Vol. 18, No. 2 (Winter, 1968-69), pp. 44-46.

4. Henry Kurtz, *The Brethren's Encyclopedia* (Columbiana, Ohio: privately printed, 1867), p. 162.

5. J. Linwood Eisenberg, *A History of the Church of the Brethren in Southern District of Pennsylvania* (Quincy, Pa.: Quincy Orphanage Press, 1941), pp. 19-20.

6. *Minutes of the Annual Meetings of the Church of the Brethren* (Elgin, Ill.: Brethren Publishing House, 1909), p. 104.

7. Phoebe E. Gibbons, *The Plain People* (Lebanon, Pa.: Applied Arts Publishers, 1963), p. 9.

8. Kurtz, *The Brethren's Encyclopedia*, p. 162.

Chapter Five

1. *Minutes of the Annual Meetings of the Church of the Brethren* (Elgin, Ill.: Brethren Publishing House, 1909), p. 119.

2. *Ibid.*, p. 82.

3. *Ibid.*, p. 115.

4. *Ibid.*, 112.

5. From the introduction to the minutes of 1840, pp. 68-69.

6. *The Gospel-Visiter*, Vol. III (June, 1853), p. 11.

7. H. R. Holsinger, *History of the Tunkers and the*

Brethren Church (Lathrop, California: privately printed, 1901), p. 237.

Chapter Six

1. Donald F. Durnbaugh, "Henry Kurtz: Man of the Book," *Ohio History*, Vol. 76, No. 3, (Columbus, Ohio: the Ohio Historical Society, Summer, 1967), p. 115. This article was reprinted in *Brethren Life and Thought*, Vol. 16, No. 2 (Spring, 1971), pp. 103-122. I am heavily indebted to Dr. Durnbaugh's excellent research for much of the material on Henry Kurtz.

2. *Ibid.*, p. 117.

3. *The Gospel-Visitor*, I (April, 1851), p. 3.

4. H. R. Holsinger, *History of the Tunkers and The Brethren Church* (Lathrop, California: privately printed, 1901), p. 354.

5. *Ibid.*, pp. 353-354.

6. *Minutes of the Annual Meetings of the Church of the Brethren* (Elgin, Ill.: Brethren Publishing House, 1909), p. 117.

7. *The Gosepl-Visiter*, I (June, 1851) p. 40.

8. *The Gospel Messenger*, 36 (February 12, 1898), p. 110.

9. *Minutes*, p. 124.

10. *The Gospel-Visiter*, I (March, 1852), p. 191.

11. *The Gospel-Visiter*, I (April & May, 1852), p. 231.

12. *Minutes*, p. 129.

13. *Ibid.*, p. 134.

14. *The Gospel-Visiter*, III (June, 1853), p. 12.

15. *The Gospel-Visiter*, I (May, 1851), p. 25.

16. *The Gospel-Visiter,* XI (August, 1861), p. 256.

17. The sources do not all agree on the dates for Elder Hoke's moves from congregation to congregation. The dates used here are from Otho Winger, *History and Doc-*

trines of the Church of the Brethren (Elgin, Ill.: Brethren Publishing House, 1920), pp. 262-263.

18. *Ibid.*, p. 262.

19. T. S. Mohrman, *A History of the Church of the Brethren in Northeastern Ohio* (Elgin, Ill.: Brethren Publishing House, 1914), p. 42.

Chapter Seven

1. J. H. Moore, *Some Brethren Pathfinders* (Elgin, Ill.: Brethren Publishing House, 1929), pp. 39-121.

Chapter Eight

1. Landon West, *Life of Elder Samuel Weir* (Tuskegee, Ala.: Normal School Steam Press, 1897).

2. *Minutes of the Annual Meetings of the Church of the Brethren* (Elgin, Ill.: Brethren Publishing House, 1909), p. 85.

Chapter Nine

1. Benjamin Funk, "Some Reminiscences of Eld. John Kline," *The Gospel Messenger* (January 23, 1904), p. 52.

2. There are two works I would particularly recommend. Roger E. Sappington, *Courageous Prophet* (Elgin, Ill.: The Brethren Press, 1964) and Benjamin Funk, *Life and Labors of Elder John Kline the Martyr Missionary* (Elgin, Ill.: Brethren Publishing House, 1900).

3. Annie Zigler Bowman, "Memories of Elder John Kline," *The Gospel Messenger* (April 18, 1936), pp. 18-20.

4. Funk, *Life and Labors of Elder John Kline*, p. 38.

5. Dr. Peter Fahrney, *History of the House of Fahrney, 1780-1892* (Chicago: The Dr. Peter Fahrney and Sons

Co., 1892 (?)), p. 12. It is unclear if Dr. Fahrney actually wrote this large (10 ¾ x 15 ½), lavishly appointed sixteen page family history. A phrase on page thirteen refers to him as "the Dr. Fahrney who furnished this sketch." That he authorized it and published it there is no doubt. A copy exists in the historical library at the Church of the Brethren general offices, 1451 Dundee Avenue, Elgin, Illinois.

6. *Ibid.*, p. 12.

7. *Ibid.*

8. *Ibid.*, p. 13.

9. H. R. Holsinger, *History of the Tunkers and the Brethren Church* (Lathrop, California, privately printed, 1901), pp. 324-325.

10. Fahrney, p. 13.

11. *Ibid.*

12. *Minutes of the Annual Meetings of the Church of the Brethren* (Elgin, Ill.: Brethren Publishing House, 1909), p. 107.

13. Fahrney, p. 13.

14. *History of the Church of the Brethren of the Eastern District of Pennsylvania* (Lancaster, Pa.: The Committee, 1915) pp. 273-274. Hereafter referred to as *Eastern Pa.*, 1915.

15. Holsinger, *History of the Tunkers*, p. 400.

16. *Eastern Pa.*, 1915, p. 275.

17. Holsinger, *History of the Tunkers*, p. 400.

18. From a handwritten manuscript by George D. Zollers, "Partial Biography of Elder John Umsted," in the historical library of the Church of the Brethren general offices, 1451 Dundee Avenue, Elgin, Illinois. This description was printed in slightly altered form in "Elder John H. Umstad," *Brethren Family Almanac*, 1909, p. 19.

19. "Elder John H. Umstad, *Brethren Family Almanac*, 1909, p. 17.

20. Holsinger, *History of the Tunkers*, p. 399.

21. *Almanac*, 1909, p. 17.

22. Accounts of this story are to be found in the Zollers manuscript; in Holsinger, *History of the Tunkers*, pp. 399-400; in *Eastern Pa.*, 1915, pp. 276-277; and in D. L. Miller and Galen B. Royer, *Some Who Led* (Elgin, Ill.: Brethren Publishing House, 1912), p. 52.

23. *Eastern Pa.*, 1915, pp. 277-278.

24. Holsinger, *History of the Tunkers*, p. 401.

25. *Almanac*, 1909, pp. 17 and 19.

Chapter Ten

1. Dayton, Ohio: B. F. Ells, printer.

2. Staunton, Virginia: Kenton Harper, printer. This book in revised form along with some other previously published material and some new material was issued in 1850 as *Theological Writings*.

3. *The Gospel-Visiter*, I (April, 1851), p. 3.

4. Donald F. Durnbaugh, "*Vindicator* of Primitive Christianity: The Life and Diary of Peter Nead," *Brethren Life and Thought* XIV (Autumn, 1969), pp. 214-216. Nead's diary is reproduced here in full from a typed copy in the historical library, Church of the Brethren general offices, 1451 Dundee Avenue, Elgin, Ill. This typed version was perpared from the original diary in the possession of Nead's descendants.

5. There is no known copy of this.

6. Durnbaugh, p. 201.

7. *Ibid.*, p. 202.

8. Peter Nead, *Theological Writings on Various Subjects* (Dayton, Ohio: B. F. Ells, printer, 1850), p. 61.

9. Durnbaugh, p. 202.

10. *Ibid.*

11. H. R. Holsinger, *History of the Tunkers and the Brethren Church* (Lathrop: California: privately printed,

1901), p. 469.

12. John Smith, "Elder Peter Nead," *Brethren Family Almanac*, 1909, pp. 27 and 29.

13. Donald F. Durnbaugh, "The German Journalist and the Dunker Lovefeast," *Pennsylvania Folklife* Vol. 18 (Winter 1968-69), p. 48.

14. *Minutes of the Annual Meetings of the Church of the Brethren* (Elgin, Ill.: Brethren Publishing House, 1909), p. 58.

15. *Brethren's Family Almanac*, 1901, p. 5.

16. This is quoted with the permission of Edith Bonsack Barnes, Elgin, Ill. (See Note 6 on page 37, Chapter One.)

17. From the same collection as the 1840 letter. The original is reportedly in the library of Duke University. This excerpt was copied from a typed copy of the original, and printed here with the permission of Edith Bonsack Barnes, Elgin, Ill., who has possession of the typed copy.

18. *Almanac*, 1901, p. 5.

19. Edward Frantz, "A Personal Recollection," handwritten, dated April 28, 1942, at Elgin, Ill. This is in the historical library, Church of the Brethren general offices, 1451 Dundee Avenue, Elgin, Ill.

20. Quoted from a letter from Sarah Righter to Jacob Sola, Canton, Ohio, April 1, 1835. It was published in a pamphlet in 1835 by Sola. The only known copy of this pamphlet is in the possession of John A. Pritchett, Sr., Nashville, Tenn. It was most recently republished in Donald F. Durnbaugh, "She Kept on Preaching," *Messenger* 124 (April, 1975), pp. 18-21. This excerpt is from p. 20.

21. *Ibid.*, p. 21.

22. *Ibid.*

23. Holsinger, *History of the Tunkers*, pp. 360-361.

24. Durnbaugh, *Messenger*, p.21.

Chapter Eleven

1. *History of the Church of the Brethren of the Eastern District of Pennsylvania* (Lancaster, Pa.: The Committee, 1915), p. 369.

2. M. G. Brumbaugh, *A History of the German Baptist Brethren* (Mt. Morris, Ill.: Brethren Publishing House, 1899), p. 520.

3. Donald F. Durnbaugh, *The Brethren in Colonial America* (Elgin, Ill.: The Brethren Press, 1967), p. 265.

4. *Eastern Pa.*, 1915, p. 372.

5. *Ibid.*, pp. 380-386.

6. *Ibid.*, p. 386.

7. *Ibid.*, p. 425.

8. *Ibid.*, p. 424.

9. *Ibid.*, p. 389.

10. *Ibid.*

11. *Ibid.*, p. 426.

12. *Ibid.*, p. 427.

13. *Ibid.*, p. 389-390.

14. *Ibid.*, p. 390.

15. *Ibid.*

16. *Ibid.*, p. 391.

17. H. R. Holsinger. *Christian Family Companion*. Vol. VII No. 27 (July 1871), p. 434. Holsinger was born in 1832. Yearly Meeting was held in his congregation in 1849, so we will assume his experience goes back at least that far.

18. *History of the Church of the Brethren, Eastern Pennsylvania*, 1915-1965. (Lancaster, Pa.: Forry and Hacker, printer, 1965), p. 141. The chart on page 141 of *History* shows ten congregations; however, East Petersburg and Salunga merged in 1974. The resulting congregation is

called the Hempfield Church of the Brethren.
19. *Eastern Pa.*, 1915, pp. 354-355.
20. *Ibid.*, pp. 355-356.
21. *Ibid.*, pp. 568-570.

Chapter Twelve

1. *History of the Church of the Brethren of the Southern District of Ohio* (Dayton, Ohio: The Otterbein Press, 1921), p. 252. Hereafter referred to as *Southern Ohio*, 1921.

2. *Ibid.*

3. Levi Minnich, *History of the Painter Creek Church* (Greenville, Ohio; Frank H. Jobes and Son, printer, 1841), pp. 5-11. A booklet of 28 pages.

4. Ralph G. Rarick, *History of the Mississinewa Church of the Brethren, Delaware County, Indiana* (Elgin, Ill.: Brethren Publishing House, 1917), p. 133. This book contains biographical information on Philip Younce because he was the father of Mississinewa Elder John Younce.

5. *Southern Ohio*, 1921, p. 594.

6. Rarick, *History of the Mississinewa Church*, p. 23.

7. *Ibid.*, p. 24. This passage is quoted by Rarick from John S. Ellis, *History of Delaware County*, 1898.

8. Rarick, *History of the Mississinewa Church*, p. 121.

9. *Ibid.*

Chapter Thirteen

1. I surveyed the histories of all the districts that had a congregation in or before 1850, in order to estimate how many congregations existed in 1840 and how many in 1850, to determine the founding date of all congregations existing in 1850, and to estimate the number

of meetinghouses in 1840 and in 1850 and when each house was built. The figure of thirty-six congregations in 1800 I extrapolated from that data and the estimate for membership is based on between fifty-five and seventy members per congregation. Hereafter all references to that data will be designated *District Histories Survey*.

2. Donald F. Durnbaugh, ed., *The Church of the Brethren Past and Present* (Elgin, Ill.: The Brethren Press, 1971), p. 143.

3. *District Histories Survey*.

4. *The Brethren's Family Almanac*, 1900 (Elgin, Ill.: Brethren Publishing House, 1900), pp. 32-33.

5. *District Histories Survey*.

6. Durnbaugh, *The Church of the Brethren*, p. 143.

7. *District Histories Survey*.

8. *Ibid*.

9. Peter Nead, *Theological Writings on Various Subjects, or A Vindication of Primitive Christianity* (Dayton, Ohio: B. F. Ellis, printer, 1850), p. 61.

10. *Minutes of the Annual Meetings of the Church of the Brethren* (Elgin, Ill.: Brethren Publishing House, 1909), p. 85.

11. *Ibid*., p. 91.

12. *Ibid*., p. 98.

13. *Ibid*., p. 104.

14. *Ibid*., p. 108.

15. *Proceedings of the Annual Meeting of the Brethren for 1877* (Huntingdon, Pa.: Quinter and Brumbaugh, 1877), p. 30.

16. Esther Fern Rupel, *An Investigation of the Origin, Significance, and Demise of the Prescribed Dress Worn by the Members of the Church of the Brethren* (Unpublished Dissertation, December 1971), pp. 97-98.

17. *Proceedings*, p. 29.

18. Rupel, *An Investigation of the Origin of Dress*, p. 87.

19. *Ibid.*, pp. 87-88.

20. *Minutes*, 1909, p. 98.

21. This paragraph is based on Rupel, *An Investigation of the Origin of Dress*, pp. 128-200.

22. Otho Winger, *History of the Church of the Brethren in Indiana* (Elgin, Ill.: Brethren Publishing House, 1917), p. 28.

23. L. Edward Plum, (Unpublished manuscript), pp. 13-15.

24. *Ibid.*, pp. 12-14.

25. Winger, *History of the Church of the Brethren*, p. 29. There is not complete agreement among the historians what the issues were. Winger's list seemed the best to me.

26. *Minutes*, 1909, pp. 103-104.

Index

A Brief and Simple Exhibition of the Word of God (Nead), 268
Alcohol, 360
Anointing Service, 88
Antietam Congregation, 118
Arnold, Daniel, 268-70
Arnold, Samuel, 268-69
Attics, 103
Avoidance, 159-60
Bachelor Run Congregation, 356-59
Baptism, 65-89
Bond, Shadrach, 203, 204
Bowman, Annie Zigler, 240
Bowman, Benjamin, 176, 177, 182
Brethren's Encyclopedia, 133, 172
Brower, Daniel, 176
Brower, Jacob, 176
Brumbaugh, M. G., 292
Brush Creek Church, 318
Bryant, Catherine Long, 221-22
Bryant, William, 220-21
Busch, Julius, 96-97, 122-23
Bush, John, 220
Byrd, William, 216
Byrket, Margaret, 324
Cadwallader, John, 219

Calvert, Robert, 219, 220
Calvin, John, 69
Carter, Harvey, 225, 226, 227, 228
Carter, Martha, 225, 228
Cassel, Abraham, 24, 27, 28, 281, 310
Cassel, George, 28
Cassel, Sally, 27
Cassel, Yelles, 24, 27
Church Council
   directing business, 154
   election of officers, 150-52
   enforcing the order, 153-54
   examining applicants, 152-53
   installation of officers, 152
Civil War, 236
Concordia, 168, 170
Conestoga Church, 300-310
Creed
   defenselessness, 54-58
   nonconformity to the world, 48-54
   nonlitigation, 58-59
   nonswearing, 59-61
Daguerrotype, 250, 253
Dasher, Isaac, 31
Deacon's bench, 112-13
Defenselessness, 54-58

Dickey, Elias P., 180
Die Grosse Versammlung,
    359-63
Divorce, 360
Dress, 347-56
Eldership, 156-58
Election of officers,
    150-52
Emmings, Jacob, 222
Enforcing the order,
    153-54
Examining applicants,
    152-53
Eyeman, Jacob, 220
Eyman, Peter, 356-59
Fahrney, Abraham,
    244-45
Fahrney, Jacob, 243-53,
    354
Fahrney, Peter, 244, 245
Far Western Brethren,
    82, 188-89, 207, 208
Feet-washing, 72, 188,
    189, 357
Fisher, David, 357-59
Fitchner, Mr., 68-69
Fitzwater, Isabella,
    254, 281
Fitzwater, William, 31
Flory, Emanuel, 32
Fonfield, Dr., 29
Foritz, David, 182
Frankfort, Ohio, 225-26,
    228-31
Frantz, Edward, 279

Frantz, George, 305
Frantz, Henry, 228, 229
Fraternity of German
    Baptists, 46
Fretz, Daniel, 294
Funk, Benjamin, 30, 238
Furry, S. B., 68
Geographical spread, 339,
    342-47
    growth, 342-43
    meetinghouses, 343-46
Gerlach, David, 299
German Baptist Brethren,
    46, 68
"German Baptist
    Meetinghouses," 304
Gibbel, Abraham, 310
Gibson, Daniel B., 209
Gibson, Isham, 34, 37
Grammar, John, 201
Gump, Jacob, 326-27
Haller, Jacob, 294-96
Hardman, David, 208
Harmony Society, 168
Harshberger, John. 177
Hedrick, George R.,
    30-31, 32
Hendricks, James, 201,
    206
Hendricks, John, 197-98,
    201
*History of the Tunkers
    and the Brethren
    Church,* 96
Hoke, George, 170,

180-82, 358
Holsinger, H. R.
  description of Henry
    Kurtz, 172-74
  feet-washing, 82
  New Testament, 46-47
  Ordinances of the Lord,
    68, 74
  progressivism, 250
  prosperity, 122
  relations with elders,
    253, 254
  and Sarah Major, 284
  spirit of worship, 93-97
Holy Kiss, 84
Hostetler, Adam, 198
Hummer, Catherine,
  292-93
Hummer, Peter, 292
Hunsaker, Abraham, 196,
  197, 200
Hunsaker, Anna, 190, 196
Hunsaker, Jacob, 201
Hymnbooks, 115
Installation of officers,
  152
Jones, John, 228, 230
Keller, Sebastian, 293
Kelso, Joseph, 223, 224
Keyser, John, 275
Kinsey, Samuel, 271-72
Kline, John
  biography of, 237-43
  deaconship, 270
  as farmer, 333

leadership of, 29-30
  trip of, 30-33
  Yearly Meeting, 176
Kurtz, Henry
  baptism, 69
  biography of, 165-83
  frontier, 333
  and George Wolfe, 207
  and John Kline, 31
  order of worship, 133
  prayer, 116
  quoted, 55-56, 57
  Yearly Meeting, 358
Laying hands, 86-88
Leedy, John, 176
"Liberty," 118
"Life of Elder Samuel
    Weir" (West), 215
Lightner, Sophia, 37,
  276, 278
Litigation, 58-59
Livermore, Harriet, 274
Long, Christian, 182,
  207, 208
Longenecker, Christian,
  294-95, 297
Lord's Supper, 77-81,
  83, 84
Love Feast, 72-76, 82,
  209, 225-26, 227
Lower White Oak
  Church, 296
Luther, Martin, 69
Major, Sarah Righter, 39,
  219, 225, 274-85, 333

Major, Thomas, 219, 225, 226, 276, 278
Mallow, William D., 227, 228, 229, 230
Martin, David, 305
Martyr's Mirror, 181
McClure, Andrew, 216, 217, 231
Mellinger, Christian, 180
Mennonites, 245, 246
Metzger, John, 20-24, 33, 333, 358
Meyers, Jacob, 298
Military service, 55-57, 237
Minister's seating arrangement, 112
Minnich, Levi, 318, 322
Mississinewa Church, 325-32
Mohler, John, 219, 222
Moomaw, B. F., 216, 218, 219, 220
Montgomery County, Pennsylvania, 27
Nead, Daniel, 264
Nead, Peter
  biography of, 261-72
  and dress, 352, 353, 354
  and geography, 346
  New Testament, 48, 51, 52, 53, 59
  Ohio Brethren, 182
  Ordinances of the Lord, 69, 70, 82, 84, 88

schism, 358, 361
slavery, 217, 218, 227
Western Brethren, 333
New Brethren, 46
New Dunkards, 356-59
New Testament, 43, 46-48, 361-62
Nonconformity of the World, 46-54, 350
Nonlitigation, 58-59
Nonswearing, 59-61
Nonviolence, 54-58
Officers of the Church, 154
  eldership, 156-58
  speaker, 155
"Old Order," 264
Order, 139-43
Owen, Robert, 168
Painter Creek Church, 318-25, 335
  members, 318-19
  Philip Younce, 320-25
Paradise Regained (Kurtz), 168
Patton, George, 356-59
Paulson, Israel, 275
Peddler's Bar, 126
Pfautz, Jacob, 301
Piatt County, Illinois, 22-23
Price, Isaac, 247, 254
Primitive Christianity (Nead), 261
Profanity, 60

Quinter, James, 68, 281, 282
Rapp, George, 168
Rench, David, 328-29
Replogle, Peter, 356, 357
Richardson, William, 206
Righter, John, 274
River Brethren, 46
Saylor, D. P., 176, 350-52, 353
Schism, 356-59
Schwarzenau, Germany, 43, 361
Sermon on the Mount, 57, 60
Slavery, 216-19, 225
Snider, Joseph, 326-27, 329
Some Brethren Path-finders (Moore), 54, 189
Spanogle, Andrew, 182
Spartan life, 48-54
Speaker, 155
Standing Committee, 148
Stauffer, Jacob, 321, 322
Steinmetz, Isaac, 301, 304
Stoner, Rachel, 37, 39
Studebaker, George, 327, 330, 332, 333
Studebaker, John, 327, 330
Sturgis, Daniel B., 33-37
Sunday Schools, 109
Swearing, 59-61
Testimony, 121

The Gospel Visitor (Kurtz), 174-78
The Messenger of Concordia (Kurtz), 168
Theological Writings (Nead), 261, 271, 353, 354
Thomas, Jacob, 31
Tippecanoe County, Indiana, 21
Tracy, Henry, 176
Tracy, James H., 275
Ulery, Hannah, 21
Umstad, John, 24, 182, 208, 253-57, 281
Upper White Oak Church, 296
Waddams Grove Conference, 209
Wampler, Anna, 238, 242
Wampole, Isaac, 27
Warstler, J. H., 278
Weir, Samuel, 215-33, 284
Werner, Peter, 299
Wesley, John, 69
West, Dan, 215
West, Landon, 215
White Coats, 123
White Oak Church, 292-300
White, Thomas J., 28
Winger, Otho, 182
Wolfe, George
  biography of, 189-211
  Black Hawk War, 237

defenselessness,
    54-56, 57
leadership of, 187-89,
    215, 264
Old Brethren, 36, 37,
    253
Western Brethren, 333
Wolfe, Jacob, 189, 191,
    196, 197, 198

Yearly Meeting, 143-50
Younce, Abraham, 325
Younce, John, 327, 330
Younce, Philip, 318,
    320-25, 335
Young, Barbara, 270
Yount, Daniel, 177
Zollers, George D., 254-55
Zug, Johannes, 294-95